The Nature, Power, Deceit, and Prevalency of the Remainders of Indwelling Sin in Believers;

By John Owen (1616-1683)

Edited by Anthony Uyl

Devoted Publishing

Woodstock, Ontario, 2017

The Nature, Power, Deceit, and Prevalency of the Remainders of Indwelling Sin in Believers;

together with The Ways of its Working and Means of Prevention Opened, Evinced, and Applied:

with

A Resolution of Sundry Cases of Conscience Thereunto Appertaining.
By John Owen (1616-1683)
Edited By Anthony Uyl

"O wretched man that I am! who shall deliver me from the body of this death? I thank God through Jesus Christ our Lord." -- Rom. vii. 24, 25.

What kind of philosophies do you have?
Let us know!

Contact us at: devotedpub@hotmail.com
Visit our shop on Facebook: @DevotedPublishing
Published in Woodstock, Ontario, Canada 2017

For bulk educational rates, please contact us at the above email address.

ISBN: 978-1-77356-015-1

This version orginally published in 1825

Table of Contents

Prefatory note

While the Government was enforcing stringent measures against Nonconformity, while dissenting ministers if they ventured to preach the gospel of salvation became liable to the penalties of the Conventicle or Five-mile Act, and when Owen himself on a visit to some old friends at Oxford narrowly escaped arrest, and imprisonment, our author did not abandon himself to inactivity, but employed the leisure of the concealment into which the rigour of the times had driven him in the preparation of some of his most valuable works. In one year (1668) the two treatises which conclude this volume were published, together with the first volume of his colossal and elaborate work, the "Exposition of the Epistle to the Hebrews."

His treatise on "Indwelling Sin" has always ranked high among the productions of our author. The opinion which Dr Chalmers entertained of it will be seen in the "Life of Owen," vol. i. p. lxxxiv. That such a work should have been prepared under the gloom of public trials, and the hardship of personal exposure to civil penalties, evinces not merely great industry, but a strength of religious principle with which no outward commotions were permitted to intermeddle. Temptations were strong at that time to merge all duty into a secular struggle for the rights of conscience and liberty of worship. Owen issued various tracts which had some share in securing these blessings for his country. But he was intent, with engrossing zeal, on the advancement of vital piety; and his treatise on "Indwelling Sin" is a specimen of the discourses which he preached whenever a safe opportunity occurred. It is avowedly designed for believers, to aid and guide them in the exercise of self-examination. There is uncommon subtilty of moral analysis in many of its statements, -- an exposure, irksome it may be thought, in its fulness and variety, of the manifold deceitfulness of the human heart. A question may even be raised, if it be altogether a healthful process, for the mind to be conducted through this laborious and acute unvailing of the hidden mysteries of sin, and if it may not tend to exclude from the view the objective truths of the Word. But the process is in itself supremely needful, -- essential to the life of faith and the growth of holiness; and with no guide can we be safer than with Owen. The reader is never suffered to lose sight of the fact, amid the most searching investigation into human motives, that our acceptance with God cannot depend upon the results of any scrutiny into our internal condition, and that the guilt of all lurking corruption which we may detect is remitted only by the blood of the cross.

The basis of the treatise is taken from Rom. vii. 21. After a brief explanation of the passage, he considers indwelling sin under the light and character of "a law;" -- the seat and subject of this law, the heart; -- its nature generally, as enmity against God; -- its actings and operations; first, in withdrawing the mind from what is good; secondly, exciting positive opposition to God; thirdly, ensnaring the soul into captivity; and lastly, filling it with insensate hatred to the principles and claims of holiness. The power of indwelling sin is next illustrated from its deceitfulness, chap. viii. A lengthened exposition follows, of three stages along which indwelling sin may beguile us; first, when the mind is withdrawn from a course of obedience and holiness; secondly, when the affections are enticed and ensnared: and, lastly, when actual sin is conceived and committed. With chap. xiv. a new demonstration begins of the power of indwelling sin, as exhibited, first, in the lives of Christians; and, secondly, in unregenerate persons, in the last chapter evidence to the same effect is adduced from the resistance which sin offers to the authority of the moral law, and from the fruitless and unavailing endeavours of men in their own strength to subdue and mortify it. As to the way in which it is really to be mortified, the author refers to his treatise on the "Mortification of Sin." -- Ed.

Preface

That the doctrine of original sin is one of the fundamental truths of our Christian profession hath been always owned in the church of God; and all especial part it is of that peculiar possession of truth which they enjoy whose religion towards God is built upon and resolved into divine revelation. As the world by its wisdom never knew God aright, so the wise men of it were always utterly ignorant of this inbred evil in themselves and others. With us the doctrine and conviction of it lie in the very foundation of all wherein we have to do with God, in reference unto our pleasing of him here, or obtaining the enjoyment of him hereafter, it is also known what influence it hath into the great truths concerning the person of Christ, his mediation, the fruits and effects of it, with all the benefits that we are made partakers of thereby. Without a supposition of it, not any of them can be truly known or savingly believed. For this cause hath it been largely treated of by many holy and learned men, both of old and of latter days. Some have laboured in the discovery of its nature, some of its guilt and demerit; by whom also the truth concerning it hath been vindicated from the opposition made unto it in the past and present ages. By most these things have been considered in their full extent and latitude, with respect unto all men by nature, with the estate and condition of them who are wholly under the power and guilt of it. How thereby men are disenabled and incapacitated in themselves to answer the obedience required either in the law or the gospel, so as to free themselves from the curse of the one or to make themselves partakers of the blessing of the other, hath been by many also fully evinced. Moreover, that there are remainders of it abiding in believers after their regeneration and conversion to God, as the Scripture abundantly testifies, so it hath been fully taught and confirmed; as also how the guilt of it is pardoned unto them, and by what means the power of it is weakened in them. All these things, I say, have been largely treated on, to the great benefit and edification of the church. In what we have now in design we therefore take them all for granted, and endeavour only farther to carry on the discovery of it in its actings and oppositions to the law and grace of God in believers. Neither do I intend the discussing of any thing that hath been controverted about it. What the Scripture plainly revealeth and teacheth concerning it, -- what believers evidently find by experience in themselves, -- what they may learn from the examples and acknowledgments of others, shall be represented in a way suited unto the capacity of the meanest and weakest who is concerned therein. And many things seem to render the handling of it at this season not unnecessary. The effects and fruits of it, which we see in the apostasies and backslidings of many, the scandalous sins and miscarriages of some, and the course and lives of the most, seem to call for a due consideration of it. Besides, of how great concernment a full and clear acquaintance with the power of this indwelling sin (the matter designed to be opened) is unto believers, to stir them up to watchfulness and diligence, to faith and prayer, to call them to repentance, humility, and self-abasement, will appear in our progress. These, in general, were the ends aimed at in the ensuing discourse, which, being at first composed and delivered for the use and benefit of a few, is now by the providence of God made public. And if the reader receive any advantage by these weak endeavours, let him know that it is his duty, as to give glory unto God, so to help them by his prayers who in many temptations and afflictions are willing to labour in the vineyard of the Lord, unto which work they are called.

Chapter I

Indwelling sin in believers treated of by the apostle, Romans vii. 21 -- The place explained.

It is of indwelling sin, and that in the remainders of it in persons after their conversion to God, with its power, efficacy, and effects, that we intend to treat. This also is the great design of the apostle to manifest and evince in chap. vii. of the Epistle to the Romans. Many, indeed, are the contests about the principal scope of the apostle in that chapter, and in what state the person is, under the law or under grace, whose condition he expresseth therein. I shall not at present enter into that dispute, but take that for granted which may be undeniably proved and evinced, -- namely, that it is the condition of a regenerate person, with respect unto the remaining power of indwelling sin which is there proposed and exemplified, by and in the person of the apostle himself. In that discourse, therefore, of his, shall the foundation be laid of what we have to offer upon this subject. Not that I shall proceed in an exposition of his revelation of this truth as it lies in its own contexture, but only make use of what is delivered by him as occasion shall offer itself. And here first occurreth that which he affirms, verse 21: "I find then a law, that, when I would do good, evil is present with me."

There are four things observable in these words:--

First, The appellation he gives unto indwelling sin, whereby he expresseth its power and efficacy: it is "a law;" for that which he terms "a law" in this verse, he calls in the foregoing, "sin that dwelleth in him."

Secondly, The way whereby he came to the discovery of this law; not absolutely and in its own nature, but in himself he found it: "I find a law."

Thirdly, The frame of his soul and inward man with this law of sin, and under its discovery: "he would do good."

Fourthly, The state and activity of this law when the soul is in that frame when it would do good: it "is present with him." For what ends and purposes we shall show afterward.

The first thing observable is the compellation here used by the apostle, he calls indwelling sin "a law." It is a law.

A law is taken either properly for a directive rule, or improperly for an operative effective principle, which seems to have the force of a law. In its first sense, it is a moral rule which directs and commands, and sundry ways moves and regulates, the mind and the will as to the things which it requires or forbids. This is evidently the general nature and work of a law. Some things it commands, some things it forbids, with rewards and penalties, which move and impel men to do the one and avoid the other. Hence, in a secondary sense, an inward principle that moves and inclines constantly unto any actions is called a law. The principle that is in the nature of every thing, moving and carrying it towards its own end and rest, is called the law of nature. In this respect, every inward principle that inclineth and urgeth unto operations or actings suitable to itself is a law. So, Rom. viii. 2, the powerful and effectual working of the Spirit and grace of Christ in the hearts of believers is called "The law of the Spirit of life." And for this reason doth the apostle here call indwelling sin a law. It is a powerful and effectual indwelling principle, inclining and pressing unto actions agreeable and suitable unto its own nature. This, and no other, is the intention of the apostle in this expression: for although that term, "a law," may sometimes intend a state and condition, -- and if here so used, the meaning of the words should be, "I find that this is my condition, this is the state of things with me, that when I would do good evil is present with me," which makes no great alteration in the principal intendment of the place, -- yet properly it can denote nothing here but the chief subject treated of; for although the name of a law be variously used by the apostle in this chapter, yet when it relates unto sin it is nowhere applied by him to the condition of the person, but only to express either the nature or the power of sin itself. So, chap. vii. 23, "I see another law in my members, warring against the law of my mind, and bringing me into captivity to the law of sin which is in my members." That which he here calls the "law of his mind," from the principal subject and seat of it, is in itself no other but the "law of the Spirit of life which is in Christ Jesus," chap. viii. 2; or the effectual operation of the Spirit of grace, as was said. But "the law," as applied unto sin, hath a double sense: for as, in the first place, "I see a law in my members," it denotes the being and nature of sin; so, in the latter, "Leading into captivity to the law of sin which is in my members," it signifies its power and efficacy. And both these are comprised in the same name, singly used, chap. vii. 21. Now, that which we observe from this name or term of a "law" attributed unto sin is, That there is an exceeding efficacy and power in the remainders of indwelling sin in believers, with a constant working towards evil.

Thus it is in believers; it is a law even in them, though not to them. Though its rule be broken, its strength weakened and impaired, its root mortified, yet it is a law still of great force and efficacy. There, where it is least felt, it is most powerful. Carnal men, in reference unto spiritual and moral duties, are nothing but this law; they do nothing but from it and by it. It is in them a ruling and prevailing principle of all moral actions, with reference unto a supernatural and eternal end. I shall not consider it in them in whom it hath most power, but in them in whom its power is chiefly discovered and discerned, -- that is, in believers; in the others only in order to the farther conviction and manifestation thereof.

Secondly, The apostle proposeth the way whereby he discovered this law in himself: Ηευρισξηο αρα του νομον, "I find then," or therefore, "a law." He found it. It had been told him there was such a law; it had been preached unto him. This convinced him that there was a law of sin. But it is one thing for a man to know in general that there is a law of sin; another thing for a man to have an experience of the power of this law of sin in himself. It is preached to all; all men that own the Scripture acknowledge it, as being declared therein. But they are but few that know it in themselves; we should else have more complaints of it than we have, and more contendings against it, and less fruits of it in the world. But this is that which the apostle affirms, -- not that the doctrine of it had been preached unto him, but that he found it by experience in himself. "I find a law;" -- "I have experience of its power and efficacy." For a man to find his sickness, and danger thereon from its effects, is another thing than to hear a discourse about a disease from its causes. And this experience is the great preservative of all divine truth in the soul. This it is to know a thing indeed, in reality, to know it for ourselves, when, as we are taught it from the word, so we find it in ourselves. Hence we observe, secondly, Believers have experience of the power and efficacy of indwelling sin. They find it in themselves; they find it as a law. It hath a self evidencing efficacy to them that are alive to discern it. They that find not its power are under its dominion. Whosoever contend against it shall know and find that it is present with them, that it is powerful in them. He shall find the stream to be strong who swims against it, though he who rolls along with it be insensible of it.

Thirdly, The general frame of believers, notwithstanding the inhabitation of this law of sin, is here also expressed. They "would do good." This law is "present:" Τηελοντι εμοι ποιειν το ξηαλον. The habitual inclination of their will is unto good. The law in them is not a law unto them, as it is to unbelievers. They are not wholly obnoxious to its power, nor morally unto its commands. Grace hath the sovereignty in their souls: this gives them a will unto good. They "would do good," that is, always and constantly. 1 John iii. 9, Ποιειν ηαμαρτιαν, "To commit sin," is to make a trade of sin, to make it a man's business to sin. So it is said a believer "doth not commit sin;" and so poiein to kalon, "to do that which is good." To will to do so -- is to have the habitual bent and inclination of the will set on that which is good, -- that is, morally and spiritually good, which is the proper subject treated of: whence is our third observation, -- There is, and there is through grace, kept up in believers a constant and ordinarily prevailing will of doing good, notwithstanding the power and efficacy of indwelling sin to the contrary.

This, in their worst condition, distinguisheth them from unbelievers in their best. The will in unbelievers is under the power of the law of sin. The opposition they make to sin, either in the root or branches of it, is from their light and their consciences; the will of sinning in them is never taken away. Take away all other considerations and hinderances, whereof we shall treat afterward, and they would sin willingly always. Their faint endeavours to answer their convictions are far from a will of doing that which is good. They will plead, indeed, that they would leave their sins if they could, and they would fain do better than they do. But it is the working of their light and convictions, not any spiritual inclination of their wills, which they intend by that expression: for where there is a will of doing good, there is a choice of that which is good for its own excellency's sake, -- because it is desirable and suitable to the soul, and therefore to be preferred before that which is contrary. Now, this is not in any unbelievers. They do not, they cannot, so choose that which is spiritually good, nor is it so excellent or suitable unto any principle that is in them; only they have some desires to attain that end whereunto that which is good doth lead, and to avoid that evil which the neglect of it tends unto. And these also are for the most part so weak and languid in many of them, that they put them not upon any considerable endeavours. Witness that luxury, sloth, worldliness, and security, that the generality of men are even drowned in. But in believers there is a will of doing good, an habitual disposition and inclination in their wills unto that which is spiritually good; and where this is, it is accompanied with answerable effects. The will is the principle of our moral actions; and therefore unto the prevailing disposition thereof will the general course of our actings be suited. Good things will proceed from the good treasures of the heart. Nor can this disposition be evidenced to be in any but by its fruits. A will of doing good, without doing good, is but pretended.

Fourthly, There is yet another thing remaining in these words of the apostle, arising from that respect that the presence of sin hath unto the time and season of duty: "When I would do good," saith he, "evil is present with me."

There are two things to be considered in the will of doing good that is in believers:--

1. There is its habitual residence in them. They have always an habitual inclination of will unto that which is good. And this habitual preparation for good is always present with them; as the apostle expresses it, verse 18 of this chapter.

2. There are especial times and seasons for the exercise of that principle. There is a "When I would do good," -- a season wherein this or that good, this or that duty, is to be performed and accomplished suitably unto the habitual preparation and inclination of the will.

Unto these two there are two things in indwelling sin opposed. To the gracious principle residing in the will, inclining unto that which is spiritually good, it is opposed as it is a law, -- that is, a contrary principle, inclining unto evil, with an aversation from that which is good. Unto the second, or the actual willing of this or that good in particular, unto this "When I would do good," is opposed the presence of this law: "Evil is present with me," -- Εμοι το κακον παρακειται· evil is at hand, and ready to oppose the actual accomplishment of the good aimed at. Whence, fourthly, Indwelling sin is effectually operative in rebelling and inclining to evil, when the will of doing good is in a particular manner active and inclining unto obedience.

And this is the description of him who is a believer and a sinner, as every one who is the former is the latter also. These are the contrary principles and the contrary operations that are in him. The principles are, a will of doing good on the one hand, from grace, and a law of sin on the other. Their adverse actings and operations are insinuated in these expressions: "When I would do good, evil is present with me." And these both are more fully expressed by the apostle, Gal. v. 17, "For the flesh lusteth against the Spirit, and the Spirit against the flesh: and these are contrary the one to the other; so that I cannot do the things that I would."

And here lie the springs of the whole course of our obedience. An acquaintance with these several principles and their actings is the principal part of our wisdom. They are upon the matter, next to the free grace of God in our justification by the blood of Christ, the only things wherein the glory of God and our own souls are concerned. These are the springs of our holiness and our sins, of our joys and troubles, of our refreshments and sorrows. It is, then, all our concernments to be thoroughly acquainted with these things, who intend to walk with God and to glorify him in this world.

And hence we may see what wisdom is required in the guiding and management of our hearts and ways before God. Where the subjects of a ruler are in feuds and oppositions one against another, unless great wisdom be used in the government of the whole, all things will quickly be ruinous in that state. There are these contrary principles in the hearts of believers. And if they labour not to be spiritually wise, how shall they be able to steer their course aright? Many men live in the dark to themselves all their days; whatever else they know, they know not themselves. They know their outward estates, how rich they are, and the condition of their bodies as to health and sickness they are careful to examine; but as to their inward man, and their principles as to God and eternity, they know little or nothing of themselves. Indeed, few labour to grow wise in this matter, few study themselves as they ought, are acquainted with the evils of their own hearts as they ought; on which yet the whole course of their obedience, and consequently of their eternal condition, doth depend. This, therefore, is our wisdom; and it is a needful wisdom, if we have any design to please God, or to avoid that which is a provocation to the eyes of his glory.

We shall find, also, in our inquiry hereinto, what diligence and watchfulness is required unto a Christian conversation. There is a constant enemy unto it in every one's own heart; and what an enemy it is we shall afterward show, for this is our design, to discover him to the uttermost. In the meantime, we may well bewail the woful sloth and negligence that is in the most, even in professors. They live and walk as though they intended to go to heaven hood-winked and asleep, as though they had no enemy to deal withal. Their mistake, therefore, and folly will be fully laid open in our progress.

That which I shall principally fix upon, in reference unto our present design, from this place of the apostle, is that which was first laid down, -- namely, that there is an exceeding efficacy and power in the remainder of indwelling sin in believers, with a constant inclination and working towards evil.

Awake, therefore, all of you in whose hearts is any thing of the ways of God! Your enemy is not only upon you, as on Samson of old, but is in you also. He is at work, by all ways of force and craft, as we shall see. Would you not dishonour God and his gospel; would you not scandalize the saints and ways of God; would you not wound your consciences and endanger your souls; would you not grieve the good and holy Spirit of God, the author of all your comforts; would you keep your garments undefiled, and escape the woful temptations and pollutions of the days wherein we live; would you be preserved from the number of the apostates in these latter days; -- awake to the consideration of this cursed enemy, which is the spring of all these and innumerable other evils, as also of the ruin of all the souls that perish in this world!

Chapter II

Indwelling sin a law -- In what sense it is so called -- What kind of law it is -- An inward effective principle called a law -- The power of sin thence evinced.

That which we have proposed unto consideration is the power and efficacy of indwelling sin. The ways whereby it may be evinced are many. I shall begin with the appellation of it in the place before mentioned. It is a law. "I find a law," saith the apostle. It is because of its power and efficacy that it is so called. So is also the principle of grace in believers the "law of the Spirit of life," as we observed before, Rom. viii. 2; which is the "exceeding greatness of the power of God" in them, Eph. i. 19. Where there is a law there is power.

We shall, therefore, show both what belongs unto it as it is a law in general, and also what is peculiar or proper in it as being such a law as we have described.

There are in general two things attending every law, as such:--

First, Dominion. Rom. vii. 1, "The law hath dominion over a man whilst he liveth:" Κυριευει του αντηροπου· -- "It lordeth it over a man." Where any law takes place, κυριευει, it hath dominion. It is properly the act of a superior, and it belongs to its nature to exact obedience by way of dominion. Now, there is a twofold dominion, as there is a twofold law. There is a moral authoritative dominion over a man, and there is a real effective dominion in a man. The first is an affection of the law of God, the latter of the law of sin. The law of sin hath not in itself a moral dominion, -- it hath not a rightful dominion or authority over any man; but it hath that which is equivalent unto it; whence it is said βασιλευειν, "to reign as a king," Rom. vi. 12, and κυριευειν "to lord it," or have dominion, verse 14, as a law in general is said to have, chap. vii. 1. But because it hath lost its complete dominion in reference unto believers, of whom alone we speak, I shall not insist upon it in this utmost extent of its power. But even in them it is a law still; though not a law unto them, yet, as was said, it is a law in them. And though it have not a complete, and, as it were, a rightful dominion over them, yet it will have a domination as to some things in them. It is still a law, and that in them; so that all its actings are the actings of a law, -- that is, it acts with power, though it have lost its complete power of ruling in them. Though it be weakened, yet its nature is not changed. It is a law still, and therefore powerful. And as its particular workings, which we shall afterward consider, are the ground of this appellation, so the term itself teacheth us in general what we are to expect from it, and what endeavours it will use for dominion, to which it hath been accustomed.

Secondly, A law, as a law, hath an efficacy to provoke those that are obnoxious unto it unto the things that it requireth. A law hath rewards and punishments accompanying of it. These secretly prevail on them to whom they are proposed, though the things commanded be not much desirable. And generally all laws have their efficacy on the minds of men, from the rewards and punishments that are annexed unto them. Nor is this law without this spring of power: it hath its rewards and punishments. The pleasures of sin are the rewards of sin; a reward that most men lose their souls to obtain. By this the law of sin contended in Moses against the law of grace. Heb. xi. 25, 26, "He chose rather to suffer affliction with the people of God, than to enjoy the pleasures of sin for a season; for he looked unto the recompense of reward." The contest was in his mind between the law of sin and the law of grace. The motive on the part of the law of sin, wherewith it sought to draw him over, and wherewith it prevails on the most, was the reward that it proposed unto him, -- namely, that he should have the present enjoyment of the pleasures of sin. By this it contended against the reward annexed unto the law of grace, called "the recompense of reward."

By this sorry reward doth this law keep the world in obedience to its commands; and experience shows us of what power it is to influence the minds of men. It hath also punishments that it threatens men with who labour to cast off its yoke. Whatever evil, trouble, or danger in the world, attends gospel obedience, -- whatever hardship or violence is to be offered to the sensual part of our natures in a strict course of mortification, -- sin makes use of, as if they were punishments attending the neglect of its commands. By these it prevails on the "fearful," who shall have no share in life eternal, Rev. xxi. 8. And it is hard to say by whether of these, its pretended rewards or pretended punishments, it doth most prevail, in whether of them its greatest strength doth lie. By its rewards it enticeth men to sins of commission, as they are called, in ways and actions tending to the satisfaction of its lusts. By its punishments it induceth men to the omitting of duties; a course tending to no less a pernicious event than the former. By which of these the law of sin hath its greatest success in and upon the souls of men is not evident; and that because they are seldom or never separated, but equally take place on the same persons. But this is certain, that by tenders and promises of the pleasures of sin on the one hand, by threats of the deprivation of all sensual contentments and the infliction of temporal evils on the other, it hath an exceeding efficacy on the minds of men, oftentimes on believers themselves. Unless a man be prepared to reject the reasonings that will offer themselves from the one and the other of these, there is no standing before the power of the law. The world falls before them every day. With what deceit and violence they are urged and imposed on the minds of men we shall afterward declare; as also what advantages they have to prevail upon them. Look on the generality of men, and you shall find them wholly by these means at sin's disposal. Do the profits and pleasures of sin lie before them? -- nothing can withhold them from reaching after them. Do difficulties and inconveniences attend the duties of the gospel? -- they will have nothing to do with them; and so are wholly given up to the rule and dominion of this law.

And this light in general we have into the power and efficacy of indwelling sin from the general nature of a law, whereof it is partaker.

We may consider, nextly, what kind of law in particular it is; which will farther evidence that power of it which we are inquiring after. It is not an outward, written, commanding, directing law, but an inbred, working, impelling, urging law. A law proposed unto us is not to be compared, for efficacy, to a law inbred in us. Adam had a law of sin proposed to him in his temptation; but because he had no law of sin inbred and working in him, he might have withstood it. An inbred law must needs be effectual. Let us take an example from that law which is contrary to this law of sin. The law of God was at first inbred and natural unto man; it was concreated with his faculties, and was their rectitude, both in being and operation, in reference to his end of living unto God and glorifying of him. Hence it had an especial power in the whole soul to enable it unto all obedience, yea, and to make all obedience easy and pleasant. Such is the power of an inbred law. And though this law, as to the rule and dominion of it, be now by nature cast out of the soul, yet the remaining sparks of it, because they are inbred, are very powerful and effectual; as the apostle declares, Rom. ii. 14, 15. Afterward God renews this law, and writes it in tables of stone. But what is the efficacy of this law? Will it now, as it is external and proposed unto men, enable them to perform the things that it exacts and requires? Not at all. God knew it would not, unless it were turned to an internal law again; that is, until, of a moral outward rule, it be turned into an inward real principle. Wherefore God makes his law internal again, and implants it on the heart as it was at first, when he intends to give it power to produce obedience in his people: Jer. xxxi. 31-33, "I will put my law in their inward parts, and write it in their hearts." This is that which God fixeth on, as it were, upon a discovery of the insufficiency of an outward law leading men unto obedience. "The written law," saith he, "will not do it; mercies and deliverances from distress will not effect it; trials and afflictions will not accomplish it. "Then," saith the Lord, "will I take another course: I will turn the written law into an internal living principle in their hearts; and that will have such an efficacy as shall assuredly make them my people, and keep them so." Now, such is this law of sin. It is an indwelling law: Rom. vii. 17, "It is sin that dwelleth in me;" verse 20, "Sin that dwelleth in me;" verse 21, "It is present with me;" verse 23, "It is in my members;" -- yea, it is so far in a man, as in some sense it is said to be the man himself; verse 18, "I know that in me (that is, in my flesh) dwelleth no good thing." The flesh, which is the seat and throne of this law, yea, which indeed is this law, is in some sense the man himself, as grace also is the new man. Now, from this consideration of it, that it is an indwelling law inclining ánd moving to sin, as an inward habit or principle, it hath sundry advantages increasing its strength and furthering its power; as,

1. It always abides in the soul, -- it is never absent. The apostle twice useth that expression, "It dwelleth in me." There is its constant residence and habitation. If it came upon the soul only at certain seasons, much obedience might be perfectly accomplished in its absence; yea, and as they deal with usurping tyrants, whom they intend to thrust out of a city, the gates might be sometimes shut against it, that it might not return, -- the soul might fortify itself against it. But the soul is its home; there it dwells, and is no wanderer. Wherever you are, whatever you are about, this law of sin is always in you; in the best that You do, and in the worst. Men little consider what a dangerous companion is always at home with them. When they are in company, when alone, by night or by day, all is one, sin is with them. There is a living coal continually in their houses; which, if it be not looked unto, will fire them, and it may be consume them. Oh, the woful security of poor souls! How little do the most of men think of this inbred enemy that is never from home! How little, for the most part, doth the watchfulness of any professors answer the danger of their state and condition!

2. It is always ready to apply itself to every end and purpose that it serves unto. "It doth not only dwell in me," saith the apostle, "but when I would do good, it is present with me." There is somewhat more in that expression than mere indwelling. An inmate may dwell in a house, and yet not be always meddling with what the good-man of the house hath to do (that so we may keep to the allusion of

indwelling, used by the apostle): but it is so with this law, it doth so dwell in us, as that it will be present with us in every thing we do; yea, oftentimes when with most earnestness we desire to be quit of it, with most violence it will put itself upon us: "When I would do good, it is present with me." Would you pray, would you hear, would you give alms, would you meditate, would you be in any duty acting faith on God and love towards him, would you work righteousness, would you resist temptations, -- this troublesome, perplexing indweller will still more or less put itself upon you and be present with you; so that you cannot perfectly and completely accomplish the thing that is good, as our apostle speaks, verse 18. Sometimes men, by hearkening to their temptations, do stir up, excite, and provoke their lusts; and no wonder if then they find them present and active. But it will be so when with all our endeavours we labour to be free from them. This law of sin "dwelleth" in us; -- that is, it adheres as a depraved principle, unto our minds in darkness and vanity, unto our affections in sensuality, unto our wills in a loathing of and aversation from that which is good; and by some, more, or all of these, is continually putting itself upon us, in inclinations, motions, or suggestions to evil, when we would be most gladly quit of it.

3. It being an indwelling law, it applies itself to its work with great facility and easiness, like "the sin that doth so easily beset us," Heb. xii. 1. It hath a great facility and easiness in the application of itself unto its work; it needs no doors to be opened unto it; it needs no engines to work by. The soul cannot apply itself to any duty of a man but it must be by the exercise of those faculties wherein this law hath its residence. Is the understanding or the mind to be applied unto any thing? -- there it is, in ignorance, darkness, vanity, folly, madness. Is the will to be engaged? -- there it is also, in spiritual deadness, stubbornness, and the roots of obstinacy. Is the heart and affections to be set on work? -- there it is, in inclinations to the world and present things, and sensuality, with proneness to all manner of defilements. Hence it is easy for it to insinuate itself into all that we do, and to hinder all that is good, and to further all sin and wickedness. It hath an intimacy, an inwardness with the soul; and therefore, in all that we do, doth easily beset us. It possesseth those very faculties of the soul whereby we must do what we do, whatever it be, good or evil. Now, all these advantages it hath as it is a law, as an indwelling law, which manifests its power and efficacy. It is always resident in the soul, it puts itself upon all its actings, and that with easiness and facility.

This is that law which the apostle affirms that he found in himself; this is the title that he gives unto the powerful and effectual remainder of indwelling sin even in believers; and these general evidences of its power, from that appellation, have we. Many there are in the world who find not this law in them, -- who, whatever they have been taught in the word, have not a spiritual sense and experience of the power of indwelling sin; and that because they are wholly under the dominion of it. They find not that there is darkness and folly in their minds; because they are darkness itself, and darkness will discover nothing. They find not deadness and an indisposition in their hearts and wills to God; because they are dead wholly in trespasses and sins. They are at peace with their lusts, by being in bondage unto them. And this is the state of most men in the world; which makes them wofully despise all their eternal concernments. Whence is it that men follow and pursue the world with so much greediness, that they neglect heaven, and life, and immortality for it, every day? Whence is it that some pursue their sensuality with delight? -- they will drink and revel, and have their sports, let others say what they please. Whence is it that so many live so unprofitably under the word, that they understand so little of what is spoken unto them, that they practice less of what they understand, and will by no means be stirred up to answer the mind of God in his calls unto them? It is all from this law of sin and the power of it, that rules and bears sway in men, that all these things do proceed; but it is not such persons of whom at present we particularly treat.

From what hath been spoken it will ensue, that, if there be such a law in believers, it is doubtless their duty to find it out, to find it so to be.

The more they find its power, the less they will feel its effects. It will not at all advantage a man to have an hectical distemper and not to discover it, -- a fire lying secretly in his house and not to know it. So much as men find of this law in them, so much they will abhor it and themselves, and no more. Proportionably also to their discovery of it will be their earnestness for grace, nor will it rise higher. All watchfulness and diligence in obedience will be answerable also thereunto. Upon this one hinge, or finding out and experiencing the power and the efficacy of this law of sin, turns the whole course of our lives. Ignorance of it breeds senselessness, carelessness, sloth, security, and pride; all which the Lord's soul abhors. Eruptions into great, open, conscience-wasting, scandalous sins, are from want of a due spiritual consideration of this law. Inquire, then, how it is with your souls. What do you find of this law? what experience have you of its power and efficacy? Do you find it dwelling in you, always present with you, exciting itself, or putting forth its poison with facility and easiness at all times, in all your duties, "when you would do good?" What humiliation, what self-abasement, what intenseness in prayer, what diligence, what watchfulness, doth this call for at your hands! What spiritual wisdom do you stand in need of! What supplies of grace, what assistance of the Holy Ghost, will be hence also discovered! I fear we have few of us a diligence proportionable to our danger.

Chapter III

The seat or subject of the law of sin, the heart -- What meant thereby -- Properties of the heart as possessed by sin, unsearchable, deceitful -- Whence that deceit ariseth -- Improvement of these considerations.

Having manifested indwelling sin, whereof we treat in the remainders of it in believers, to be a law, and evinced in general the power of it from thence, we shall now proceed to give particular instances of its efficacy and advantages from some things that generally relate unto it as such. And these are three:-- First, Its seat and subject; Secondly, Its natural properties; and, Thirdly, Its operations and the manner thereof; -- which principally we aim at and shall attend unto.

First, For the seat and subject of this law of sin, the Scripture everywhere assigns it to be the heart. There indwelling sin keeps its especial residence. It hath invaded and possessed the throne of God himself: Eccles. ix. 3, "Madness is in the heart of men while they live." This is their madness, or the root of all that madness which appears in their lives. Matt. xv. 19, "Out of the heart proceed evil thoughts, murders, adulteries, fornications, thefts, false witness, blasphemies," etc. There are many outward temptations and provocations that befall men, which excite and stir them up unto these evils; but they do but as it were open the vessel, and let out what is laid up and stored in it. The root, rise, and stirring of all these things is in the heart. Temptations and occasions put nothing into a man, but only draw out what was in him before, Hence is that summary description to the whole work and effect of this law of sin, Gen. vi. 5, "Every imagination of the thoughts of man's heart is only evil continually;" so also chap. viii. 21. The whole work of the law of sin, from its first rise, its first coining of actual sin, is here described. And its seat, its work-house, is said to be the heart; and so it is called by our Saviour "The evil treasure of the heart:" Luke vi. 45, "An evil man, out of the evil treasure of his heart, bringeth forth evil things." This treasure is the prevailing principle of moral actions that is in men. So, in the beginning of the verse, our Saviour calls grace "The good treasure of the heart" of a good man, whence that which is good doth proceed. It is a principle constantly and abundantly inciting and stirring up unto, and consequently bringing forth, actions conformable and like unto it, of the same kind and nature with itself. And it is also called a treasure for its abundance. It will never be exhausted; it is not wasted by men's spending on it; yea, the more lavish men are of this stock, the more they draw out of this treasure, the more it grows and abounds! As men do not spend their grace, but increase it, by its exercise, no more do they their indwelling sin. The more men exercise their grace in duties of obedience, the more it is strengthened and increased; and the more men exert and put forth the fruits of their lust, the more is that enraged and increased in them; -- it feeds upon itself, swallows up its own poison, and grows thereby. The more men sin, the more are they inclined unto sin. It is from the deceitfulness of this law of sin, whereof we shall speak afterward at large, that men persuade themselves that by this or that particular sin they shall so satisfy their lusts as that they shall need to sin no more. Every sin increaseth the principle, and fortifieth the habit of sinning. It is an evil treasure, that increaseth by doing evil. And where doth this treasure lie? It is in the heart; there it is laid up, there it is kept in safety. All the men in the world, all the angels in heaven, cannot dispossess a man of this treasure, it is so safely stored in the heart.

The heart in the Scripture is variously used; sometimes for the mind and understanding, sometimes for the will, sometimes for the affections, sometimes for the conscience, sometimes for the whole soul. Generally, it denotes the whole soul of man and all the faculties of it, not absolutely, but as they are all one principle of moral operations, as they all concur in our doing good or evil. The mind, as it inquireth, discerneth, and judgeth what is to be done, what refused; the will, as it chooseth or refuseth and avoids; the affections, as they like or dislike, cleave to or have an aversation from, that which is proposed to them; the conscience, as it warns and determines, -- are all together called the heart. And in this sense it is that we say the seat and subject of this law of sin is the heart of man. Only, we may add that the Scripture, speaking of the heart as the principle of men's good or evil actions, doth usually insinuate together with it two things belonging unto the manner of their performance:--

1. A suitableness and pleasingness unto the soul in the things that are done. When men take delight and are pleased in and with what they do, they are said to do it heartily, with their whole hearts. Thus, when God himself blesseth his people in love and delight, he says the doth it "with his whole

heart, and with his whole soul," Jer. xxxii. 41.

2. Resolution and constancy in such actions. And this also is denoted in the metaphorical expression before used of a treasure, from whence men do constantly take out the things which either they stand in need of or do intend to use.

This is the subject, the seat, the dwelling-place of this law of sin, -- the heart; as it is the entire principle of moral operations, of doing good or evil, as out of it proceed good or evil. Here dwells our enemy; this is the fort, the citadel of this tyrant, where it maintains a rebellion against God all our days. Sometimes it hath more strength, and consequently more success; sometimes less of the one and of the other; but it is always in rebellion whilst we live.

That we may in our passage take a little view of the strength and power of sin from this seat and subject of it, we may consider one or two properties of the heart that exceedingly contribute thereunto. It is like an enemy in war, whose strength and power lie not only in his numbers and force of men or arms, but also in the unconquerable forts that he doth possess. And such is the heart to this enemy of God and our souls; as will appear from the properties of it, whereof one or two shall be mentioned.

1. It is unsearchable: Jer. xvii. 9, 10, "Who can know the heart? I the Lord search it." The heart of man is pervious to God only; hence he takes the honour of searching the heart to be as peculiar to himself, and as fully declaring him to be God, as any other glorious attribute of his nature. We know not the hearts of one another; we know not our own hearts as we ought. Many there are that know not their hearts as to their general bent and disposition, whether it be good or bad, sincere and sound, or corrupt and naught; but no one knows all the secret intrigues, the windings and turnings, the actings and aversations of his own heart. Hath any one the perfect measure of his own light and darkness? Can any one know what actings of choosing or aversation his will will bring forth, upon the proposal of that endless variety of objects that it is to be exercised with? Can any one traverse the various mutability of his afflictions? Do the secret springs of acting and refusing in the soul lie before the eyes of any man? Doth any one know what will be the motions of the mind or will in such and such conjunctions of things, such a suiting of objects, such a pretension of reasonings, such an appearance of things desirable? All in heaven and earth, but the infinite, all-seeing God, are utterly ignorant of these things. In this unsearchable heart dwells the law of sin; and much of its security, and consequently of its strength, lies in this, that it is past our finding out. We fight with an enemy whose secret strength we cannot discover, whom we cannot follow into its retirements. Hence, oftentimes, when we are ready to think sin quite ruined, after a while we find it was but out of sight. It hath coverts and retreats in an unsearchable heart, whither we cannot pursue it. The soul may persuade itself all is well, when sin may be safe in the hidden darkness of the mind, which it is impossible that he should look into; for whatever makes manifest is light. It may suppose the will of sinning is utterly taken away, when yet there is an unsearchable reserve for a more suitable object, a more vigorous temptation, than at present it is tried withal. Hath a man had a contest with any lust, and a blessed victory over it by the Holy Ghost as to that present trial? -- when he thinks it is utterly expelled, he ere long finds that it was but retired out of sight. It can lie so close in the mind's darkness, in the will's indisposition, in the disorder and carnality of the affections, that no eye can discover it. The best of our wisdom is but to watch its first appearances, to catch its first under-earth heavings and workings, and to set ourselves in opposition to them; for to follow it into the secret corners of the heart, that we cannot do. It is true, there is yet a relief in this case, -- namely, that he to whom the work of destroying the law of sin and body of death in us is principally committed, namely, the Holy Ghost, comes with his axe to the very root; neither is there any thing in an unsearchable heart that is not "naked and open unto him," Heb. iv. 13; but we in a way of duty may hence see what an enemy we have to deal withal.

2. As it is unsearchable, so it is deceitful, as in the place above mentioned: "It is deceitful above all things," -- incomparably so. There is great deceit in the dealings of men in the world; great deceit in their counsels and contrivances in reference to their affairs, private and public; great deceit in their words and actings: the world is full of deceit and fraud. But all this is nothing to the deceit that is in man's heart towards himself; for that is the meaning of the expression in this place, and not towards others. Now, incomparable deceitfulness, added to unsearchableness, gives a great addition and increase of strength to the law of sin, upon the account of its seat and subject. I speak not yet of the deceitfulness of sin itself, but the deceitfulness of the heart where it is seated. Prov. xxvi. 25, "There are seven abominations in the heart;" that is, not only many, but an absolute complete number, as seven denotes. And they are such abominations as consist in deceitfulness; so the caution foregoing insinuates, "Trust him not:" for it is only deceit that should make us not to trust in that degree and measure which the object is capable of.

Now, this deceitfulness of the heart, whereby it is exceedingly advantaged in its harbouring of sin, lies chiefly in these two things:--

(1.) That it abounds in contradictions, so that it is not to be found and dealt withal according to any constant rule and way of procedure. There are some men that have much of this, from their natural constitution, or from other causes, in their conversation. They seem to be made up of contradictions;

sometimes to be very wise in their affairs, sometimes very foolish; very open, and very reserved; very facile, and very obstinate; very easy to be entreated, and very revengeful, -- all in a remarkable height. This is generally accounted a bad character, and is seldom found but when it proceeds from some notable predominant lust. But, in general, in respect of moral good or evil, duty or sin, it is so with the heart of every man, -- flaming hot, and key cold; weak, and yet stubborn; obstinate, and facile. The frame of the heart is ready to contradict itself every moment. Now you would think you had it all for such a frame, such a way; anon it is quite otherwise: so that none know what to expect from it. The rise of this is the disorder that is brought upon all its faculties by sin. God created them all in a perfect harmony and union. The mind and reason were in perfect subjection and subordination to God and his will; the will answered, in its choice of good, the discovery made of it by the mind; the affections constantly and evenly followed the understanding and will. The mind's subjection to God was the spring of the orderly and harmonious motion of the soul and all the wheels in it. That being disturbed by sin, the rest of the faculties move cross and contrary one to another. The will chooseth not the good which the mind discovers; the affections delight not in that which the will chooseth; but all jar and interfere, cross and rebel against each other. This we have got by our falling from God. Hence sometimes the will leads, the judgment follows. Yea, commonly the affections, that should attend upon all, get the sovereignty, and draw the whole soul captive after them. And hence it is, as I said, that the heart is made up of so many contradictions in its actings. Sometimes the mind retains its sovereignty, and the affections are in subjection, and the will ready for its duty. This puts a good face upon things. Immediately the rebellion of the affections or the obstinacy of the will takes place and prevails, and the whole scene is changed. This, I say, makes the heart deceitful above all things: it agrees not at all in itself, is not constant to itself, hath no order that it is constant unto, is under no certain conduct that is stable; but, if I may so say, hath a rotation in itself, where ofttimes the feet lead and guide the whole.

(2.) Its deceit lies in its full promisings upon the first appearance of things; and this also proceeds from the same principle with the former. Sometimes the affections are touched and wrought upon; the whole heart appears in a fair frame; all promiseth to be well. Within a while the whole frame is changed; the mind was not at all affected or turned; the affections a little acted their parts and are gone off, and all the fair promises of the heart are departed with them. Now, add this deceitfulness to the unsearchableness before mentioned, and we shall find that at least the difficulty of dealing effectually with sin in its seat and throne will be exceedingly increased. A deceiving and a deceived heart, who can deal with it? -- especially considering that the heart employs all its deceits unto the service of sin, contributes them all to its furtherance. All the disorder that is in the heart, all its false promises and fair appearances, promote the interest and advantages of sin. Hence God cautions the people to look to it, lest their own hearts should entice and deceive them.

Who can mention the treacheries and deceits that lie in the heart of man? It is not for nothing that the Holy Ghost so expresseth it, "It is deceitful above all things," -- uncertain in what it doth, and false in what it promiseth. And hence moreover it is, amongst other causes, that, in the pursuit of our war against sin, we have not only the old work to go over and over, but new work still while we live in this world, still new stratagems and wiles to deal withal; as the manner will be where unsearchableness and deceitfulness are to be contended with.

There are many other properties of this seat and subject of the law of sin which might be insisted on to the same end and purpose, but that would too far divert us from our particular design, and therefore I shall pass these over with sonic few considerations:--

First, Never let us reckon that our work in contending against sin, in crucifying, mortifying, and subduing of it, is at an end. The place of its habitation is unsearchable; and when we may think that we have thoroughly won the field, there is still some reserve remaining that we saw not, that we knew not of. Many conquerors have been ruined by their carelessness after a victory, and many have been spiritually wounded after great successes against this enemy. David was so; his great surprisal into sin was after a long profession, manifold experiences of God, and watchful keeping himself from his iniquity. And hence, in part, hath it come to pass that the profession of many hath declined in their old age or riper time; which must more distinctly be spoken to afterward. They have given over the work of mortifying of sin before their work was at an end. There is no way for us to pursue sin in its unsearchable habitation but by being endless in our pursuit. And that command of the apostle which we have, Col. iii. 5, on this account is as necessary for them to observe who are towards the end of their race, as those that are but at the beginning of it: "Mortify therefore your members which are upon the earth;" be always doing it whilst you live in this world. It is true, great ground is obtained when the work is vigorously and constantly carried on; sin is much weakened, so that the soul presseth forwards towards perfection: but yet the work must be endless; I mean, whilst we are in this world. If we give over, we shall quickly see this enemy exerting itself with new strength and vigour. It may be under some great affliction, it may be in some eminent enjoyment of God, in the sense of the sweetness of blessed communion with Christ, we have been ready to say that there was an end of sin, that it was dead and gone for ever; but have we not found the contrary by experience? hath it not manifested that it was only retired into some unsearchable recesses of the heart, as to its in-being and nature, though, it may be, greatly weakened in its power? Let us, then, reckon on it, that there is no way to have our work done but by always doing of it; and he who dies fighting in this warfare dies assuredly a conqueror.

Secondly, Hath it its residence in that which is various, inconstant, deceitful above all things? This calls for perpetual watchfulness against it. An open enemy, that deals by violence only, always gives some respite. You know where to have him and what he is doing, so as that sometimes you may sleep quietly without fear. But against adversaries that deal by deceit and treachery (which are long swords, and reach at the greatest distance) nothing will give security but perpetual watchfulness. It is impossible we should in this case be too jealous, doubtful, suspicious, or watchful. The heart hath a thousand wiles and deceits; and if we are in the least off from our watch, we may, be sure to be surprised. Hence are those reiterated commands and cautions given for watching, for being circumspect, diligent, careful, and the like. There is no living for them who have to deal with an enemy deceitful above all things, unless they persist in such a frame. All cautions that are given in this case are necessary, especially that, "Remember not to believe." Doth the heart promise fair? -- rest not on it, but say to the Lord Christ, "Lord, do thou undertake for me." Doth the sun shine fair in the morning? -- reckon not therefore on a fair day; the clouds may arise and fall. Though the morning give a fair appearance of serenity and peace, turbulent affections may arise, and cloud the soul with sin and darkness.

Thirdly then, commit the whole matter with all care and diligence unto Him who can search the heart to the uttermost, and knows how to prevent all its treacheries and deceits. In the firings before mentioned lies our duty, but here lies our safety. There is no treacherous corner in our hearts but he can search it to the uttermost; there is no deceit in them but he can disappoint it. This course David takes, Psalm cxxxix. After he had set forth the omnipresence of God and his omniscience, verses 1-10, he makes improvement of it: verse 23, "Search me, O God, and try me." As if he had said, "It is but a little that I know of my deceitful heart, only I would be sincere; I would not have reserves for sin retained therein. Wherefore, do thou, who art present with my heart, who knowest my thoughts long before, undertake this work, perform it thoroughly, for thou alone art able so to do."

There are yet other arguments for the evidencing of the power and strength of indwelling sin, from whence it is termed a "law," which we must pass through, according to the order wherein before we laid them down.

Chapter IV

Indwelling sin enmity against God -- Thence its power -- Admits of no peace nor rest -- Is against God himself -- Acts itself in aversation from God, and propensity to evil -- Is universal -- To all of God -- In all of the soul -- Constant.

Secondly. We have seen the seat and subject of this law of sin. In the next place we might take a view of its nature in general, which also will manifest its power and efficacy; but this I shall not enlarge upon, it being not my business to declare the nature of indwelling sin: it hath also been done by others. I shall therefore only, in reference unto our special design in hand, consider one property of it that belongs unto its nature, and this always, wherever it is. And this is that which is expressed by the apostle, Rom. viii. 7, "The carnal mind is enmity against God." That which is here called πηρονεμα τες σαρκος, "the wisdom of the flesh," is the same with "the law of sin" which we insist on. And what says he hereof? Why, it is εξητηρα εις Τηεον, -- "enmity against God." It is not only an enemy, -- for so possibly some reconciliation of it unto God might be made, -- but it is enmity itself, and so not capable of accepting any terms of peace. Enemies may be reconciled, but enmity cannot; yea, the only way to reconcile enemies is to destroy the enmity. So the apostle in another case tells us, Rom. v. 10, "We, who were enemies, are reconciled to God;" that is, a work compassed and brought about by the blood of Christ, -- the reconciling of the greatest enemies. But when he comes to speak of enmity, there is no way for it, but it must be abolished and destroyed: Eph. ii. 15, "Having abolished in his flesh the enmity." There is no way to deal with any enmity whatever but by its abolition or destruction.

And this also lies in it as it is enmity, that every part and parcel of it, if we may so speak, the least degree of it that can possibly remain in any one, whilst and where there is any thing of its nature, is enmity still. It may not be so effectual and powerful in operation as where it hath more life and vigour, but it is enmity still As every drop of poison is poison, and will infect, and every spark of fire is fire, and will burn; so is every thing of the law of sin, the last, the least of it, -- it is enmity, it will poison, it will burn. That which is any thing in the abstract is still so whilst it hath any being at all. Our apostle, who may well be supposed to have made as great a progress in the subduing of it as any one on the earth, yet after all cries out for deliverance, as from an irreconcilable enemy, Rom. vii. 24. The meanest acting, the meanest and most imperceptible working of it, is the acting and working of enmity. Mortification abates of its force, but doth not change its nature. Grace changeth the nature of man, but nothing can change the nature of sin. Whatever effect be wrought upon it, there is no effect wrought in it, but that it is enmity still, sin still. This then, by it, is our state and condition:-- "God is love," 1 John iv. 8. He is so in himself, eternally excellent, and desirable above all. He is so to us, he is so in the blood of his Son and in all the inexpressible fruits of it, by which we are what we are, and wherein all our future hopes and expectations are wrapped up. Against this God we carry about us an enmity all our days; an enmity that hath this from its nature, that it is incapable of cure or reconciliation. Destroyed it may be, it shall be, but cured it cannot be. If a man hath an enemy to deal withal that is too mighty for him, as David had with Saul, he may take the course that he did, -- consider what it is that provoked his enemy against him, and so address himself to remove the cause and make up his peace: 1 Sam. xxvi. 19, "If the Lord have stirred thee up against me, let him accept an offering: but if they be the children of men, cursed be they before the Lord." Come it from God or man, there is yet hope of peace. But when a man hath enmity itself to deal withal, nothing is to be expected but continual fighting, to the destruction of the one party. If it be not overcome and destroyed, it will overcome and destroy the soul.

And herein lies no small part of its power, which we are inquiring after, -- it can admit of no terms of peace, of no composition. There may be a composition where there is no reconciliation, -- there may be a truce where there is no peace; but with this enemy we can obtain neither the one nor the other. It is never quiet, conquering nor conquered; which was the only kind of enemy that the famous warrior complained of old. It is in vain for a man to have any expectation of rest from his lust but by its death; of absolute freedom but by his own. Some, in the tumultuating of their corruptions, seek for quietness by labouring to satisfy them, "making provision for the flesh, to fulfil the lusts thereof," as the apostle speaks, Rom. xiii. 14. This is to aslake fire by wood and oil. As all the fuel in the world, all the fabric of the creation that is combustible, being cast into the fire, will not at all satisfy it, but increase it; so is it with satisfaction given to sin by sinning, -- it doth but inflame and increase. If a man will part with some of his goods unto an enemy, it may satisfy him; but enmity will have all, and is not one whit the more satisfied than if he had received nothing at all, -- like the lean cattle that were never the less hungry for having devoured the fat. You cannot bargain with the fire to take but so much of your houses; ye have no way but to quench it. It is in this case as it is in the contest between a wise man and a fool: Prov. xxix. 9, "Whether he rage or laugh, there is no rest." Whatever frame or temper he be in, his importunate folly makes him troublesome. It is so with this indwelling sin: whether it violently tumultuate, as it will do on provocations and temptations, it will be outrageous in the soul; or whether it seem to be pleased and contented, to be satisfied, all is one, there is no peace, no rest to be had with it or by it. Had it, then, been of any other nature, some other way might have been fixed on; but seeing it consists in enmity, all the relief the soul hath must lie in its ruin.

Secondly, It is not only said to be "enmity," but it is said to be "enmity against God." It hath chosen a great enemy indeed. It is in sundry places proposed as our enemy: 1 Pet. ii. 11, "Abstain from fleshly lusts, which war against the soul;" they are enemies to the soul, that is, to ourselves. Sometimes as an enemy to the Spirit that is in us: "The flesh lusteth" or fighteth "against the Spirit," Gal. v. 17. It fights against the Spirit, or the spiritual principle that is in us, to conquer it; it fights against our souls, to destroy them. It hath special ends and designs against our souls, and against the principle of grace that is in us; but its proper formal object is God: it is "enmity against God." It is its work to oppose grace; it is a consequent of its work to oppose our souls, which follows upon what it doth more than what it intends; but its nature and formal design is to oppose God, -- God as the lawgiver, God as holy, God as the author of the gospel, a way of salvation by grace, and not by works, -- this is the direct object of the law of sin. Why doth it oppose duty, so that the good we would do we do not, either as to matter or manner? Why doth it render the soul carnal, indisposed, unbelieving, unspiritual, weary, wandering? It is because of its enmity to God, whom the soul aims to have communion withal in duty. It hath, as it were, that command from Satan which the Assyrians had from their king: "Fight neither with small nor great, save only with the king of Israel," 1 Kings xxii. 31. It is neither great nor small, but God himself, the King of Israel, that sin sets itself against. There lies the secret formal reason of all its opposition to good, -- even because it relates unto God. May a road, a trade, a way of duties be set up, where communion with God is not aimed at, but only the duty itself, as is the manner of men in most of their superstitious worship, the opposition that will lie against it from the law of sin will be very weak, easy, and gentle. Or, as the Assyrians, because of his show of a king, assaulted Jehoshaphat, but when they found that it was not Ahab, they turned back from pursuing of him; so because there is a show and appearance of the worship of God, sin may make head against it at first, but when the duty cries out in the heart that indeed God is not there, sin turns away to seek out its proper enemy, even God himself, elsewhere. And hence do many poor creatures spend their days in dismal, tiring superstitions, without any great reluctancy from within, when others cannot be suffered freely to watch with Christ in a spiritual manner one hour. And it is no wonder that men fight with carnal weapons for their superstitious worship without, when they have no fighting against it within; for God is not in it, and the law of sin makes not opposition to any duty, but to God in every duty. This is our state and condition:-- All the opposition that ariseth in us unto any thing that is spiritually good, whether it be from darkness in the mind, or aversation in the will, or sloth in the affections, all the secret arguings and reasonings that are in the soul in pursuit of them, the direct object of them is God himself. The enmity lies against him; which consideration surely should influence us to a perpetual, constant watchfulness over ourselves.

It is thus also in respect of all propensity unto sin, as well as aversation from God. It is God himself that is aimed at. It is true, the pleasures, the wages of sin, do greatly influence the sensual, carnal affections of men: but it is the holiness and authority of God that sin itself rises up against; it hates the yoke of the Lord. "Thou hast been weary of me," saith God to sinners; and that during their performance of abundance of duties. Every act of sin is a fruit of being weary of God. Thus Job tells us what lies at the bottom in the heart of sinners: "They say to God, Depart from us;" -- it is enmity against him and aversation from him. Here lies the formal nature of every sin:-- it is an opposition to God, a casting off his yoke, a breaking off the dependence which the creature ought to have on the Creator. And the apostle, Rom. viii. 7, gives the reason why he affirms "the carnal mind to be enmity against God," -- namely, "because it is not subject to the will of God, nor indeed can be." It never is, nor will, nor can be subject to God, its whole nature consisting in an opposition to him. The soul wherein it is may be subject to the law of God; but this law of sin sets up in contrariety unto it, and will not be in subjection.

To manifest a little farther the power of this law of sin from this property of its nature, that it is enmity against God, one or two inseparable adjuncts of it may be considered, which will farther evince it:--

1. It is universal. Some contentions are bounded unto some particular concernments; this is about one thing, that about another. It is not so here; the enmity is absolute and universal, as are all enmities that are grounded in the nature of the things themselves. Such enmity is against the whole kind of that

which is its object. Such is this enmity: for, (1.) It is universal to all of God; and, (2.) It is universal in all of the soul.

(1.) It is universal to all of God. If there were any thing of God, his nature, properties, his mind or will, his law or gospel, any duty of obedience to him, of communion with him, that sin had not an enmity against, the soul might have a constant shelter and retreat within itself, by applying itself to that of God, to that of duty towards him, to that of communion with him, that sin would make no opposition against. But the enmity lies against God, and all of God, and every thing wherein or whereby we have to do with him. It is not subject to the law, nor any part or parcel, word or tittle of the law. Whatever is opposite to any thing as such, is opposite unto all of it. Sin is enmity to God as God, and therefore to all of God. Not his goodness, not his holiness, not his mercy, not his grace, not his promises: there is not any thing of him which it doth not make head against; nor any duty, private, public, in the heart, in external works, which it opposeth not. And the nearer (if I may so say) any thing is to God, the greater is its enmity unto it. The more of spirituality and holiness is in any thing, the greater is its enmity. That which hath most of God hath most of its opposition. Concerning them in whom this law is most predominant, God says, "Ye have set at nought all my counsel, and would none of my reproof," Prov. i. 25. Not this or that part of God's counsel, his mind, or will is opposed, but all his counsel; whatever he calleth for or guideth unto, in every particular of it, all is set at nought, and nothing of his reproof attended unto. A man would think it not very strange that sin should maintain an enmity against God in his law, which comes to judge it, to condemn it; but it raiseth a greater enmity against him in his gospel, wherein he tenders mercy and pardon as a deliverance from it; and that merely because more of the glorious properties of God's nature, more of his excellencies and condescension, is manifested therein than in the other.

(2.) It is universal in all of the soul. Would this law of sin have contented itself to have subdued any one faculty of the soul, -- would it have left any one at liberty, any one affection free from its yoke and bondage, -- it might possibly have been with more ease opposed or subdued. But when Christ comes with his spiritual power upon the soul, to conquer it to himself, he hath no quiet landing-place. He can set foot on no ground but what he must fight for and conquer. Not the mind, not an affection, not the will, but all is secured against him. And when grace hath made its entrance, yet sin will dwell in all its coasts. Were any thing in the soul at perfect freedom and liberty, there a stand might be made to drive it from all the rest of its holds; but it is universal, and wars in the whole soul. The mind hath its own darkness and vanity to wrestle with, -- the will its own stubbornness, obstinacy, and perverseness; every affection its own frowardness and aversation from God, and its sensuality, to deal withal: so that one cannot yield relief unto another as they ought; they have, as it were, their hands full at home. Hence it is that our knowledge is imperfect, our obedience weak, love not unmixed, fear not pure, delight not free and noble. But I must not insist on these particulars, or I could abundantly show how diffused this principle of enmity against God is through the whole soul.

2. Hereunto might be added its constancy. It is constant unto itself, it wavers not, it hath no thoughts of yielding or giving over, notwithstanding the powerful opposition that is made unto it both by the law and gospel; as afterward shall be showed.

This, then, is a third evidence of the power of sin, taken from its nature and properties, wherein I have fixed but On one instance for its illustration, -- namely, that it is "enmity against God," and that universal and constant. Should we eater upon a full description of it, it would require more space and time than we have allotted to this whole subject. What hath been delivered might give us a little sense of it, if it be the will of God, and stir us up unto watchfulness. What can be of a more sad consideration than that we should carry about us constantly that which is enmity against God, and that not in this or that particular, but in all that he is and in all wherein he hath revealed himself? I cannot say it is well with them who find it not. It is well with them, indeed, in whom it is weakened, and the power of it abated; but yet, for them who say it is not in them, they do but deceive themselves, and there is no truth in them.

Chapter V

Nature of sin farther discovered as it is enmity against God -- Its aversation from all good opened -- Means to prevent the effects of it prescribed.

Thirdly. We have considered somewhat of the nature of indwelling sin, not absolutely, but in reference unto the discovery of its power; but this more clearly evidenceth itself in its actings and operations. Power is an act of life, and operation is the only discoverer of life. We know not that any thing lives but by the effects and works of life; and great and strong operations discover a powerful and vigorous life. Such are the operations of this law of sin, which are all demonstrations of its power.

That which we have declared concerning its nature is, that it consists in enmity. Now, there are two general heads of the working or operation of enmity, -- first, Aversation; secondly, Opposition.

First, Aversation. Our Saviour, describing the enmity that was between himself and the teachers of the Jews, by the effects of it, saith in the prophet, "My soul loathed them, and their soul also abhorred me," Zech. xi. 8. Where there is mutual enmity, there is mutual aversation, loathing, and abomination. So it was between the Jews and the Samaritans, -- they were enemies, and abhorred one another; as John iv. 9.

Secondly, Opposition, or contending against one another, is the next product of enmity. Isa. lxiii. 10, "He was turned to be their enemy, and he fought against them;" speaking of God towards the people. Where there is enmity, there will be fighting; it is the proper and natural product of it. Now, both these effects are found in this law of sin:--

First, For aversation. There is an aversation in it unto God and every thing of God, as we have in part discovered in handling the enmity itself, and so shall not need much to insist upon it again. All indisposition unto duty, wherein communion with God is to be obtained; all weariness of duty; all carnality, or formality unto duty, -- it all springs from this root. The wise man cautions us against this evil: Eccles. v. 1, "Keep thy foot when thou goest to the house of God;" -- "Hast thou any spiritual duty to perform, and dost thou design the attaining of any communion with God? look to thyself, take care of thy affections; they will be gadding and wandering, and that from their aversation to what thou hast in hand." There is not any good that we would do wherein we may not find this aversation exercising itself. "When I would do good, evil is present with me;" -- "At any time, at all times, when I would do any thing that is spiritually good, it is present, -- that is, to hinder me, to obstruct me in my duty; because it abhors and loathes the thing which I have in hand, it will keep me off from it if it be possible." In them in whom it prevails, it comes at length unto that frame which is expressed, Ezek. xxxiii. 31. It will allow an outward, bodily presence unto the worship of God, wherein it is not concerned, but it keeps the heart quite away.

It may be some will pretend they find it not so in themselves, but they have freedom and liberty in and unto all the duties of obedience that they attend unto. But I fear this pretended liberty will be found, upon examination, to arise from one or both of these causes:-- First, Ignorance of the true state and condition of their own souls, of their inward man and its actings towards God. They know not how it is with them, and therefore are not to be believed in what they report. They are in the dark, and neither know what they do nor whither they are going. It is like the Pharisee knew little of this matter; which made him boast of his duties to God himself. Or, secondly, It may be, whatever duties of worship or obedience such persons perform, they may, through want of faith and an interest in Christ, have no communion with them; and if so, sin will make but little opposition unto them therein. We speak of them whose hearts are exercised with these things. And if under their complaints of them, and groanings for deliverance from them, others cry out unto them, "Stand off, we are holier than ye," they are willing to bear their condition, as knowing that their way may be safe, though it be troublesome; and being willing to see their own dangers, that they may avoid the ruin which others fall into.

Let us, then, a little consider this aversation in such acts of obedience as wherein there is no concernment but that of God and the soul. In public duties there may be a mixture of other considerations; they may be so influenced by custom and necessity, that a right judgment cannot from them be made of this matter. But let us take into consideration the duties of retirement, as private prayer and meditation, and the like; or else extraordinary duties, or duties to be performed in an extraordinary manner:--

1. In these will this aversation and loathing oftentimes discover itself in the affections. A secret striving will be in them about close and cordial dealing with God, unless the hand of God in his Spirit be high and strong upon his soul. Even when convictions, sense of duty, dear and real esteem of God and communion with him, have carried the soul into its closet, yet if there be not the vigour and power of a spiritual life constantly at work, there will be a secret loathness in them unto duty; yea, sometimes there will be a violent inclination to the contrary, so that the soul had rather do any thing, embrace any diversion, though it wound itself thereby, than vigorously apply itself unto that which in the inward man it breathes after. It is weary before it begins, and says, "When will the work be over?" Here God and the soul are immediately concerned; and it is a great conquest to do what we would, though we come exceedingly short of what we should do.

2. It discovers itself in the mind also. When we address ourselves to God in Christ, we are, as Job speaks, to "fill our mouths with arguments," Job xxiii. 4, that we may be able to plead with him, as he calls upon us to do: Isa. xliii. 26, "Put me in remembrance; let us plead together." Whence the church is called upon to take unto itself words or arguments in going to God, Hos. xiv. 2. The sum is, that the mind should be furnished with the considerations that are prevailing with God, and be in readiness to plead them, and to manage them in the most spiritual manner, to the best advantage. Now, is there no difficulty to get the mind into such a frame as to lay out itself to the utmost in this work; to be clear, steady, and constant in its duty; to draw out and make use of its stores and furniture of promises and experiences? It starts, wanders, flags, -- all from this secret aversation unto communion with God, which proceeds from the law of indwelling sin. Some complain that they can make no work of meditation, -- they cannot bend their minds unto it. I confess there may be a great cause of this in their want of a right understanding of the duty itself, and of the ways of managing the soul in it; which therefore I shall a little speak to afterward: but yet this secret enmity hath its hand in the loss they are at also, and that both in their minds and in their affections. Others are forced to live in family and public duties, they find such little benefit and success in private. And here hath been the beginning of the apostasy of many professors, and the source of many foolish, sensual opinions. Finding this aversation in their minds and affections from closeness and constancy in private spiritual duties, not knowing how to conquer and prevail against these difficulties through Him who enables us, they have at first been subdued to a neglect of them, first partial, then total, until, having lost all conscience of them, they have had a door opened unto all sin and licentiousness, and so to a full and utter apostasy. I am persuaded there are very few that apostatize from a profession of any continuance, such as our days abound withal, but their door of entrance into the folly of backsliding was either some great and notorious sin that blooded their consciences, tainted their affections, and intercepted all delight of having any thing more to do with God; or else it was a course of neglect in private duties, arising from a weariness of contending against that powerful aversation which they found in themselves unto them. And this also, through the craft of Satan, hath been improved into many foolish and sensual opinions of living unto God without and above any duties of communion. And we find, that after men have for a while choked and blinded their consciences with this pretence, cursed wickedness or sensuality hath been the end of their folly. And the reason of all this is, that the giving way to the law of sin in the least is the giving strength unto it. To let it alone, is to let it grow; not to conquer it, is to be conquered by it.

As it is in respect of private, so it is also in respect of public duties, that have any thing extraordinary in them. What strivings, strugglings, and pleadings are there in the heart about them, especially against the spirituality of them! Yea, in and under them, will not the mind and affections sometimes be entangled with things uncouth, new, and strange unto them, such as, at the time of the least serious business, a man would not deign to take into his thoughts? But if the least loose, liberty, or advantage be given unto indwelling sin, if it be not perpetually watched over, it will work to a strange and unexpected issue. In brief, let the soul unclothe any duty whatever, private or public, any thing that is called good, -- let a man divest it of all outward respects which secretly insinuate themselves into the mind and give it some complacency in what it is about, but do not render it acceptable unto God -- and he shall assuredly find somewhat of the power and some of the effects of this aversation. It begins in loathness and indisposition; goes on with entangling the mind and affections with other things; and will end, if not prevented, in weariness of God, which he complains of in his people, Isa. xliii. 22. They ceased from duty because they were "weary of God."

But this instance being of great importance unto professors in their walking with God, we must not pass it over without some intimations of directions for them in their contending against it and opposition to it. Only this must be premised, that I am not giving directions for the mortifying of indwelling sin in general, -- which is to be done alone by the Spirit of Christ, by virtue of our union with him, Rom. viii. 13, -- but only of our particular duty with reference unto this especial evil or effect of indwelling sin that we have a little insisted on, or what in this single case the wisdom of faith seems to direct unto and call for; which will be our way and course in our process upon the consideration of other effects of it.

1. The great means to prevent the fruits and effects of this aversation is the constant keeping of the soul in a universally holy frame. As this weakens the whole law of sin, so answerably all its properties,

and particularly this aversation. It is this frame only that will enable us to say with the Psalmist, Ps. lvii. 7, "My heart is fixed, O God, my heart is fixed." It is utterly impossible to keep the heart in a prevailing holy frame in any one duty, unless it be so in and unto all and every one. If sin-entanglements get hold in any one thing, they will put themselves upon the soul in every thing. -- A constant, even frame and temper in all duties, in all ways, is the only preservative for any one way. Let not him who is neglectful in public persuade himself that all will be clear and easy in private, or on the contrary. There is a harmony in obedience; break but one part, and you interrupt the whole. Our wounds in particular arise generally from negligence as to the whole course; so David informs us, Ps. cxix. 6, "Then shall I not be ashamed, when I have respect unto all thy commandments." A universal respect to all God's commandments is the only preservative from shame; and nothing have we more reason to be ashamed of than the shameful miscarriages of our hearts in point of duty, which are from the principle before mentioned.

2. Labour to prevent the very beginnings of the workings of this aversation; let grace be beforehand with it in every duty. We are directed, 1 Pet. iv. 7, to "watch unto prayer;" and as it is unto prayer, so unto every duty, -- that is, to consider and take care that we be not hindered from within nor from without as to a due performance of it. Watch against temptations, to oppose them; watch against the aversation that is in sin, to prevent it. As we are not to give place to Satan, no more are we to sin. If it be not prevented in its first attempts it will prevail. My meaning is: Whatever good, as the apostle speaks, we have to do, and find evil present with us (as we shall find it present), prevent its parleying with the soul, its insinuating of poison into the mind and affections, by a vigorous, holy, violent stirring up of the grace or graces that are to be acted and set at work peculiarly in that duty. Let Jacob come first into the world; or, if prevented by the violence of Esau, let him lay hold on his heel, to overthrow him and obtain the birthright. Upon the very first motion of Peter to our Saviour, crying, "Master, spare thyself," he immediately replies, "Get thee behind me, Satan." So ought we to say, "Get thee gone, thou law of sin, thou present evil;" and it may be of the same use unto us. Get grace, then, up betimes unto duty, and be early in the rebukes of sin.

3. Though it do its worst, yet be sure it never prevail to a conquest. Be sure you be not wearied out by its pertinacity, nor driven from your hold by its importunity; do not faint by its opposition. Take the apostle's advice, Heb. vi. 11, 12, "We desire that every one of you do show the same diligence to the full assurance of hope unto the end: that ye be not slothful." Still hold out in the same diligence. There are many ways whereby men are driven from a constant holy performance of duties, all of them dangerous, if not pernicious to the soul. Some are diverted by business, some by company, some by the power of temptations, some discouraged by their own darkness; but none so dangerous as this, when the soul gives over in part or in whole, as wearied by the aversation of sin unto it, or to communion with God in it. This argues the soul's giving up of itself unto the power of sin; which, unless the Lord break the snare of Satan therein, will assuredly prove ruinous. Our Saviour's instruction is, that "we ought always to pray, and not to faint," Luke xviii. 1. Opposition will arise, -- none so bitter and keen as that from our own hearts; if we faint, we perish. "Take heed lest ye be wearied," saith the apostle, "and faint in your minds," Heb. xii. 3. Such a fainting as attended with a weariness, and that with a giving place to the aversation working in our hearts, is to be avoided, if we would not perish. The caution is the same with that of the same apostle, Rom. xii. 12, "Rejoicing in hope, patient in tribulation, continuing instant in prayer;" and in general with that of chap. vi. 12, "Let not sin therefore reign in your mortal body, that ye should obey it in the lusts thereof." To cease from duty, in part or in whole, upon the aversation of sin unto its spirituality, is to give sin the rule, and to obey it in the lusts thereof. Yield not, then, unto it, but hold out the conflict; wait on God, and ye shall prevail: Isa. xl. 31, "They that wait upon the Lord shall renew their strength; they shall mount up with wings as eagles; they shall run, and not be weary; and they shall walk, and not faint." But that which is now so difficult will increase in difficulty if we give way unto it; but if we abide in our station, we shall prevail. The mouth of the Lord hath spoken it.

4. Carry about a constant, humbling sense of this close aversation unto spiritualness that yet lies in our nature. If men find the efficacy of it, what should, what consideration can, be more powerful, to bring them unto humble walking with God? That after all the discoveries that God hath made of himself unto them, all the kindness they have received from him, his doing of them good and not evil in all things, there should yet be such a heart of unkindness and unbelief still abiding as to have an aversation lying in it to communion with him, -- how ought the thoughts of it to cast us into the dust! to fill us with shame and self-abhorrency all our days! What have we found in God, in any of our approaches or addresses unto him, that it should be thus with us? What iniquity have we found in him? Hath he been a wilderness unto us, or a land of darkness? Did we ever lose any thing by drawing nigh unto him? nay, hath not therein lain all the rest and peace which we have obtained? Is not he the fountain and spring of all our mercies, of all our desirable things? Hath he not bid us welcome at our coming? Have we not received from him more than heart can conceive or tongue express? What ails, then, our foolish and wretched hearts, to harbour such a cursed secret dislike of him and his ways? Let us be ashamed and astonished at the consideration of it, and walk in an humbling sense of it all our days. Let us carry it

about with us in the most secret of our thoughts. And as this is a duty in itself acceptable unto God, who delights to dwell with them that are of an humble and contrite spirit, so it is of exceeding efficacy to the weakening of the evil we treat of.

5. Labour to possess the mind with the beauty and excellency of spiritual things, that so they may be presented lovely and desirable to the soul; and this cursed aversation of sin will be weakened thereby. It is an innate acknowledged principle, that the soul of man will not keep up cheerfully unto the worship of God unless it have a discovery of a beauty and comeliness in it. Hence, when men had lost all spiritual sense and savour of the things of God, to supply the want that was in their own souls, they invented outwardly pompous and gorgeous ways of worship, in images, paintings, pictures, and I know not what carnal ornaments; which they have called "The beauties of holiness!" Thus much, however, was discovered therein, that the mind of man must see a beauty, a desirableness in the things of God's worship, or it will not delight in it; aversation will prevail. Let, then, the soul labour to acquaint itself with the spiritual beauty of obedience, of communion with God, and of all duties of immediate approach to him, that it may be rifled with delight in them. It is not my present work to discover the heads and springs of that beauty and desirableness which is in spiritual duties, in their relation to God, the eternal spring of all beauty, -- to Christ, the love, desire, and hope of all nations, -- to the Spirit, the great beautifier of souls, rendering them by his grace all glorious within; in their suitableness to the souls of men, as to their actings towards their last end, in the rectitude and holiness of the rule in attendance whereunto they are to be performed. But I only say at present, in general, that to acquaint the soul throughly with these things is an eminent way of weakening the aversation spoken of.

Chapter VI

The work of this enmity against God by way of opposition -- First, It lusteth -- Wherein the lusting of sin consisteth -- Its surprising of the soul -- Readiness to close with temptations -- Secondly, Its fighting and warring -- 1. In rebellion against the law of grace -- 2. In assaulting the soul.

How this enmity worketh by way of aversation hath been declared, as also the means that the soul is to use for the preventing of its effects and prevalency. The second way whereby it exerts itself is opposition. Enmity will oppose and contend with that wherewith it is at enmity; it is so in things natural and moral. As light and darkness, heat and cold, so virtue and vice oppose each other. So is it with sin and grace; saith the apostle, "These are contrary one to the other," Gal. v. 17; -- Αλλελοις αντικειται. They are placed and set in mutual opposition, and that continually and constantly, as we shall see.

Now, there are two ways whereby enemies manage an opposition, -- first, by force; and, secondly, by fraud and deceit. So when the Egyptians became enemies to the children of Israel, and managed an enmity against them, Exod. i. 10, Pharaoh saith, "Let us deal wisely," or, rather cunningly and subtilely, "with this people;" for so Stephen, with respect to this word, expresseth it, Acts vii. 19, by κατασοπητισαμενος, -- he used "all manner of fraudulent sophistry." And unto this deceit they added force in their grievous oppressions. This is the way and manner of things where there is a prevailing enmity; and both these are made use of by the law of sin in its enmity against God and our souls.

I shall begin with the first, or its actings, as it were, in a way of force, in an open downright opposition to God and his law, or the good that a believing soul would do in obedience unto God and his law. And in this whole matter we must be careful to steer our course aright, taking the Scripture for our guide, with spiritual reason and experience for our companions; for there are many shelves in our course which must diligently be avoided, that none who consider these things be troubled without cause, or comforted without a just foundation.

In this first way, whereby this sin exerts its enmity in opposition, -- namely, as it were by force or strength, -- there are four things, expressing so many distinct degrees in its progress and procedure in the pursuit of its enmity:--

First, Its general inclination: It "lusteth," Gal. v. 17.

Secondly, Its particular way of contending: It "fights or wars," Rom. vii. 23; James iv. 1; 1 Pet. ii. 11.

Thirdly, Its success in this contest: It "brings the soul into captivity to the law of sin," Rom. vii. 23.

Fourthly, Its growth and rage upon success: It comes up to "madness," as an enraged enemy will do, Eccles. ix. 3. All which we must speak to in order.

First, In general it is said to lust: Gal. v. 17, "The flesh lusteth against the Spirit." This word expresseth the general nature of that opposition which the law of sin maketh against God and the rule of his Spirit or grace in them that believe; and, therefore, the least degree of that opposition is expressed hereby. When it doth any thing, it lusteth; as, because burning is the general acting of fire, whatever it doth else, it doth also burn. When fire doth any thing it bums; and when the law of sin doth any thing it lusts.

Hence, all the actings of this law of sin are called "The lusts of the flesh:" Gal. v. 16, "Ye shall not fulfil the lust of the flesh;" Rom. xiii. 14, "Make no provision for the flesh, to fulfil the lusts thereof." Nor are these lusts of the flesh those only whereby men act their sensuality in riot, drunkenness, uncleanness, and the like; but they comprehend all the actings of the law of sin whatever, in all the faculties and affections of the soul. Thus, Eph. ii. 3, we have mention of the desires, or wills, or "lusts of the mind," as well as of the "flesh." The mind, the most spiritual part of the soul, hath its lusts, no less than the sensual appetite, which seems sometimes more properly to be called the "flesh." And in the products of these lusts there are "defilements of the spirit" as well as of the "flesh," 2 Cor. vii. 1, -- that is, of the mind and understanding, as well of the appetite and affections, and the body that attends their service. And in the blamelessness of all these consists our holiness: 1 Thess. v. 23, "The God of peace sanctify you wholly; and I pray God, your whole spirit, and soul, and body, be preserved blameless unto the coming of our Lord Jesus Christ." Yea, by the "flesh" in this matter the whole old man, or the law of sin, is intended: John iii. 6, "That which is born of the flesh is flesh," -- that is, it is all so, and nothing else; and whatever remains of the old nature in the new man is flesh still. And this flesh lusteth, -- this law of sin cloth so; which is the general bottom and foundation of all its opposition unto God. And this it doth two ways:--

1. In a hidden, close propensity unto all evil. This lies in it habitually. Whilst a man is in the state of nature, fully under the power and dominion of this law of sin, it is said that "every figment of his heart is evil, and that continually," Gen. vi. 5. It can frame, fashion, produce, or act nothing but what is evil; because this habitual propensity unto evil that is in the law of sin is absolutely predominant in such a one. It is in the heart like poison that hath nothing to allay its venomous qualities, and so infects whatever it touches. And where the power and dominion of it is broken, yet in its own nature it hath still an habitual propensity unto that which is evil, wherein its lusting doth consist.

But here we must distinguish between the habitual frame of the heart and the natural propensity or habitual inclination of the law of sin in the heart. The habitual inclination of the heart is denominated from the principle that bears chief or sovereign rule in it; and therefore in believers it is unto good, unto God, unto holiness, unto obedience. The heart is not habitually inclined unto evil by the remainders of indwelling sin; but this sin in the heart hath a constant, habitual propensity unto evil in itself or its own nature. This the apostle intends by its being present with us: "It is present with me;" that is, always and for its own end, which is to lust unto sin.

It is with indwelling sin as with a river. Whilst the springs and fountains of it are open, and waters are continually supplied unto its streams, set a dam before it, and it causeth it to rise and swell until it bear down all or overflow the banks about it. Let these waters be abated, dried up in some good measure in the springs of them, and the remainder may be coerced and restrained. But still, as long as there is any running water, it will constantly press upon what stands before it, according to its weight and strength, because it is its nature so to do; and if by any means it make a passage, it will proceed. So is it with indwelling sin; whilst the springs and fountains of it are open, in vain is it for men to set a clam before it by their convictions, resolutions, vows, and promises. They may check it for a while, but it will increase, rise high, and rage, at one time or another, until it bears down all those convictions and resolutions, or makes itself an under-ground passage by some secret lust, that shall give a full vent unto it. But now, suppose that the springs of it are much dried up by regenerating grace, the streams or actings of it abated by holiness, yet whilst any thing remains of it, it will be pressing constantly to have vent, to press forward into actual sin; and this is its lusting.

And this habitual propensity in it is discovered two ways:--

(1.) In its unexpected surprisals of the soul into foolish, sinful figments and imaginations, which it looked not for, nor was any occasion administered unto them. It is with indwelling sin as it is with the contrary principle of sanctifying grace. This gives the soul, if I may so say, many a blessed surprisal. It oftentimes ingenerates and brings forth a holy, spiritual frame in the heart and mind, when we have had no previous rational considerations to work them thereunto. And this manifests it to be an habitual principle prevailing in the mind: so Cant. vi. 12, "Or ever I was aware, my soul made me as the chariots of Ammi-nadib; that is, free, willing, and ready for communion with Christ. I' ydty?; -- "I knew not; it was done by the power of the Spirit of grace; so that I took no notice of it, as it were, until it was done." The frequent actings of grace in this manner, exciting acts of faith, love, and complacency in God, are evidences of much strength and prevalency of it in the soul. And thus, also, is it with indwelling sin; ere the soul is aware, without any provocation or temptation, when it knows not, it is cast into a vain and foolish frame. Sin produceth its figments secretly in the heart, and prevents the mind's consideration of what it is about. I mean hereby those "actus primo primi," first acts of the soul; which are thus far involuntary, as that they have not the actual consent of the will unto them, but are voluntary as far as sin hath its residence in the will. And these surprisals, if the soul be not awake to take speedy care for the prevention of their tendency, do oftentimes set all as it were on fire, and engage the mind and affections into actual sin: for as by grace we are oftentimes, ere we are aware, "made as the chariots of a willing people," and are far engaged in heavenly-mindedness and communion with Christ, making speed in it as in a chariot; so by sin are we oftentimes, ere we are aware, carried into distempered affections, foolish imaginations, and pleasing delightfulness in things that are not good nor profitable. Hence is that caution of the apostle, Gal. vi. 1, Εας προλεπητηε· -- "If a man be surprised at unawares with a fault, or in a transgression." I doubt not but the subtlety of Satan and the power of temptation are here taken into consideration by the apostle, which causeth him to express a man's falling into sin by προλεπητηε, -- "if he be surprised." So this working of indwelling sin also hath its consideration in it, and that in the chiefest place, without which nothing else could surprise us; for without the help thereof, whatever comes from without, from Satan or the world, must admit of some parley in the mind before it be received, but it is from within, from ourselves, that we are surprised. Hereby are we disappointed and wrought over to do that which we would not, and hindered from the doing of that which we would.

Hence it is, that when the soul is oftentimes doing as it were quite another thing, engaged quite upon another design, sin starts that in the heart or imaginations of it that carries it away into that which is evil and sinful. Yea, to manifest its power, sometimes, when the soul is seriously engaged in the mortification of any sin, it will, by one means or other, lead it away into a dalliance with that very sin whose ruin it is seeking, and whose mortification it is engaged in! But as there is in this operation of the law of sin a special enticing or entangling, we shall speak unto it fully afterward. Now, these surprisals can be from nothing but an habitual propensity unto evil in the principle from whence they proceed; not an habitual inclination unto actual sin in the mind or heart, but an habitual propensity unto evil in the sin that is in the mind or heart. This prevents the soul with its figments. How much communion with God is hereby prevented, how many meditations are disturbed, how much the minds and consciences of men have been defiled by this acting of sin, some may have observed. I know no greater burden in the life of a believer than these involuntary surprisals of soul; involuntary, I say, as to the actual consent of the will, but not so in respect of that corruption which is in the will, and is the principle of them. And it is in respect unto these that the apostle makes his complaint, Rom. vii. 25.

(2.) This habitual inclination manifests itself in its readiness and promptness, without dispute or altercation, to join and close with every temptation whereby it may possibly be excited. As we know it is in the nature of fire to burn, because it immediately lays hold on whatever is combustible, let any temptation whatever be proposed unto a man, the suitableness of whose matter unto his corruptions, or manner of its proposal, makes it a temptation; immediately he hath not only to do with the temptation as outwardly proposed, but also with his own heart about it. Without farther consideration or debate, the temptation hath got a friend in him. Not a moment's space is given between the proposal and the necessity there is incumbent on the soul to look to its enemy within. And this also argues a constant, habitual propensity unto evil. Our Saviour said of the assaults and temptations of Satan, "The prince of this world cometh, and he hath no part in me," John xiv. 30. He had more temptations, intensively and extensively, in number, quality, and fierceness, from Satan and the world, than ever had any of the sons of men; but yet in all of them he had to deal only with that which came from without. His holy heart had nothing like to them, suited to them, or ready to give them entertainment: "The prince of this world had nothing in him." So it was with Adam. When a temptation befell him, he had only the outward proposal to look unto; all was well within until the outward temptation took place and prevailed. With us it is not so. In a city that is at unity in itself, compact and entire, without divisions and parties, if an enemy approach about it, the rulers and inhabitants have no thoughts at all but only how they may oppose the enemy without, and resist him in his approaches. But if the city be divided in itself, if there be factions and traitors within, the very first thing they do is to look to the enemies at home, the traitors within, to cut off the head of Sheba, if they will be safe. All was well with Adam within doors when Satan came, so that he had nothing to do but to look to his assaults and approaches. But now, on the access of any temptation, the soul is instantly to look in, where it shall find this traitor at work, closing with the baits of Satan, and stealing away the heart; and this it doth always, which evinceth an habitual inclination. Ps. xxxviii. 17, saith David, "I am ready to halt," or for halting: ky'ny ltsl nkvn?; -- "I am prepared and disposed unto hallucination, to the slipping of my foot into sin," verse 16, as he expounds the meaning of that phrase, Ps. lxxviii. 2, 3. There was from indwelling sin a continual disposition in him to be slipping, stumbling, halting, on every occasion or temptation. There is nothing so vain, foolish, ridiculous, fond, nothing so vile and abominable, nothing so atheistical or execrable, but, if it be proposed unto the soul in a way of temptation, there is that in this law of sin which is ready to answer it before it be decried by grace. And this is the first thing in this lusting of the law of sin, -- it consists in its habitual propensity unto evil, manifesting itself by the involuntary surprisals of the soul unto sin, and its readiness, without dispute or consideration, to join in all temptations whatever.

2. Its lusting consists in its actual pressing after that which is evil, and actual opposition unto that which is good. The former instance showed its constant readiness to this work; this now treats of the work itself. It is not only ready, but for the most part always engaged. "It lusteth," saith the Holy Ghost. It doth so continually. It stirreth in the soul by one act or other constantly, almost as the spirits in the blood, or the blood in the veins. This apostle calls its tempting: James i. 14, "Every man is tempted of his own lust." Now, what is it to be tempted? It is to have that proposed to a man's consideration which, if he close withal, it is evil, it is sin unto him. This is sin's trade: Επιτηυμει· -- "It lusteth." It is raising up in the heart, and proposing unto the mind and affections, that which is evil; trying, as it were, whether the soul will close with its suggestions, or how far it will carry them on, though it do not wholly prevail. Now, when such a temptation comes from without, it is unto the soul an indifferent thing, neither good nor evil, unless it be consented unto; but the very proposal from within, it being the soul's own act, is its sin. And this is the work of the law of sin, -- it is restlessly and continually raising up and proposing innumerable various forms and appearances of evil, in this or that kind, indeed in every kind that the nature of man is capable to exercise corruption in. Something or other, in matter, or manner, or circumstance, inordinate, unspiritual, unanswerable unto the rule, it hatcheth and proposeth unto the soul. And this power of sin to beget figments and ideas of actual evil in the heart the apostle may have respect unto, 1 Thess. v. 22, Apo pantos eidous ponerou apechesthe· -- "Keep yourselves from every figment or idea of sin in the heart;" for the word there used doth not anywhere signify an outward form or appearance: neither is it the appearance of evil, but an evil idea or figment that is intended. And this

lusting of sin is that which the prophet expresseth in wicked men, in whom the law of it is predominant: Isa. lvii. 20, "The wicked are like the troubled sea, when it cannot rest, whose waters cast up mire and dirt;" a similitude most lively, expressing the lustings of the law of sin, restlessly and continually bubbling up in the heart, with wicked, foolish, and filthy imaginations and desires. This, then, is the first thing in the opposition that this enmity makes to God, -- namely, in its general inclination, it "lusteth."

Secondly, There is its particular way of contending, -- it fights or wars; that is, it acts with strength and violence, as men do in war. First, it lusts, stirring and moving inordinate figments in the mind, desires in the appetite and the affections, proposing them to the will. But it rests not there, it cannot rest; it urgeth, presseth, and pursueth its proposals with earnestness, strength, and vigour, fighting, and contending, and warring to obtain its end and purpose. Would it merely stir up and propose things to the soul, and immediately acquiesce in the sentence, and judgment of the mind, that the thing is evil, against God and his will, and not farther to be insisted on, much sin might be prevented that is now produced; but it rests not here, -- it proceeds to carry on its design, and that with earnestness and contention. By this means wicked men "inflame themselves," Isa. lvii. 5. They are self-inflamers, as the word signifies, unto sin; every spark of sin is cherished in them until it grows into a flame: and so it will do in others, where it is so cherished.

Now, this fighting or warring of sin consists in two things:-- 1. In its rebellion against grace, or the law of the mind. 2. In its assaulting the soul, contending for rule and sovereignty over it.

1. The first is expressed by the apostle, Rom. vii. 23: "I find," says he, "another law," αντιστρατευομενον το νομο του νοος μου, "rebelling against the law of my mind." There are, it seems, two laws in us, -- the "law of the flesh," or of sin; and the "law of the mind," or of grace. But contrary laws cannot both obtain sovereign power over the same person, at the same time. The sovereign power in believers is in the hand of the law of grace; so the apostle declares, verse 22, "I delight in the law of God in the inward man." Obedience unto this law is performed with delight and complacency in the inward man, because its authority is lawful and good. So more expressly, chap. vi. 14, "For sin shall not have dominion over you, for ye are not under the law, but under grace." Now, to war against the law that hath a just sovereignty is to rebel; and so Αντιστρατευεστηαι signifies, it is to rebel, and ought to have been so translated, "Rebelling against the law of my mind." And this rebellion consists in a stubborn, obstinate opposition unto the commands and directions of the law of grace. Doth the "law of the mind" command any thing as duty? doth it severely rise up against any thing that is evil? When the lusting of the law of sin rises up to this degree, it contends against obedience with all its might; the effect whereof, as the apostle tells us, is "the doing of that which we would not, and the not doing of that which we would," chap. vii. 15, 16. And we may gather a notable instance of the power of sin in this its rebellion from this place. The law of grace prevails upon the will, so that it would do that which is good: "To will is present with me," verse 18; "When I would do good," verse 21; and again, verse 19, "And I would not do evil." And it prevails upon the understanding, so that it approves or disapproves, according to the dictates of the law of grace: Verse 16, "I consent unto the law that it is good;" and verse 15. The judgment always lies on the side of grace. It prevails also on the affections: Verse 22, "I delight in the law of God in the inward man." Now, if this be so, that grace hath the sovereign power in the understanding, will, and affections, whence is it that it doth not always prevail, that we do not always do that which we would, and abstain from that which we would not? Is it not strange that a man should not do that which he chooseth, willeth, liketh, delighteth in? Is there any thing more required to enable us unto that which is good? The law of grace doth all, as much as can be expected from it, that which in itself is abundantly sufficient for the perfecting of all holiness in the fear of the Lord. But here lies the difficulty, in the entangling opposition that is made by the rebellion of this "law of sin." Neither is it expressible with what vigour and variety sin acts itself in this matter. Sometimes it proposeth diversions, sometimes it causeth weariness, sometimes it finds out difficulties, sometimes it stirs up contrary affections, sometimes it begets prejudices, and one way or other entangles the soul; so that it never suffers grace to have an absolute and complete success in any duty. Verse 18, To katergazesthai to kalon ouch heurisko· -- "I find not the way perfectly to work out, or accomplish, that which is good," so the word signifies; and that from this opposition and resistance that is made by the law of sin. Now, this rebellion appears in two things:-- (1.) In the opposition that it makes unto the general purpose and course of the soul. (2.) In the opposition it makes unto particular duties.

(1.) In the opposition it makes to the general purpose and course of the soul. There is none in whom is the Spirit of Christ, that is his, but it is his general design and purpose to walk in a universal conformity unto him in all things. Even from the inward frame of the heart to the whole compass of his outward actions, so it is with him. This God requires in his covenant: Gen. xvii. 1, "Walk before me, and be thou perfect." Accordingly, his design is to walk before God; and his frame is sincerity and uprightness therein. This is called, "Cleaving unto the Lord with purpose of heart," Acts xi. 23, -- that is, in all things; and that not with a slothful, dead, ineffectual purpose, but such as is operative, and sets the whole soul at work in pursuit of it. This the apostle sets forth, Phil. iii. 12-14, "Not as though I had already attained, either were already perfect: but I follow after, if that I may apprehend that for which also I am apprehended of Christ Jesus. Brethren, I count not myself to have apprehended: but this one thing I do, forgetting those things which are behind, and reaching forth unto those things which are before, I press toward the mark for the prize of the high calling of God in Christ Jesus." He useth three words excellently expressing the soul's universal pursuit of this purpose of heart in cleaving unto God: First, saith he, Διοκο, verse 12, -- "I follow after," prosecute; the word signifies properly to persecute, which with what earnestness and diligence it is usually done we know. Secondly, Επεκτεινομαι, -- "I reach forward," reaching with great intension of spirit and affections. It is a great and constant endeavour that is expressed in that word. Thirdly, Κατα σκοπον διοκο, -- say we, "I press towards the mark;" that is, even as men that are running for a prize. All set forth the vigour, earnestness, diligence, and constancy that is used in the pursuit of this purpose. And this the nature of the principle of grace requireth in them in whom it is. But yet we see with what failings, yea failings, their pursuit of this course is attended. The frame of the heart is changed, the heart is stolen away, the affections entangled, eruptions of unbelief and distempered passions discovered, carnal wisdom, with all its attendancies, are set on work; all contrary to the general principle and purpose of the soul. And all this is from the rebellion of this law of sin, stirring up and provoking the heart unto disobedience. The prophet gives this character of hypocrites, Hos. x. 2, "Their heart is divided; therefore shall they be found faulty." Now, though this be wholly so in respect of the mind and judgment in hypocrites only, yet it is partially so in the best, in the sense described. They have a division, not of the heart, but in the heart; and thence it is that they are so often found faulty. So saith the apostle, "So that we cannot do the things that we would," Gal. v. 17. We cannot accomplish the design of close walking according to the law of grace, because of the contrariety and rebellion of this law of sin.

(2.) It rebels also in respect unto particular duties. It raiseth a combustion in the soul against the particular commands and designings of the law of grace. "You cannot do the things that you would;" that is, "The duties which you judge incumbent on you, which you approve and delight in in the inward man, you cannot do them as you would." Take an instance in prayer. A man addresseth himself unto that duty; he would not only perform it, but he would perform it in that manner that the nature of the duty and his own condition do require. He would "pray in the spirit," fervently, "with sighs and groans that cannot be uttered;" in faith, with love and delight, pouring forth his soul unto the Lord. This he aims at. Now, oftentimes he shall find a rebellion, a fighting of the law of sin in this matter. He shall find difficulty to get any thing done who thought to do all things. I do not say that it is thus always, but it is so when sin "wars and rebels;" which expresseth an especial acting of its power. Woful entanglements do poor creatures oftentimes meet withal upon this account. Instead of that free, enlarged communion with God that they aim at, the best that their souls arrive unto is but to go away mourning for their folly, deadness, and indisposition. In a word, there is no command of the law of grace that is known, liked of, and approved by the soul, but when it comes to be observed, this law of sin one way or other makes head and rebels against it. And this is the first way of its fighting.

2. It doth not only rebel and resist, but it assaults the soul. It sets upon the law of the mind and grace; which is the second part of its warring: 1 Pet. ii. 11, Στρατευονται κατα τες πσυξηες,.-- "They fight," or war, "against the soul;" James iv. 1, Strateuontai en tois melesin humon, -- "They fight," or war, "in your members." Peter shows what they oppose and fight against, -- namely, the "soul" and the law of grace therein; James, what they fight with or by, -- namely, the "members," or the corruption that is in our mortal bodies. Αντιστρατευεστηαι is to rebel against a superior; στρατευστηαι is to assault or war for a superiority. It takes the part of an assailant as well as of a resister. It makes attempts for rule and sovereignty, as well as opposeth the rule of grace. Now, all war and fighting hath somewhat of violence in it; and there is therefore some violence in that acting of sin which the Scripture calls "fighting and warring." And this assailing efficacy of sin, as distinguished from its rebelling, before treated of, consists in these things that ensue:--

(1.) All its positive actings in stirring up unto sin belong to this head. Oftentimes, by the vanity of the mind, or the sensuality of the affections, the folly of the imaginations, it sets upon the soul then when the law of grace is not actually putting it on duty; so that therein it doth not rebel but assault. Hence the apostle cries out, Rom. vii. 24, "Who shall deliver me from it?" "Who shall rescue me out of its hand?" as the word signifies. When we pursue an enemy, and he resists us, we do not cry out, "Who shall deliver us?" for we are the assailants; but, "Who shall rescue me?" is the cry of one who is set upon by an enemy. So it is here; a man is assaulted by his "own lust," as James speaks. By the wayside, in his employment, under a duty, sin sets upon the soul with vain imaginations, foolish desires, and would willingly employ the soul to make provision for its satisfaction; which the apostle cautions us against, Rom. xiii. 14, Tes sarkos pronoian me poieisthe eis epithumias· -- "Do not accomplish the providence or projection of the flesh for its own satisfaction."

(2.) Its importunity and urgency seems to be noted in this expression, of its warring. Enemies in war are restless, pressing, and importunate; so is the law of sin. Doth it set upon the soul? -- Cast off its motions; it returns again. Rebuke them by the power of grace; they withdraw for a while, and return again. Set before them the cross of Christ; they do as those that came to take him, -- at sight of him they went backwards and fell unto the ground, but they arose again and laid hands on him -- sin gives place for a season, but returns and presseth on the soul again. Mind it of the love of God in Christ; though it be stricken, yet it gives not over. Present hell-fire unto it; it rusheth into the midst of those flames. Reproach it with its folly and madness; it knows no shame, but presseth on still. Let the thoughts of the mind strive to fly from it; it follows as on the wings of the wind. And by this importunity it wearies and wears out the soul; and if the great remedy, Rom. viii. 3, come not timely, it prevails to a conquest. There is nothing more marvellous nor dreadful in the working of sin than this of its importunity. The soul knows not what to make of it; it dislikes, abhors, abominates the evil it tends unto; it despiseth the thoughts of it, hates them as hell; and yet is by itself imposed on with them, as if it were another person, an express enemy got within him. All this the apostle discovers, Rom. vii. 15-17: "The things that I do I hate." It is not of outward actions, but the inward risings of the mind that he treats. "I hate them," saith he; "I abominate them." But why, then, will he have any thing more to do with them? If he hate them, and abhor himself for them, let them alone, have no more to do with them, and so end the matter. Alas! saith he, verse 17, "It is no more I that do it, but sin that dwelleth in me;" -- "I have one within me that is my enemy, that with endless, restless importunity puts these things upon me, even the things that I hate and abominate. I cannot be rid of them, I am weary of myself, I cannot fly from them. O wretched man that I am! who shall deliver me?'?" I do not say that this is the ordinary condition of believers, but thus it is often when this law of sin riseth up to war and fighting. It is not thus with them in respect of particular sins, -- this or that sin, outward sins, sins of life and conversation, -- but yet in respect of vanity of mind, inward and spiritual distempers, it is often so. Some, I know, pretend to great perfection; but I am resolved to believe the apostle before them all and every one.

(3.) It carries on its war by entangling of the affections, and drawing them into a combination against the mind. Let grace be enthroned in the mind and judgment, yet if the law of sin lays hold upon and entangles the affections, or any of them, it hath gotten a fort from whence it continually assaults the soul. Hence the great duty of mortification is chiefly directed to take place upon the affections: Col. iii. 5, "Mortify therefore your members which are upon the earth; fornication, uncleanness, inordinate affection, concupiscence, and covetousness, which is idolatry." The "members that are upon the earth" are our affections: for in the outward part of the body sin is not seated; in particular, not "covetousness," which is there enumerated, to be mortified amongst our members that are on the earth. Yea, after grace hath taken possession of the soul, the affections do become the principal seat of the remainders of sin; -- and therefore Paul saith that this law is "in our members," Rom. vii. 23; and James, that it "wars in our members," James iv. 1, -- that is, our affections. And there is no estimate to be taken of the work of mortification aright but by the affections. We may every day see persons of very eminent light, that yet visibly have unmortified hearts and conversations; their affections have not been crucified with Christ. Now, then, when this law of sin can possess any affection, whatever it be, love, delight, fear, it will make from it and by it fearful assaults upon the soul. For instance, hath it got the love of any one entangled with the world or the things of it, the lust of the flesh, the lust of the eyes, or the pride of life, -- how will it take advantage on every occasion to break in upon the soul! It shall do nothing, attempt nothing, be in no place or company, perform no duty, private or public, but sin will have one blow or other at it; it will be one way or other soliciting for itself.

This is the sum of what we shall offer unto this acting of the law of sin, in a way of fighting and warring against our souls, which is so often mentioned in the Scripture; and a due consideration of it is of no small advantage unto us, especially to bring us unto self-abasement, to teach us to walk humbly and mournfully before God. There are two things that are suited to humble the souls of men, and they are, first, a due consideration of God, and then of themselves; -- of God, in his greatness, glory, holiness, power, majesty, and authority; of ourselves, in our mean, abject, and sinful condition. Now, of all things in our condition, there is nothing so suited unto this end and purpose as that which lies before us; namely, the vile remainders of enmity against God which are yet in our hearts and natures. And it is no small evidence of a gracious soul when it is willing to search itself in this matter, and to be helped therein from a word of truth; when it is willing that the word should dive into the secret parts of the heart, and rip open whatever of evil and corruption lies therein. The prophet says of Ephraim, Hos. x. 11, "He loved to tread out the corn;" he loved to work when he might eat, to have always the corn before him: but God, says he, would "cause him to plough;" a labour no less needful, though at present not so delightful. Most men love to hear of the doctrine of grace, of the pardon of sin, of free love, and suppose they find food therein; however, it is evident that they grow and thrive in the life and notion of them. But to be breaking up the fallow ground of their hearts, to be inquiring after the weeds and briers that grow in them, they delight not so much, though this be no less necessary than the other. This path is not so beaten as that of grace, nor so trod in, though it be the only way to come to a true knowledge of grace itself. It may be some, who are wise and grown in other truths, may yet be so little skilled in searching their own hearts, that they may be slow in the perception and understanding of these things. But this sloth and neglect is to be shaken off, if we have any regard unto our own souls. It is more than probable that many a false hypocrite, who have deceived themselves as well as others, because they thought the doctrine of the gospel pleased them, and therefore supposed they believed it, might be delivered from their soul-ruining deceits if they would diligently apply themselves unto this search of their own hearts. Or, would other professors walk with so much boldness and security as some do, if they considered aright what a deadly watchful enemy they continually carry about with them and in them? would they so much indulge as they do carnal joys and pleasures, or pursue their perishing affairs with so much delight and greediness as they do? It were to be wished that we would all apply our hearts more to this work, even to come to a true understanding of the nature, power, and subtlety of this our adversary, that our souls may be humbled; and that, --

1. In walking with God. His delight is with the humble and contrite ones, those that tremble at his word, the mourners in Zion; and such are we only when we have a due sense of our own vile condition. This will beget reverence of God, a sense of our distance from him, admiration of his grace and condescension, a due valuation of mercy, far above those light, verbal, airy attainments, that some have boasted of.

2. In walking with others. It lays in provision to prevent those great evils of judging, spiritual unmercifulness, harsh censuring, which I have observed to have been pretended by many, who, at the same time, as afterward hath appeared, have been guilty of greater or worse crimes than those which they have raved against in others. This, I say, will lead us to meekness, compassion, readiness to forgive, to pass by offences; even when we shall "consider" what is our state, as the apostle plainly declares, Gal. vi. 1. The man that understands the evil of his own heart, how vile it is, is the only useful, fruitful, and solid believing and obedient person. Others are fit only to delude themselves, to disquiet families, churches, and all relations whatever. Let us, then, consider our hearts wisely, and then go and see if we can be proud of our gifts, our graces, our valuation and esteem amongst professors, our enjoyments. Let us go then and judge, condemn, reproach others that have been tempted; we shall find a great inconsistency in these things. And many things of the like nature might be here added upon the consideration of this woful effect of indwelling sin. The way of opposing and defeating its design herein shall be afterward considered.

Chapter VII

The captivating power of indwelling sin, wherein it consisteth -- The prevalency of sin, when from itself, when from temptation -- The rage and madness that is in sin.

The third thing assigned unto this law of sin in its opposition unto God and the law of his grace is, that it leads the soul captive: Rom. vii. 23, "I find a law leading me captive" (captivating me) "unto the law of sin." And this is the utmost height which the apostle in that place carries the opposition and warring of the remainders of indwelling sin unto; closing the consideration of it with a complaint of the state and condition of believers thereby, and an earnest prayer for deliverance from it: Verse 24, "O wretched man that I am! who shall deliver me from this body of death?" What is contained in this expression and intended by it shall be declared in the ensuing observations:--

1. It is not directly the power and actings of the law of sin that are here expressed, but its success in and upon its actings. But success is the greatest evidence of power, and leading captive in war is the height of success. None can aim at greater success than to lead their enemies captive; and it is a peculiar expression in the Scripture of great success. So the Lord Christ, on his victory over Satan, is said to "lead captivity captive," Eph. iv. 8, -- that is, to conquer him who had conquered and prevailed upon others; and this he did when "by death he destroyed him that had the power of death, that is, the devil," Heb. ii. 14. Here, then, a great prevalency and power of sin in its warring against the soul is discovered. It so wars as to "lead captive;" which, had it not great power, it could not do, especially against that resistance of the soul which is included in this expression.

2. It is said that it leads the soul captive "unto the law of sin;" -- not to this or that sin, particular sin, actual sin, but to the "law of sin." God, for the most part, ordereth things so, and gives out such supplies of grace unto believers, as that they shall not be made a prey unto this or that particular sin, that it should prevail in them and compel them to serve it in the lusts thereof, that it should have dominion over them, that they should be captives and slaves unto it. This is that which David prays so earnestly against: Ps. xix. 12, 13, "Cleanse thou me from secret faults. Keep back thy servant also from presumptuous sins; let them not have dominion over me: then shall I be upright." He supposeth the continuance of the law of sin in him, verse 12, which will bring forth errors of life and secret sins; against which he findeth relief in pardoning and cleansing mercy, which he prays for. "This," saith he, "will be my condition. But for sins of pride and boldness, such as all sins are that get dominion in a man, that make a captive of a man, the Lord restrain thy servant from them." For what sin soever gets such power in a man, be it in its own nature small or great, it becomes in him in whom it is a sin of boldness, pride, and presumption; for these things are not reckoned from the nature or kind of the sin, but from its prevalency and customariness, wherein its pride, boldness, and contempt of God doth consist. To the same purpose, if I mistake not, prays Jabez: 1 Chron. iv. 10, "Oh that thou wouldest bless me indeed, and enlarge my coast, and that thine hand might be with me, and that thou wouldest keep me from evil, that it may not grieve me!" The holy man took occasion from his own name to pray against sin, that that might not be a grief and sorrow to him by its power and prevalency. I confess, sometimes it may come to this with a believer, that for a season he may be led captive by some particular sin; it may have so much prevalency in him as to have power over him. So it seems to have been with David, when he lay so long in his sin without repentance; and was plainly so with those in Isa. lvii. 17, 18, "For the iniquity of his covetousness was I wroth, and smote him: I hid me, and was wroth, and he went on frowardly in the way of his heart. I have seen his ways, and will heal him." They continued under the power of their covetousness, so that no dealings of God with them, for so long a time, could reclaim them. But, for the most part, when any lust or sin doth so prevail, it is from the advantage and furtherance that it hath got by some powerful temptation of Satan. He hath poisoned it, inflamed it, and entangled the soak So the apostle, speaking of such as through sin were fallen off from their holiness, says, "They were in the snare of the devil, being taken captive by him at his will," 2 Tim. ii. 26. Though it were their own lusts that they served, yet they were brought into bondage thereunto by being entangled in some snare of Satan; and thence they are said to be "taken alive," as a poor beast in a toil.

And here, by the way, we may a little inquire, whether the prevailing power of a particular sin in any be from itself, or from the influence of temptation upon it; concerning which at present take only these two observations:--

(1.) Much of the prevalency of sin upon the soul is certainly from Satan, when the perplexing and captivating sin hath no peculiar footing nor advantage in the nature, constitution, or condition of the sinner. When any lust grows high and prevailing more than others, upon its own account, it is from the peculiar advantage that it hath in the natural constitution, or the station or condition of the person in the world; for otherwise the law of sin gives an equal propensity unto all evil, an equal vigour unto every lust. When, therefore, it cannot be discerned that the captivating sin is peculiarly fixed in the nature of the sinner, or is advantaged from his education or employment in the world, the prevalency of it is peculiarly from Satan. He hath got to the root of it, and hath given it poison and strength. Yea, perhaps, sometimes that which may seem to the soul to be the corrupt lusting of the heart, is nothing but Satan's imposing his suggestions on the imagination. If, then, a man find an importunate rage from any corruption that is not evidently seated in his nature, let him, as the Papists say, cross himself, or fly by faith to the cross of Christ, for the devil is nigh at hand.

(2.) When a lust is prevalent unto captivity, where it brings in no advantage to the flesh, it is from Satan. All that the law of sin doth of itself is to serve the providence of the flesh, Rom. xiii. 14; and it must bring in unto it somewhat of the profits and pleasures that are its object. Now, if the prevailing sin do not so act in itself, if it be more spiritual and inward, it is much from Satan by the imagination, more than the corruption of the heart itself. But this by the way.

I say, then, that the apostle treats not here of our being captivated unto this or that sin, but unto the law of sin; that is, we are compelled to bear its presence and burden whether we will or no. Sometimes the soul thinks or hopes that it may through grace be utterly freed from this troublesome inmate. Upon some sweet enjoyment of God, some full supply of grace, some return from wandering, some deep affliction, some thorough humiliation, the poor soul begins to hope that it shall now be freed from the law of sin; but after a while it perceives that it is quite otherwise. Sin acts again, makes good its old station; and the soul finds that, whether it will or no, it must bear its yoke. This makes it sigh and cry out for deliverance.

3. This leading captive argues a prevalency against the renitency or contrary actings of the will. This is intimated plainly in this expression, -- namely, that the will opposeth and makes head, as it were, against the working of sin. This the apostle declares in those expressions which he uses, Rom. vii. 15, 19, 20. And herein consists the "lusting of the Spirit against the flesh," Gal. v. 17; that is, the contending of grace to expel and subdue it. The spiritual habits of grace that are in the will do so resist and act against it; and the excitation of those habits by the Spirit are directed to the same purpose. This leading captive is contrary, I say, to the inclinations and actings of the renewed will. No man is made a captive but against his will. Captivity is misery and trouble, and no man willingly puts himself into trouble. Men choose it in its causes, and in the ways and means leading unto it, but not in itself. So the prophet informs us, Hos. v. 11, "Ephraim was," not willingly, "oppressed and broken in judgment," -- that was his misery and trouble; but he "willingly walked after the commandment" of the idolatrous kings, which brought him thereunto. Whatever consent, then, the soul may give unto sin, which is the means of this captivity, it gives none to the captivity itself; that is against the will wholly. Hence these things ensue:--

(1.) That the power of sin is great, -- which is that which we are in demonstration of; and this appears in its prevalency unto captivity against the actings and contendings of the will for liberty from it. Had it no opposition made unto it, or were its adversary weak, negligent, slothful, it were no great evidence of its power that it made captives; but its prevailing against diligence, activity, watchfulness, the constant renitency of the will, this evinceth its efficacy.

(2.) This leading captive intimates manifold particular successes. Had it not success in particular, it could not be said at all to lead captive. Rebel it might, assail it might; but it cannot be said to lead captive without some successes. And there are several degrees of the success of the law of sin in the soul. Sometimes it carries the person unto outward actual sin, which is its utmost aim; sometimes it obtaineth the consent of the will, but is cast out by grace, and proceeds no farther; sometimes it wearies and entangles the soul, that it turns aside, as it were, and leaves contending, -- which is a success also. One or more, or all of these, must be, where captivity takes place. Such a kind of course doth the apostle ascribe unto covetousness, 1 Tim. vi. 9, 10.

(3.) This leading captive manifests this condition to be miserable and wretched. To be thus yoked and dealt withal, against the judgment of the mind, the choice and consent of the will, its utmost strivings and contendings, how sad is it! When the neck is sore and tender with former pressures, to be compelled to bear the yoke again, this pierces, this grieves, this even breaks the heart. When the soul is principled by grace unto a loathing of sin, of every evil way, to a hatred of the least discrepancy between itself and the holy will of God, then to be imposed on by this law of sin, with all that enmity and folly, that deadness and filth wherewith it is attended, what more dreadful condition? All captivity is dreadful in its own nature. The greatest aggravation of it is from the condition of the tyrant unto whom any one is captivated. Now, what can be worse than this law of sin? Hence the apostle, having once mentioned this captivity, cries out, as one quite weary and ready to faint, Rom. vii. 24.

(4.) This condition is peculiar to believers. Unregenerate men are not said to be led captive to the law of sin. They may, indeed, be led captive unto this or that particular sin or corruption, -- that is, they may be forced to serve it against the power of their convictions. They are convinced of the evil of it, -- an adulterer of his uncleanness, a drunkard of his abomination, -- and make some resolutions, it may be, against it; but their lust is too hard for them, they cannot cease to sin, and so are made captives or slaves to this or that particular sin. But they cannot be said to be led captive to the law of sin, and that because they are willingly subject thereunto. It hath, as it were, a rightful dominion over them, and they oppose it not, but only when it hath irruptions to the disturbance of their consciences; and then the opposition they make unto it is not from their wills, but is the mere acting of an affrighted conscience and a convinced mind. They regard not the nature of sin, but its guilt and consequences. But to be brought into captivity is that which befalls a man against his will; which is all that shall be spoken unto this degree of the actings of the power of sin, manifesting itself in its success.

The fourth and last degree of the opposition made by the law of sin to God and the law of his will and grace, is in its rage and madness. There is madness in its nature: Eccles. ix. 3, "The heart of the sons of men is full of evil, and madness is in their heart." The evil that the heart of man is full of by nature is that indwelling sin whereof we speak; and this is so in their heart, that it riseth up unto madness. The Holy Ghost expresseth this rage of sin by a fit similitude, which he useth in sundry places: as Jer. ii. 24; Hos. viii. 9. It maketh men as "a wild ass;" "she traverseth her ways," and "snuffeth up the wind," and runneth whither her mind or lust leads her. And he saith of idolaters, enraged with their lusts, that they are "mad upon their idols," Jer. l. 38. We may a little consider what lies in this madness and rage of sin, and how it riseth up thereunto:--

1. For the nature of it; it seems to consist in a violent, heady, pertinacious pressing unto evil or sin. Violence, importunity, and pertinacy are in it. It is the tearing and torturing of the soul by any sin to force its consent and to obtain satisfaction. It riseth up in the heart, is denied by the law of grace, and rebuked; -- it returns and exerts its poison again; the soul is startled, casts it off; -- it returns again with new violence and importunity; the soul cries out for help and deliverance, looks round about to all springs of gospel grace and relief, trembles at the furious assaults of sin, and casts itself into the arms of Christ for deliverance. And if it be not able to take that course, it is foiled and hurried up and down through the mire and filth of foolish imaginations, corrupt and noisome lusts, which rend and tear it, as if they would devour its whole spiritual life and power. See 1 Tim. vi. 9, 10; 2 Pet. ii. 14. It was not much otherwise with them whom we instanced in before, Isa. lvii. 17. They had an inflamed, enraged lust working in them, even "covetousness," or the love of this world; by which, as the apostle speaks, men "pierce themselves through with many sorrows." God is angry with them, and discovereth his wrath by all the ways and means that it was possible for them to be made sensible thereof. He was "wroth, and smote them;" but though, it may be, this staggered them a little, yet they "went on." He is angry, and "hides himself" from them, -- deserts them as to his gracious, assisting, comforting presence. Doth this work the effect? No; they go on frowardly still, as men mad on their covetousuess. Nothing can put a stop to their raging lusts. This is plain madness and fury. We need not seek far for instances. We see men mad on their lusts every day; and, which is the worst kind of madness, their lusts do not rage so much in them, as they rage in the pursuit of them. Are those greedy pursuits of things in the world, which we see some men engaged in, though they have other pretences, indeed any thing else but plain madness in the pursuit of their lusts? God, who searcheth the hearts of men, knows that the most of things that are done with other pretences in the world, are nothing but the actings of men mad and furious in the pursuit of their lusts.

2. That sin ariseth not unto this height ordinarily, but when it hath got a double advantage:--

(1.) That it be provoked, enraged, and heightened by some great temptation. Though it be a poison in itself, yet, being inbred in nature, it grows not violently outrageous without the contribution of some new poison of Satan unto it, in a suitable temptation. It was the advantage that Satan got against David, by a suitable temptation, that raised his lust to that rage and madness which it went forth unto in the business of Bath-sheba and Uriah. Though sin be always a fire in the bones, yet it flames not unless Satan come with his bellows to blow it up. And let any one in whom the law of sin ariseth to this height of rage seriously consider, and he may find out where the devil stands and puts in in the business.

(2.) It must be advantaged by some former entertainment and prevalency. Sin grows not to this height at its first assault. Had it not been suffered to make its entrance, had there not been some yielding in the soul, this had not come about. The great wisdom and security of the soul in dealing with indwelling sin is to put a violent stop unto its beginnings, its first motions and actings. Venture all on the first attempt. Die rather than yield one step unto it. If, through the deceit of sin, or the negligence of the soul, or its carnal confidence to give bounds to lust's actings at other seasons, it makes any entrance into the soul, and finds any entertainment, it gets strength and power, and insensibly ariseth to the frame under consideration. Thou hadst never had the experience of the fury of sin, if thou hadst not been content with some of its dalliance. Hadst thou not brought up this servant, this slave, delicately, it would not have now presumed beyond a son. Now, when the law of sin in any particular hath got this double advantage, -- the furtherance of a vigorous temptation, and some prevalency formerly obtained, whereby it is let into the strengths of the soul, -- it often riseth up to this frame whereof we speak.

3. We may see what accompanies this rage and madness, what are the properties of it, and what effects it produceth:--

(1.) There is in it the casting off, for a time at least, of the yoke, rule, and government of the Spirit and law of grace. Where grace hath the dominion, it will never utterly be expelled from its throne, it will still keep its right and sovereignty; but its influences may for a season be intercepted, and its government be suspended, by the power of sin. Can we think that the law of grace had any actual influence of rule on the heart of David, when, upon the provocation received from Nabal, he was so hurried with the desire of self-revenge that he cried, "Gird on your swords," to his companions, and resolved not to leave alive one man of his whole household? 1 Sam. xxv. 34; or that Asa was in any better frame when he smote the prophet and put him in prison, that spake unto him in the name of the Lord? Sin in this case is like an untamed horse, which, having first cast off his rider, runs away with fierceness and rage. It first casts off a present sense of the yoke of Christ and the law of his grace, and then hurries the soul at its pleasure. Let us a little consider how this is done.

The seat and residence of grace is in the whole soul. It is in the inner man; it is in the mind, the will, and the affections: for the whole soul is renewed by it into the image of God, Eph. iv. 23, 24, and the whole man is a "new creature," 2 Cor. v. 17. And in all these doth it exert its power and efficacy. Its rule or dominion is the pursuit of its effectual working in all the faculties of the soul, as they are one united principle of moral and spiritual operations. So, then, the interrupting of its exercise, of its rule and power, by the law of sin, must consist in its contrary acting in and upon the faculties and affections of the soul, whereon and by which grace should exert its power and efficacy. And this it doth. It darkens the mind; partly through innumerable vain prejudices and false reasonings, as we shall see when we come to consider its deceitfulness; and partly through the steaming of the affections, heated with the noisome lusts that have laid hold on them. Hence that saving light that is in the mind is clouded and stifled, that it cannot put forth its transforming power to change the soul into the likeness of Christ discovered unto it, which is its proper work, Rom. xii. 2. The habitual inclination of the will to obedience, which is the next way of the working of the law of grace, is first weakened, then cast aside and rendered useless, by the continual solicitations of sin and temptation; so that the will first lets go its hold, and disputes whether it shall yield or no, and at last gives up itself to its adversary. And for the affections, commonly the beginning of this evil is in them. They cross one another, and torture the soul with their impetuous violence. By this way is the rule of the law of grace intercepted by the law of sin, even by imposing upon it in the whole seat of its government. When this is done, it is sad work that sin will make in the soul. The apostle warns believers to take heed hereof, Rom. vi. 12, "Let not sin therefore reign in your mortal body, that ye should obey it in the lusts thereof." Look to it that it get not the dominion, that it usurp not rule, no, not for a moment. It will labour to intrude itself unto the throne; watch against it, or a woful state and condition lies at the door. This, then, accompanies this rage and madness of the law of sin:-- It casts off, during its prevalency, the rule of the law of grace wholly; it speaks in the soul, but is not heard; it commands the contrary, but is not obeyed; it cries out, "Do not this abominable thing which the Lord hateth," but is not regarded, -- that is, not so far as to be able to put a present stop to the rage of sin, and to recover its own rule, which God in his own time restores to it by the power of his Spirit dwelling in us.

(2.) Madness or rage is accompanied with fearlessness and contempt of danger. It takes away the power of consideration, and all that influence that it ought to have upon the soul. Hence sinners that are wholly under the power of this rage are said to "run upon God, and the thick bosses of his buckler," Job xv. 26; -- that wherein he is armed for their utter ruin. They despise the utmost that he can do to them, being secretly resolved to accomplish their lusts, though it cost them their souls. Some few considerations will farther clear this unto us:--

[1.] Ofttimes, when the soul is broken loose from the power of renewing grace, God deals with it, to keep it within bounds, by preventing grace. So the Lord declares that he will deal with Israel, Hos. ii. 6; -- "Seeing thou hast rejected me, I will take another course with thee. I will lay obstacles before thee that thou shalt not be able to pass on whither the fury of thy lusts would drive thee." He will propose that to them from without that shall obstruct them in their progress.

[2.] These hinderances that God lays in the way of sinners, as shall be afterward at large declared, are of two sorts:--

1st. Rational considerations, taken from the consequence of the sin and evil that the soul is solicited unto and perplexed withal. Such are the fear of death, judgment, and hell, -- falling into the hands of the living God, who is a consuming fire. Whilst a man is under the power of the law of the Spirit of life, the "love of Christ constraineth him," 2 Cor. v. 14. The principle of his doing good and abstaining from evil is faith working by love, accompanied with a following of Christ because of the sweet savour of his name. But now, when this blessed, easy yoke is for a season cast off, so as was manifested before, God sets a hedge of terror before the soul, minds it of death and judgment to come, flashes the flames of hell-fire in the face, fills the soul with consideration of all the evil consequence of sin, to deter it from its purpose. To this end doth he make use of all threatenings recorded in the law and gospel. To this head also may be referred all the considerations that may be taken from things temporal, as shame, reproach, scandal, punishments, and the like. By the consideration of these things, I say, doth God set a hedge before them.

2dly. Providential dispensations are used by the Lord to the same purpose, and these are of two sorts:--

(1st.) Such as are suited to work upon the soul, and to cause it to desist and give over in its lustings and pursuit of sin. Such are afflictions and mercies: Isa. lvii. 17, "I was wroth, and I smote them;" -- "I testified my dislike of their ways by afflictions." So Hos. ii. 9, 11, 12. God chastens men with pains on their bodies; saith he in Job, "To turn them from their purpose, and to hide sin from them," Job xxxiii. 17-19. And other ways he hath to come to them and touch them, as in their names, relations, estates, and desirable things; or else he heaps mercies on them, that they may consider whom they are rebelling against. It may be signal distinguishing mercies are made their portion for many days.

(2dly.) Such as actually hinder the soul from pursuing sin, though it be resolved so to do. The various ways whereby God doth this we must afterward consider.

These are the ways, I say, whereby the soul is dealt withal, afar the law of indwelling sin hath cast off for a season the influencing power of the law of grace. But now, when lust rises up to rage or madness, it will also contemn all these, even the rod, and Him that hath appointed it. It will rush on shame, reproaches, wrath, and whatever may befall it; that is, though they be presented unto it, it will venture upon them all. Rage and madness is fearless. And this it doth two ways:--

[1st.] It possesseth the mind, that it suffers not the consideration of these things to dwell upon it, but renders the thoughts of them slight and evanid; or if the mind do force itself to a contemplation of them, yet it interposeth between it and the affections, that they shall not be influenced by it in any proportion to what is required. The soul in such a condition will be able to take such things into contemplation, and not at all to be moved by them; and where they do prevail for a season, yet they are insensibly wrought off from the heart again.

[2dly.] By secret stubborn resolves to venture all upon the way wherein it is.

And this is the second branch of this evidence of the power of sin, taken from the opposition that it makes to the law of grace, as it were by the way of force, strength, and violence. The consideration of its deceit doth now follow.

Chapter VIII

Indwelling sin proved powerful from its deceit -- Proved to be deceitful -- The general nature of deceit -- James i. 14, opened -- How the mind is drawn off from its duty by the deceitfulness of sin -- The principal duties of the mind in our obedience -- The ways and means whereby it is turned from it.

The second part of the evidence of the power of sin, from its manner of operation, is taken from its deceitfulness. It adds, in its working, deceit unto power. The efficacy of that must needs be great, and is carefully to be watched against by all such as value their souls, where power and deceit are combined, especially advantaged and assisted by all the ways and means before insisted on.

Before we come to show wherein the nature of this deceitfulness of sin doth consist, and how it prevaileth thereby, some testimonies shall be briefly given in unto the thing itself, and some light into the general nature of it.

That sin, indwelling sin, is deceitful, we have the express testimony of the Holy Ghost, as Heb. iii. 13, "Take heed that ye be not hardened by the deceitfulness of sin." Deceitful it is; take heed of it, watch against it, or it will produce its utmost effect in hardening of the heart against God. It is on the account of sin that the heart is said to be "deceitful above all things," Jer. xvii. 9. Take a man in other things, and, as Job speaks, though he "would be wise and crafty, he is like the wild ass's colt," Job xi. 12, -- a poor, vain, empty nothing; but consider his heart on the account of this law of sin, -- it is crafty and deceitful above all things. "They are wise to do evil," saith the prophet, "but to do good they have no knowledge," Jer. iv. 22. To the same purpose speaks the apostle, Eph. iv. 22, "The old man is corrupt according to the deceitful lusts." Every lust, which is a branch of this law of sin, is deceitful; and where there is poison in every stream, the fountain must needs be corrupt. No particular lust hath any deceit in it, but what is communicated unto it from this fountain of all actual lust, this law of sin. And, 2 Thess. ii. 10, the coming of the "man of sin" is said to be in and with the "deceivableness of unrighteousness." Unrighteousness is a thing generally decried and evil spoken of amongst men, so that it is not easy to conceive how any man should prevail himself of a reputation thereby. But there is a deceivableness in it, whereby the minds of men are turned aside from a due consideration of it; as we shall manifest afterward. And thus the account which the apostle gives concerning those who are under the power of sin is, that they are "deceived," Titus iii. 3. And the life of evil men is nothing but "deceiving, and being deceived," 2 Tim. iii. 13. So that we have sufficient testimony given unto this qualification of the enemy with whom we have to deal. He is deceitful; which consideration of all things puts the mind of man to a loss in dealing with an adversary. He knows he can have no security against one that is deceitful, but in standing upon his own guard and defence all his days.

Farther to manifest the strength and advantage that sin hath by its deceit, we may observe that the Scripture places it for the most part as the head and spring of every sin, even as though there were no sin followed after but where deceit went before. So 1 Tim. ii. 13, 14. The reason the apostle gives why Adam, though he was first formed, was not first in the transgression, is because he was not first deceived. The woman, though made last, yet being first deceived, was first in the sin. Even that first sin began in deceit, and until the mind was deceived the soul was safe. Eve, therefore, did truly express the matter, Gen. iii. 13, though she did it not to a good end. "The serpent beguiled me," saith she, "and I did eat." She thought to extenuate her own crime by charging the serpent; and this was a new fruit of the sin she had cast herself into. But the matter of fact was true, -- she was beguiled before she ate; deceit went before the transgression. And the apostle shows that sin and Satan still take the same course, 2 Cor. xi. 3. "There is," saith he, "the same way of working towards actual sin as was of old: beguiling, deceiving goes before; and sin, that is, the actual accomplishment of it, followeth after." Hence, all the great works that the devil doth in the world, to stir men up to an opposition unto the Lord Jesus Christ and his kingdom, he doth them by deceit: Rev. xii. 9, "The devil, who deceiveth the whole world." It were utterly impossible men should be prevailed on to abide in his service, acting his designs to their eternal, and sometimes their temporal ruin, were they not exceedingly deceived. See also Rev. xx. 10.

Hence are those manifold cautions that are given us to take heed that we be not deceived, if we would take heed that we do not sin. See Eph. v. 6; 1 Cor. vi. 9, xv. 33; Gal. vi. 7; Luke xxi. 8. From all which testimonies we may learn the influence that deceit hath into sin, and consequently the advantage that the law of sin hath to put forth its power by its deceitfulness. Where it prevails to deceive, it fails not to bring forth its fruit.

The ground of this efficacy of sin by deceit is taken from the faculty of the soul affected with it. Deceit properly affects the mind; it is the mind that is deceived. When sin attempts any other way of entrance into the soul, as by the affections, the mind, retaining its right and sovereignty, is able to give check and control unto it. But where the mind is tainted, the prevalency must be great; for the mind or understanding is the leading faculty of the soul, and what that fixes on, the will and affections rush after, being capable of no consideration but what that presents unto them. Hence it is, that though the entanglement of the affections unto sin be ofttimes most troublesome, yet the deceit of the mind is always most dangerous, and that because of the place that it possesseth in the soul as unto all its operations. Its office is to guide, direct, choose, and lead; and "if the light that is in us be darkness, how great is that darkness!"

And this will farther appear if we consider the nature of deceit in general. It consists in presenting unto the soul, or mind, things otherwise than they are, either in their nature, causes, effects, or present respect unto the soul. This is the general nature of deceit, and it prevails many ways. It hides what ought to be seen and considered, conceals circumstances and consequences, presents what is not, or things as they are not, as we shall afterward manifest in particular. It was showed before that Satan "beguiled" and "deceived" our first parents; that term the Holy Ghost gives unto his temptation and seduction. And how he did deceive them the Scripture relates, Gen. iii. 4, 5. He did it by representing things otherwise than they were. The fruit was desirable; that was apparent unto the eye. Hence Satan takes advantage secretly to insinuate that it was merely an abridgment of their happiness that God aimed at in forbidding them to eat of it. That it was for the trial of their obedience, that certain though not immediate ruin would ensue upon the eating of it, he hides from them; only he proposeth the present advantage of knowledge, and so presents the whole case quite otherwise unto them than indeed it was. This is the nature of deceit; it is a representation of a matter under disguise, hiding that which is undesirable, proposing that which indeed is not in it, that the mind may make a false judgment of it: so Jacob deceived Isaac by his brother's raiment and the skins on his hands and neck.

Again; deceit hath advantage by that way of management which is inseparable from it. It is always carried on by degrees, by little and little, that the whole of the design and aim in hand be not at once discovered. So dealt Satan in that great deceit before mentioned; he proceeds in it by steps and degrees, First, he takes off an objection, and tells them they shall not die; then proposeth the good of knowledge to them, and their being like to God thereby. To hide and conceal ends, to proceed by steps and degrees, to make use of what is obtained, and thence to press on to farther effects, is the true nature of deceit. Stephen tells us that the king of Egypt "dealt subtilly," or deceitfully, "with their kindred," Acts vii. 19. How he did it we may see, Exod. i. He did not at first fall to killing and slaying of them, but says, verse 10, "Come, let us deal wisely," beginning to oppress them. This brings forth their bondage, verse 11. Having got this ground to make them slaves, he proceeds to destroy their children, verse 16. He fell not on them all at once, but by degrees. And this may suffice to show in general that sin is deceitful, and the advantages that it hath thereby.

For the way, and manner, and progress of sin in working by deceit, we have it fully expressed, James i. 14, 15, "Every man is tempted when he is drawn away of his own lust, and enticed. Then when lust hath conceived, it bringeth forth sin: and sin, when it is finished, bringeth forth death." This place, declaring the whole of what we aim at in this matter, must be particularly insisted on.

In the foregoing verse the apostle manifests that men are willing to drive the old trade, which our first parents at the entrance of sin set up withal, namely, of excusing themselves in their sins, and casting the occasion and blame of them on others. It is not, say they, from themselves, their own nature and inclinations, their own designings, that they have committed such and such evils, but merely from their temptations; and if they know not where to fix the evil of those temptations, they will lay them on God himself, rather than go without an excuse or extenuation of their guilt. This evil in the hearts of men the apostle rebuketh, verse 13, "Let no man say when he is tempted, I am tempted of God: for God cannot be tempted with evil, neither tempteth he any man." And to show the justness of this reproof, in the words mentioned he discovers the true causes of the rise and whole progress of sin, manifesting that the whole guilt of it lies upon the sinner, and that the whole punishment of it, if not graciously prevented, will be his lot also.

We have, therefore, as was said, in these words the whole progress of lust or indwelling sin, by the way of subtlety, fraud, and deceit, expressed and limited by the Holy Ghost. And from hence we shall manifest the particular ways and means whereby it puts forth its power and efficacy in the hearts of men by deceitfulness and subtlety; and we may observe in the words, --

First, The utmost end aimed at in all the actings of sin, or the tendency of it in its own nature, and that is death: "Sin, when it is finished, bringeth forth death," the everlasting death of the sinner; pretend what it will, this is the end it aims at and tends unto. Hiding of ends and designs is the principal property of deceit. This sin doth to the uttermost; other things innumerable it pleads, but not once declares that it aims at the death, the everlasting death of the soul And a fixed apprehension of this end of every sin is a blessed means to prevent its prevalency in its way of deceit or beguiling.

Secondly, The general way of its acting towards that end is by temptation: "Every man is tempted of his own lust." I purpose not to speak in general of the nature of temptations, it belongs not unto our present purpose; and, besides, I have done it elsewhere. [1] It may suffice at present to observe, that the life of temptation lies in deceit; so that, in the business of sin, to be effectually tempted, and to be beguiled or deceived, are the same. Thus it was in the first temptation. It is everywhere called the serpent's beguiling or deceiving, as was manifested before: "The serpent beguiled Eve;" that is, prevailed by his temptations upon her. So that every man is tempted, -- that is, every man is beguiled or deceived, -- by his own lust, or indwelling sin, which we have often declared to be the same.

The degrees whereby sin proceedeth in this work of tempting or deceiving are five; for we showed before that this belongs unto the nature of deceit, that it works by degrees, making its advantage by one step to gain another.

The first of these consists in drawing off or drawing away: "Every man is tempted when he is drawn away of his own lust."

The second is in enticing: "And is enticed."

The third in the conception of sin: "When lust hath conceived." When the heart is enticed, then lust conceives in it.

The fourth is the bringing forth of sin in its actual accomplishment: "When lust hath conceived it bringeth forth sin." In all which there is a secret allusion to an adulterous deviation from conjugal duties, and conceiving or bringing forth children of whoredom and fornication.

The fifth is the finishing of sin, the completing of it, the filling up of the measure of it, whereby the end originally designed by lust is brought about: "Sin, when it is finished, bringeth forth death." As lust conceiving naturally and necessarily bringeth forth sin, so sin finished infallibly procureth eternal death.

The first of these relates to the mind; that is drawn off or drawn away by the deceit of sin. The second unto the affections; they are enticed or entangled. The third to the will, wherein sin is conceived; the consent of the will being the formal conception of actual sin. The fourth to the conversation wherein sin is brought forth; it exerts itself in the lives and courses of men. The fifth respects an obdurate course in sinning, that finisheth, consummates, and shuts up the whole work of sin, whereon ensues death, or eternal ruin.

I shall principally consider the three first, wherein the main strength of the deceit of sin doth lie; and that because in believers whose state and condition is principally proposed to consideration, God is pleased, for the most part, graciously to prevent the fourth instance, or the bringing forth of actual sins in their conversations; and the last always and wholly, or their being obdurate in a course of sin to the finishing of it. What ways God in his grace and faithfulness makes use of to stifle the conceptions of sin in the womb, and to hinder its actual production in the lives of men, must afterward be spoken unto. The first three instances, then, we shall insist upon fully, as those wherein the principal concernment of believers in this matter doth lie.

The first thing which sin is said to do, working in a way of deceit, is to draw away or to draw off; whence a man is said to be drawn off, or "drawn away" and diverted, -- namely, from attending unto that course of obedience and holiness which, in opposition unto sin and the law thereof, he is bound with diligence to attend unto.

Now, it is the mind that this effect of the deceit of sin is wrought upon. The mind or understanding, as we have showed, is the guiding, conducting faculty of the soul It goes before in discerning, judging, and determining, to make the way of moral actions fair and smooth to the will and affections. It is to the soul what Moses told his father-in-law that he might be to the people in the wilderness, as "eyes to guide them," and keep them from wandering in that desolate place. It is the eye of the soul, without whose guidance the will and affections would perpetually wander in the wilderness of this world, according as any object, with an appearing present good, did offer or present itself unto them.

The first thing, therefore, that sin aims at in its deceitful working, is to draw off and divert the mind from the discharge of its duty.

There are two things which belong unto the duty of the mind in that special office which it hath in and about the obedience which God requireth:--

1. To keep itself and the whole soul in such a frame and posture as may render it ready unto all duties of obedience, and watchful against all enticements unto the conception of sin.

2. In particular, carefully to attend unto all particular actions, that they be performed as God requireth, for matter, manner, time and season, agreeably unto his will; as also for the obviating all particular tenders of sin in things forbidden. In these two things consists the whole duty of the mind of a believer; and from both of them doth indwelling sin endeavour to divert it and draw it off.

1. The first of these is the duty of the mind in reference unto the general frame and course of the whole soul; and hereof two things may be considered. That it is founded in a due, constant

consideration, -- (1.) Of ourselves, of sin and its vileness; (2.) Of God, of his grace and goodness: and both these doth sin labour to draw it off from. 2. In attending to those duties which are suited to obviate the working of the law of sin in an especial manner.

1. (1.) It endeavours to draw it off from a due consideration, apprehension, and sensibleness of its own vileness, and the danger wherewith it is attended. This, in the first place, we shall instance in. A due, constant consideration of sin, in its nature, in all its aggravating circumstances, in its end and tendency, especially as represented in the blood and cross of Christ, ought always to abide with us: Jer. ii. 19, "Know therefore and see that it is an evil thing and a bitter, that thou hast forsaken the Lord thy God." Every sin is a forsaking of the Lord our God. If the heart know not, if it consider not, that it is an evil thing and a bitter, -- evil in itself, bitter in its effects, fruit, and event, -- it will never be secured against it. Besides, that frame of heart which is most accepted with God in any sinner is the humble, contrite, self-abasing frame: Isa. lvii. 15, "Thus saith the high and lofty One that inhabiteth eternity, whose name is Holy; I dwell in the high and holy place, with him also that is of a contrite and humble spirit, to revive the spirit of the humble, and to revive the spirit of the contrite ones." See also Luke xviii. 13, 14. This becomes a sinner; no garment sits so decently about him. "Be clothed with humility," saith the apostle, 1 Pet. v. 5. It is that which becomes us, and it is the only safe frame. He that walketh humbly walketh safely. This is the design of Peter's advice, 1 Pet. i. 17, "Pass the time of your sojourning here in fear." After that he himself had miscarried by another frame of mind, he gives this advice to all believers. It is not a bondage, servile fear, disquieting and perplexing the soul, but such a fear as may keep men constantly calling upon the Father, with reference unto the final judgment, that they may be preserved from sin, whereof they were in so great danger, which he advises them unto: "If ye call on the Father, who without respect of persons judgeth according to every man's work, pass the time of your sojourning here in fear." This is the humble frame of soul And how is this obtained? how is this preserved? No otherwise but by a constant, deep apprehension of the evil, vileness, and danger of sin. So was it wrought, so was it kept up, in the approved publican. "God be merciful," saith he, "to me a sinner." Sense of sin kept him humble, and humility made way for his access unto a testimony of the pardon of sin.

And this is the great preservative through grace from sin, as we have an example in the instance of Joseph, Gen. xxxix. 9. Upon the urgency of his great temptation, he recoils immediately into this frame of spirit. "How," saith he, "can I do this thing, and sin against God?" A constant, steady sense of the evil of sin gives him such preservation, that he ventures liberty and life in opposition to it. To fear sin is to fear the Lord; so the holy man tells us that they are the same: Job xxviii. 28, "The fear of the Lord, that is wisdom; and to depart from evil, that is understanding."

This, therefore, in the first place, in general, doth the law of sin put forth its deceit about, -- namely, to draw the mind from this frame, which is the strongest fort of the soul's defence and security. It labours to divert the mind from a due apprehension of the vileness, abomination, and danger of sin. It secretly and insensibly insinuates lessening, excusing, extenuating thoughts of it; or it draws it off from pondering upon it, from being conversant about it in its thoughts so much as it ought, and formerly hath been. And if, after the heart of a man hath, through the word, Spirit, and grace of Christ, been made tender, soft, deeply sensible of sin, it becomes on any account, or by any means whatever, to have less, fewer, slighter, or less affecting thoughts of it or about it, the mind of that man is drawn away by the deceitfulness of sin.

There are two ways, amongst others, whereby the law of sin endeavours deceitfully to draw off the mind from this duty and frame ensuing thereon:--

[1.] It doth it by a hórrible abuse of gospel grace. There is in the gospel a remedy provided against the whole evil of sin, the filth, the guilt of it, with all its dangerous consequents. It is the doctrine of the deliverance of the souls of men from sin and death, -- a discovery of the gracious will of God towards sinners by Jesus Christ. What, now, is the genuine tendency of this doctrine, of this discovery of grace; and what ought we to use it and improve it unto? This the apostle declares, Titus ii. 11, 12, "The grace of God that bringeth salvation hath appeared to all men, teaching us that, denying ungodliness and worldly lusts, we should live soberly, righteously, and godly, in this present world." This it teacheth; this we ought to learn of it and by it. Hence universal holiness is called a "conversation that becometh the gospel," Phil. i. 27. It becomes it, as that which is answerable unto its end, aim, and design, -- as that which it requires, and which it ought to be improved unto. And accordingly it doth produce this effect where the word of it is received and preserved in a saving light, Rom. xii. 2; Eph. iv. 20-24. But herein doth the deceit of sin interpose itself:-- It separates between the doctrine of grace and the use and end of it. It stays upon its notions, and intercepts its influences in its proper application. From the doctrine of the assured pardon of sin, it insinuates a regardlessness of sin. God in Christ makes the proposition, and Satan and sin make the conclusion. For that the deceitfulness of sin is apt to plead unto a regardlessness of it, from the grace of God whereby it is pardoned, the apostle declares in his reproof and detestation of such an insinuation: Rom. vi. 1, "What shall we say then? shall we continue in sin, that grace may abound? God forbid." "Men's deceitful hearts," saith he, "are apt to make that conclusion; but far be it from us that we should give any entertainment unto it." But yet that Some have evidently improved that deceit unto their own eternal ruin, Jude declares: Verse 4, "Ungodly men, turning the grace of God into lasciviousness." And we have had dreadful instances of it in the days of temptation wherein we have lived.

Indeed, in opposition unto this deceit lies much of the wisdom of faith and power of gospel grace,. When the mind is fully possessed with, and cast habitually and firmly into, the mould of the notion and doctrine of gospel truth about the full and free forgiveness of all sins in the blood of Christ, then to be able to keep the heart always in a deep, humbling sense of sin, abhorrency of it, and self-abasement for it, is a great effect of gospel wisdom and grace. This is the trial and touchstone of gospel light:-- If it keep the heart sensible of sin, humble, lowly, and broken on that account, -- if it teach us to water a free pardon with tears, to detest forgiven sin, to watch diligently for the ruin of that which we are yet assured shall never ruin us, -- it is divine, from above, of the Spirit of grace. If it secretly and insensibly make men loose and slight in their thoughts about sin, it is adulterate, selfish, false. If it will be all, answer all ends, it is nothing.

Hence it comes to pass that sometimes we see men walking in a bondage-frame of spirit all their days, low in their light, mean in their apprehensions of grace; so that it is hard to discern whether covenant in their principles they belong unto, -- whether they are under the law or under grace; yet walk with a more conscientious tenderness of sinning than many who are advanced into higher degrees of light and knowledge than they; -- not that the saving light of the gospel is not the only principle of saving holiness and obedience; but that, through the deceitfulness of sin, it is variously abused to countenance the soul in manifold neglect of duties, and to draw off the mind from a due consideration of the nature, desert, and danger of sin. And this is done several ways:--

1st. The soul, having frequent need of relief by gospel grace against a sense of the guilt of sin and accusation of the law, comes at length to make it a common and ordinary thing, and such as may be slightly performed. Having found a good medicine for its wounds, and such as it hath had experience of its efficacy, it comes to apply it slightly, and rather skinneth over than cureth its sores, A little less earnestness, a little less diligence, serves every time, until the soul, it may be, begins to secure itself of pardon in course; and this tends directly to draw off the mind from its constant and universal watchfulness against sin. He whose light hath made his way of access plain for the obtaining of pardon, if he be not very watchful, he is far more apt to become overly formal and careless in his work than he who, by reason of mists and darkness, beats about to find his way aright to the throne of grace; as a man that hath often travelled a road passeth on without regard or inquiry, but he who is a stranger unto it, observing all turnings and inquiring of all passengers, secures his journey beyond the other.

2dly. The deceitfulness of sin takes advantage from the doctrine of grace by many ways and means to extend the bounds of the soul's liberty beyond what God hath assigned unto it. Some have never thought themselves free from a legal, bondage frame until they have been brought into the confines of sensuality, and some into the depths of it. How often will sin plead, "This strictness, this exactness, this solicitude is no ways needful; relief is provided in the gospel against such things! Would you live as though there were no need of the gospel? as though pardon of sin were to no purpose?" But concerning these pleas of sin from gospel grace, we shall have occasion to speak more hereafter in particular.

3dly. In times of temptation, this deceitfulness of sin will argue expressly for sin from gospel grace; at least, it will plead for these two things:--

(1st.) That there is not need of such a tenacious, severe contending against it, as the principle of the new creature is fixed on. If it cannot divert the soul or mind wholly from attending unto temptations to oppose them, yet it will endeavour to draw them off as to the manner of their attendance. They need not use that diligence which at first the soul apprehends to be necessary.

(2dly.) It will be tendering relief as to the event of sin, -- that it shall not turn to the ruin or destruction of the soul, because it is, it will, or may be, pardoned by the grace of the gospel. And this is true; this is the great and only relief of the soul against sin, the guilt whereof it hath contracted already, -- the blessed and only remedy for a guilty soul. But when it is pleaded and remembered by the deceitfulness of sin in compliance with temptation unto sin, then it is poison; poison is mixed in every drop of this balsam, to the danger, if not death, of the soul. And this is the first way whereby the deceitfulness of sin draws off the mind from a due attendance unto that sense of its vileness which alone is able to keep it in that humble, self-abased frame that is acceptable with God. It makes the mind careless, as though its work were needless, because of the abounding of grace; which is a soldier's neglect of his station, trusting to a reserve, provided, indeed, only in case of keeping his own proper place.

[2.] Sin takes advantage to work by its deceit, in this matter of drawing off the mind from a due sense of it, from the state and condition of men in the world. I shall give only one instance of its procedure in this kind. Men, in their younger days, have naturally their affections more quick, vigorous, and active, more sensibly working in them, than afterward. They do, as to their sensible working and operation, naturally decay, and many things befall men in their lives that take off the edge and keenness of them. But as men lose in their affections, if they are not besotted in sensuality or by the corruptions that are in the world through lust, they grow and improve in their understandings, resolutions, and judgments. Hence it is, that if what had place formerly in their affections do not take place in their minds and judgments, they utterly lose them, they have no more place in their souls. Thus men have no regard for, yea, they utterly despise, those things which their affections were set upon with delight and greediness in their childhood. But if they are things that by any means come to be fixed in their minds and judgments, they continue a high esteem for them, and do cleave as close unto them as they did when their affections were more vigorous; only, as it were, they have changed their seat in the soul. It is thus in things spiritual. The first and chiefest seat of the sensibleness of sin is in the affections. As these in natural youth are great and large, so are they spiritually in spiritual youth: Jer. ii. 2, "I remember the kindness of thy youth, the love of thine espousals." Besides, such persons are newly come off from their convictions, wherein they have been cut to the heart, and so made tender. Whatever touches upon a wound is throughly felt; so doth the guilt of sin before the wound given by conviction be throughly cured. But now, when affections begin to decay naturally, they begin to decay also as to their sensible actings and motions in things spiritual. Although they improve in grace, yet they may decay in sense. At least, spiritual sense is not radically in them, but only by way of communication. Now, in these decays, if the soul take not care to fix a deep sense of sin on the mind and judgment, thereby perpetually to affect the heart and affections, it will decay. And here the deceit of the law of sin interposeth itself. It suffers a sense of sin to decay in the affections, and diverts the mind from entertaining a due, constant, fixed consideration of it. We may consider this a little in persons that never make a progress in the ways of God beyond conviction. How sensible of sin will they be for a season! How will they then mourn and weep under a sense of the guilt of it! How will they cordially and heartily resolve against it! Affections are vigorous, and, as it were, bear rule in their souls. But they are like an herb that will flourish for a day or two with watering although it have no root: for, a while after, we see that these men, the more experience they have had of sin, the less they are afraid of it, as the wise man intimates, Eccles. viii. 11; and at length they come to be the greatest contemners of sin in the world. No sinner like him that hath sinned away his convictions of sin. What is the reason of this? Sense of sin was in their convictions, fixed on their affections. As it decayed in them, they took no care to have it deeply and graciously fixed on their minds. This the deceitfulness of sin deprived them of, and so ruined their souls. In some measure it is so with believers. If, as the sensibleness of the affections decay, if, as they grow heavy and obtuse, great wisdom and grace be not used to fix a due sense of sin upon the mind and judgment, which may provoke, excite, enliven, and stir up the affections every day, great decays will ensue. At first sorrow, trouble, grief, fear, affected the mind, and would give it no rest. If afterward the mind do not affect the heart with sorrow and grief, the whole will be cast out, and the soul be in danger of being hardened. And these are some of the ways whereby the deceit of sin diverts the mind from the first part of its safe preserving frame, or draws it off from its constant watchfulness against sin and all the effects of it.

(2.) The second part of this general duty of the mind is to keep the soul unto a constant, holy consideration of God and his grace. This evidently lies at the spring-head of gospel obedience. The way whereby sin draws off the mind from this part of its duty is open and known sufficiently, though not sufficiently watched against. Now, this the Scripture everywhere declares to be the filling of the minds of men with earthly things. This it placeth in direct opposition unto that heavenly frame of the mind which is the spring of gospel obedience: Col. iii. 2, "Set your affection on things above, not on things on the earth;" or set your minds. As if he had said, "On both together you cannot be set or fixed, so as principally and chiefly to mind them both." And the affections to the one and the other, proceeding from these different principles of minding the one and the other, are opposed, as directly inconsistent: 1 John ii. 15, "Love not the world, neither the things that are in the world. If any man love the world, the love of the Father is not in him." And actings in a course suitable unto these affections are proposed also as contrary: "Ye cannot serve God and mammon." These are two masters whom no man can serve at the same time to the satisfaction of both. Every inordinate minding, then, of earthly things is opposed unto that frame wherein our minds ought to be fixed on God and his grace in a course of gospel obedience.

Several ways there are whereby the deceitfulness of sin draws off the mind in this particular; but the chief of them is by pressing these things on the mind under the notion of things lawful, and, it may be, necessary. So all those who excuse themselves in the parable from coming in to the marriage-feast of the gospel, did it on account of their being engaged in their lawful callings, -- one about his farm, another his oxen, -- the means whereby he ploughed in this world. By this plea were the minds of men drawn off from that frame of heavenliness which is required to our walking with God; and the rules of not loving the world, or using it as if we used it not, are hereby neglected. What wisdom, what watchfulness, what serious frequent trial and examination of ourselves is required, to keep our hearts and minds in a heavenly frame, in the use and pursuit of earthly things, is not my present business to declare. This is evident, that the engine whereby the deceit of sin draws off and turns aside the mind in this matter is the pretence of the lawfulness of things about which it would have it exercise itself; against which very few are armed with sufficient diligence, wisdom, and skill. And this is the first and most general attempt that indwelling sin makes upon the soul by deceit, -- it draws away the mind from a diligent attention unto its course in a due sense of the evil of sin, and a due and constant consideration of God and his grace.

Footnote:

1. See the previous treatise on Temptation.

Chapter IX

The deceit of sin in drawing off the mind from a due attendance unto especial duties of obedience, instanced in meditation and prayer.

How [2] sin by its deceit endeavours to draw off the mind from attending unto that holy frame in walking with God wherein the soul ought to be preserved, hath been declared; proceed we now to show how it doth the same work in reference unto those especial duties by which the designs, workings, and prevalency of it may in an especial manner be obviated and prevented. Sin, indeed, maintains an enmity against all duties of obedience, or rather with God in them. "When I would do good," saith the apostle, "evil is present with me;" -- "Whenever I would do good, or what good soever I would do, (that is, spiritually good, good in reference unto God), it is present with me to hinder me from it, to oppose me in it." And, on the other side, all duties of obedience do lie directly against the actings of the law of sin; for as the flesh in all its actings lusteth against the Spirit, so the Spirit in all its actings lusteth against the flesh. And therefore every duty performed in the strength and grace of the Spirit is contrary to the law of sin: Rom. viii. 13, "If ye through the Spirit do mortify the deeds of the flesh." Actings of the Spirit of grace in duties doth this work. These two are contrary. But yet there are some duties which, in their own nature and by God's appointment, have a peculiar influence into the weakening and subduing the whole law of sin in its very principles and chiefest strengths; and these the mind of a believer ought principally in his whole course to attend unto; and these doth sin in its deceit endeavour principally to draw off the mind from. As in diseases of the body, some remedies, they say, have a specific quality against distempers; so, in this disease of the soul, there are some duties that have an especial virtue against this sinful distemper. I shall not insist on many of them, but instance only in two, which seem to me to be of this nature, -- namely, that by God's designation they have a special tendency towards the ruin of the law of sin. And then we shall show the ways, methods, and means, which the law of sin useth to divert the mind from a due attendance unto them. Now, these duties are, -- first, Prayer, especially private prayer; and, secondly, Meditation. I put them together, because they much agree in their general nature and end, differing only in the manner of their performance; for by meditation I intend meditating upon what respect and suitableness there is between the word and our own hearts, to this end, that they may be brought to a more exact conformity. It is our pondering on the truth as it is in Jesus, to find out the image and representation of it in our own hearts; and so it hath the same intent with prayer, which is to bring our souls into a frame in all things answering the mind and will of God. They are as the blood and spirits in the veins, that have the same life, motion, and use. But yet, because persons are generally at a great loss in this duty of meditation, having declared it to be of so great efficacy for the controlling of the actings of the law of sin, I shall in our passage give briefly two or three rules for the directing of believers to a right performance of this great duty, and they are these:--

1. Meditate of God with God; that is, when we would undertake thoughts and meditations of God, his excellencies, his properties, his glory, his majesty, his love, his goodness, let it be done in a way of speaking unto God, in a deep humiliation and abasement of our souls before him. This will fix the mind, and draw it forth from one thing to another, to give glory unto God in a due manner, and affect the soul until it be brought into that holy admiration of God and delight in him which is acceptable unto him. My meaning is, that it be done in a way of prayer and praise, -- speaking unto God.

2. Meditate on the word in the word; that is, in the reading of it, consider the sense in the particular passages we insist upon, looking to God for help, guidance, and direction, in the discovery of his mind and will therein, and then labour to have our hearts affected with it.

3. What we come short of in evenness and constancy in our thoughts in these things, let it be made up in frequency. Some are discouraged because their minds do not regularly supply them with thoughts to carry on their meditations, through the weakness or imperfection of their inventions. Let this be supplied by frequent returns of the mind unto the subject proposed to be meditated upon, whereby new senses will still be supplied unto it. But this by the way.

These duties, I say, amongst others (for we have only chosen them for an instance, not excluding some others from the same place, office, and usefulness with them), do make an especial opposition to the very being and life of indwelling sin, or rather faith in them doth so. They are perpetually designing its utter ruin. I shall, therefore, upon this instance, in the pursuit of our present purpose, do these two things:-- (1.) Show the suitableness and usefulness of this duty, or these duties (as I shall handle them jointly), unto the ruining of sin. (2.) Show the means whereby the deceitfulness of sin endeavours to draw off the mind from a due attendance unto them.

(1.) For the first, observe, --

[1.] That it is the proper work of the soul, in this duty, to consider all the secret workings and actings of sin, what advantages it hath got, what temptations it is in conjunction withal, what harm it hath already done, and what it is yet farther ready to do. Hence David gives that title unto one of his prayers: Psalm cii., "A prayer of the afflicted, when he is overwhelmed, and poureth out his complaint before the Lord." I speak of that prayer which is attended with a due consideration of all the wants, straits, and emergencies of the soul. Without this, prayer is not prayer; that is, whatever show or appearance of that duty it hath, it is no way useful, either to the glory of God or the good of the souls of men. A cloud it is without water, driven by the wind of the breath of men. Nor was there ever any more present and effectual poison for souls found out than the binding of them unto a constant form and usage of I know not what words in their prayers and supplications, which themselves do not understand. Bind men so in their trades or in their businesses in this world, and they will quickly find the effect of it. By this means are they disenabled from any due consideration of what at present is good for them or evil unto them; without which, to what use can prayer serve, but to mock God and delude men's own souls? But in this kind of prayer which we insist on, the Spirit of God falls in to give us his assistance, and that in this very matter of finding out and discovering the most secret actings and workings of the law of sin: Rom. viii. 26, "We know not what we should pray for as we ought, but he helpeth our infirmities;" he discovers our wants unto us, and wherein chiefly we stand in need of help and relief. And we find it by daily experience, that in prayer believers are led into such discoveries and convictions of the secret deceitful work of sin in their hearts, as no considerations could ever have led them into. So David, Psalm li., designing the confession of his actual sin, having his wound in his prayer searched by the skillful hand of the Spirit of God, he had a discovery made unto him of the root of all his miscarriages, in his original corruption, verse 5. The Spirit in this duty is as the candle of the Lord unto the soul, enabling it to search all the inward parts of the belly. It gives a holy, spiritual light into the mind, enabling it to search the deep and dark recesses of the heart, to find out the subtle and deceitful machinations, figments, and imaginations of the law of sin therein. Whatever notion there be of it, whatever power and prevalency in it, it is laid hand on, apprehended, brought into the presence of God, judged, condemned, bewailed. And what can possibly be more effectual for its ruin and destruction? for, together with its discovery, application is made unto all that relief which in Jesus Christ is provided against it, all ways and means whereby it may be ruined. Hence, it is the duty of the mind to "watch unto prayer," 1 Pet. iv. 7, to attend diligently unto the estate of our souls, and to deal fervently and effectually with God about it. The like also may be said of meditation, wisely managed unto its proper end.

[2.] In this duty there is wrought upon the heart a deep, full sense of the vileness of sin, with a constant renewed detestation of it; which, if any thing, undoubtedly tends to its ruin. This is one design of prayer, one end of the soul in it, -- namely, to draw forth sin, to set it in order, to present it unto itself in its vileness, abomination, and aggravating circumstances, that it may be loathed, abhorred, and cast away as a filthy thing; as Isa. xxx. 22. He that pleads with God for sin's remission, pleads also with his own heart for its detestation, Hos. xiv. 3. Herein, also, sin is judged in the name of God; for the soul in its confession subscribes unto God's detestation of it, and the sentence of his law against it. There is, indeed, a course of these duties which convinced persons do give up themselves unto as a mere covert to their lusts; they cannot sin quietly unless they perform duty constantly. But that prayer we speak of is a thing of another nature, a thing that will allow no composition with sin, much less will serve the ends of the deceit of it, as the other, formal prayer, doth. It will not be bribed into a secret compliance with any of the enemies of God or the soul, no, not for a moment. And hence it is that oftentimes in this duty the heart is raised to the most sincere, effectual sense of sin and detestation of it that the soul ever obtains in its whole course of obedience. And this evidently tends also to the weakening and ruin of the law of sin.

[3.] This is the way appointed and blessed of God to obtain strength and power against sin: James i. 5, "Doth any man lack? let him ask of God." Prayer is the way of obtaining from God by Christ a supply of all our wants, assistance against all opposition, especially that which is made against us by sin. This, I suppose, need not be insisted on; it is, in the notion and practice, clear to every believer. It is that wherein we call, and upon which the Lord Jesus comes in to our succour with suitable "help in time of need," Heb. iv. 16.

[4.] Faith in prayer countermines all the workings of the deceit of sin; and that because the soul doth therein constantly engage itself unto God to oppose all sin whatsoever: Ps. cxix. 106, "I have sworn, and I will perform it, that I will keep thy righteous judgments." This is the language of every gracious soul in its addresses unto God: the inmost parts thereof engage themselves to God, to cleave to him in all things, and to oppose sin in all things. He that cannot do this cannot pray. To pray with any other frame is to flatter God with our lips, which he abhorreth. And this exceedingly helps a believer in pursuing sin unto its ruin; for, --

1st. If there be any secret lust that lies lurking in the heart, he will find it either rising up against this engagement, or using its artifices to secure itself from it. And hereby it is discovered, and the conviction of the heart concerning its evil furthered and strengthened. Sin makes the most certain discovery of itself; and never more evidently than when it is most severely pursued. Lusts in men are compared to hurtful and noisome beasts; or men themselves are so because of their lusts, Isa. xi. 4-6. Now, such beasts use themselves to their dens and coverts, and never discover themselves, at least so much in their proper nature and rage, as when they are most earnestly pursued. And so it is with sin and corruption in the heart.

2dly. If any sin be prevalent in the soul, it will weaken it, and take it off from the universality of this engagement unto God; it will breed a tergiversation unto it, a slightness in it. Now, when this is observed, it will exceedingly awaken a gracious soul, and stir it up to look about it. As spontaneous lassitude, or a causeless weariness and indisposition of the body, is looked on as the sign of an approaching fever or some dangerous distemper, which stirs up men to use a timely and vigorous prevention, that they be not seized upon by it, so is it in this case. When the soul of a believer finds in itself an indisposition to make fervent, sincere engagements of universal holiness unto God, it knows that there is some prevalent distemper in it, finds the place of it, and sets itself against it.

3dly. Whilst the soul can thus constantly engage itself unto God, it is certain that sin can rise unto no ruinous prevalency. Yea, it is a conquest over sin, a most considerable conquest, when the soul doth fully and clearly, without any secret reserve, come off with alacrity and resolution in such an engagement; as Ps. xviii. 23. And it may upon such a success triumph in the grace of God, and have good hope, through faith, that it shall have a final conquest, and what it so resolves shall be done; that it hath decreed a thing, and it shall be established. And this tends to the disappointment, yea, to the ruin of the law of sin.

4thly. If the heart be not deceived by cursed hypocrisy, this engagement unto God will greatly influence it unto a peculiar diligence and watchfulness against all sin. There is no greater evidence of hypocrisy than to have the heart like the whorish woman, Prov. vii. 14, -- to say, "?I have paid my vows,' now I may take myself unto my sin;" or to be negligent about sin, as being satisfied that it hath prayed against it. It is otherwise in a gracious soul. Sense and conscience of engagements against sin made to God, do make it universally watchful against all its motions and operations. On these and sundry other accounts doth faith in this duty exert itself peculiarly to the weakening of the power and stopping of the progress of the law of sin.

If, then, the mind be diligent in its watch and charge to preserve the soul from the efficacy of sin, it will carefully attend unto this duty and the due performance of it, which is of such singular advantage unto its end and purpose. Here, therefore, --

(2.) Sin puts forth its deceit in its own defence. It labours to divert and draw off the mind from attending unto this and the like duties. And there are, among others, three engines, three ways and means, whereby it attempts the accomplishment of its design:--

[1.] It makes advantage of its weariness unto the flesh. There is an aversation, as hath been declared, in the law of sin unto all immediate communion with God. Now, this duty is such. There is nothing accompanieth it whereby the carnal part of the soul may be gratified or satisfied, as there may be somewhat of that nature in most public duties, in most that a man can do beyond pure acts of faith and love. No relief or advantage, then, coming in by it but what is purely spiritual, it becomes wearisome, burdensome to flesh and blood. It is like travelling alone without companion or diversion, which makes the way seem long, but brings the passenger with most speed to his journey's end. So our Saviour declares, when, expecting his disciples, according to their duty and present distress, should have been engaged in this work, he found them fast asleep: Matt. xxvi. 41, "The spirit," saith he, "indeed is willing, but the flesh is weak;" and out of that weakness grow their indisposition unto and weariness of their duty. So God complains of his people: Isa. xliii. 22, "Thou hast been weary of me." And it may come at length unto that height which is mentioned, Mal. i. 13, "Ye have said, Behold, what a weariness is it! and ye have snuffed at it, saith the Lord of hosts." The Jews suppose that it was the language of men when they brought their offerings or sacrifices on their shoulders, which they pretended wearied them, and they panted and blowed as men ready to faint under them, when they brought only the torn, and the lame, and the sick. But so is this duty oftentimes to the flesh. And this the deceitfulness of sin makes use of to draw the heart by insensible degrees from a constant attendance unto it. It puts in for the relief of the weak and weary flesh. There is a compliance between spiritual flesh and natural flesh in this matter, -- they help one another; and an aversation unto this duty is the effect of their compliance. So it was in the spouse, Cant. v. 2, 8. She was asleep, drowsing in her spiritual condition, and pleads her natural unfitness to rouse herself from that state. If the mind be not diligently watchful to prevent insinuations from hence, -- if it dwell not constantly on those considerations which evidence an attendance unto this duty to be indispensable, -- if it stir not up the principle of grace in the heart to retain its rule and sovereignty, and not to be dallied withal by foolish pretences, -- it will be drawn off;

which is the effect aimed at.

[2.] The deceitfulness of sin makes use of corrupt reasonings, taken from the pressing and urging occasions of life. "Should we," says it in the heart, "attend strictly unto all duties in this kind, we should neglect our principal occasions, and be useless unto ourselves and others in the world." And on this general account, particular businesses dispossess particular duties from their due place and time. Men have not leisure to glorify God and save their own souls, It is certain that God gives us time enough for all that he requires of us in any kind in this world. No duties need to jostle one another, I mean constantly. Especial occasions must be determined according unto especial circumstances. But if in any thing we take more upon us than we have time well to perform it in, without robbing God of that which is due to him and our own souls, this God calls not unto, this he blesseth us not in. It is more tolerable that our duties of holiness and regard to God should intrench upon the duties of our callings and employments in this world than on the contrary; and yet neither doth God require this at our hands, in an ordinary manner or course. How little, then, will he bear with that which evidently is so much worse upon all accounts whatever! But yet, through the deceitfulness of sin, thus are the souls of men beguiled. By several degrees they are at length driven from their duty.

[3.] It deals with the mind, to draw it off from its attendance unto this duty, by a tender of a compensation to be made in and by other duties; as Saul thought to compensate his disobedience by sacrifice. "May not the same duty performed in public or in the family suffice?" And if the soul be so foolish as not to answer, "Those things ought to be done, and this not to be lest undone," it may be ensnared and deceived. For, besides a command unto it, namely, that we should personally "watch unto prayer," there are, as hath been declared, sundry advantages in this duty so performed against the deceit and efficacy of sin, which in the more public attendance unto it it hath not. These sin strives to deprive the soul of by this commutation, which by its corrupt reasonings it tenders unto it.

[4.] I may add here that which hath place in all the workings of sin by deceit, -- namely, its feeding the soul with promises and purposes of a more diligent attendance unto this duty when occasions will permit. By this means it brings the soul to say unto its convictions of duty, as Felix did to Paul, "Go thy way for this time; when I have a convenient season, I will call for thee." And by this means oftentimes the present season and time, which alone is ours, is lost irrecoverably.

These are some of the ways and means whereby the deceit of sin endeavours to draw off the mind from its due attendance unto this duty, which is so peculiarly suited to prevent its progress and prevalency, and which aims so directly and immediately at its ruin. I might instance also in other duties of the like tendency; but this may suffice to discover the nature of this part of the deceit of sin. And this is the first way whereby it makes way for the farther entangling of the affections and the conception of sin. When sin hath wrought this effect on any one, he is said to be "drawn away," to be diverted from what in his mind he ought constantly to attend unto in his walking before the Lord.

And this will instruct us to see and discern where lies the beginning of our declensions and failings in the ways of God, and that either as to our general course or as to our attendance unto especial duties. And this is of great importance and concernment unto us. When the beginnings and occasions of a sickness or distemper of body are known, it is a great advantage to direct in and unto the cure of it. God, to recall Zion to himself, shows her where was the "beginning of her sin," Micah i. 13. Now, this is that which for the most part is the beginning of sin unto us, even the drawing off the mind from a due attendance in all things unto the discharge of its duty. The principal care and charge of the soul lies on the mind; and if that fail of its duty, the whole is betrayed, either as unto its general frame or as unto particular miscarriages. The failing of the mind is like the failing of the watchman in Ezekiel; the whole is lost by his neglect. This, therefore, in that self-scrutiny and search which we are called unto, we are most diligently to inquire after. God doth not look at what duties we perform, as to their number and tale, or as to their nature merely, but whether we do them with that intension of mind and spirit which he requireth. Many men perform duties in a road or course, and do not, as it were, so much as think of them; their minds are filled with other things, only duty takes up so much of their time. This is but an endeavour to mock God and deceive their own souls. Would you, therefore, take the true measure of yourselves, consider how it is with you as to the duty of your minds which we have inquired after. Consider whether, by any of the deceits mentioned, you have not been diverted and drawn away; and if there be any decays upon you in any kind, you will find that there hath been the beginning of them. By one way or other your minds have been made heedless, regardless, slothful, uncertain, being beguiled and drawn off from their duty. Consider the charge, Prov. iv. 23-27. May not such a soul say, "If I had attended more diligently; if I had considered more wisely the vile nature of sin; if! had not suffered my mind to be possessed with vain hopes and foolish imaginations, by a cursed abuse of gospel grace; if I had not permitted it to be filled with the things of the world, and to become negligent in attending unto especial duties, -- I had not at this day been thus sick, weak, thriftless, wounded, decayed, defiled. My careless, my deceived mind, hath been the beginning of sin and transgression unto my soul." And this discovery will direct the soul unto a suitable way for its healing and recovery; which will never be effected by a multiplying of particular duties, but by a restoring of the mind, Ps. xxiii. 3.

And this, also, doth hence appear to be the great means of preserving our souls, both as unto their general frame and particular duties, according to the mind and will of God, -- namely, to endeavour after a sound and steadfast mind. It is a signal grace to have "the spirit of power, and of love, and of a sound mind," 2 Tim. i. 7; -- a stable, solid, resolved mind in the things of God, not easily moved, diverted, changed, not drawn aside; a mind not apt to hearken after corrupt reasonings, vain insinuations, or pretences to draw it off from its duty. This is that which the apostle exhorts believers unto: 1 Cor. xv. 58, "Therefore, my beloved brethren, be ye steadfast, unmovable, always abounding in the work of the Lord." The steadfastness of our minds abiding in their duty is the cause of all our unmovableness and fruitfulness in obedience; and so Peter tells us that those who are by any means led away or enticed, "they.fall from their own steadfastness," 2 Pet. iii. 17. And the great blame that is laid upon backsliders is, that they are not steadfast: Ps. lxxviii. 37, "Their heart was not steadfast." For if the soul be safe, unless the mind be drawn off from its duty, the soundness and steadfastness of the mind is its great preservative. And there are three parts of this steadfastness of the mind:-- First, A full purpose of cleaving to God in all things; Secondly, A daily renovation and quickening of the heart unto a discharge of this purpose; Thirdly, Resolutions against all dalliances or parleys about negligences in that discharge; -- which are not here to be spoken unto.

Footnote:

2. At the head of this paragraph the numeral 2. ought to have stood, in order to unfold the division begun on page 217, line 20. Great complexity would be occasioned in the subsequent numeration if it were inserted, and it does not appear in the original edition. Each chapter is generally made to contain its own series of numerals. -- Ed.

Chapter X

The deceit of sin, in drawing off the mind from its attendance unto particular duties, farther discovered -- Several things required in the mind of believers with respect unto particular duties of obedience -- The actings of sin, in a way of deceit, to divert the mind from them.

We have not as yet brought unto an issue the first way of the working of the deceit of sin, -- namely, in its drawing away of the mind from the discharge of its duty, which we insist upon the longer upon a double account:--

First, Because of its importance and concernment. If the mind be drawn off, if it be tainted, weakened, turned aside from a due and strict attendance unto its charge and office, the whole soul, will, and affections are certainly entangled and drawn into sin; as hath been in part declared, and will afterward farther appear. This we ought therefore to give diligent heed unto; which is the design of the apostle's exhortation: Heb. ii. 1, "Therefore we ought to give the more earnest heed to the things which we have heard, lest at any time we should let them slip." It is a failure of our minds, by the deceitfulness of sin, in losing the life, power, sense, and impression of the word, which he cautions us against. And there is no way to prevent it but by giving of most "earnest heed unto the things which we have heard;" which expresseth the whole duty of our minds in attending unto obedience.

Secondly, Because the actings and workings of the mind being spiritual, are such as the conscience, unless clearly enlightened and duly excited and stirred up, is not affected withal, so as to take due notice of them. Conscience is not apt to exercise reflex acts upon the mind's failures, as principally respecting the acts of the whole soul. When the affections are entangled with sin (of which afterward), or the will begins to conceive it by its express consent, conscience is apt to make an uproar in the soul, and to give it no rest or quiet until the soul be reclaimed, or itself be one way or other bribed or debauched; but these neglects of the mind being spiritual, without very diligent attendance they are seldom taken notice of. Our minds are often in the Scriptures called our spirits, -- as Rom. i. 9, "Whom I serve with my spirit;" and are distinguished from the soul, which principally intends the affections in that distribution, 1 Thess. v. 23, "Sanctify you wholly, your whole spirit and soul," -- that is, your mind and affections. It is true, where the [word] "spirit" is used to express spiritual gifts, it is, as unto those gifts, opposed to our "understanding," 1 Cor. xiv. 15, which is there taken for the first act of the mind in a rational perception of things; but as that word is applied unto any faculty of our souls, it is the mind that it expresseth. This, then, being our spirit, the actings of it are secret and hidden, and not to be discovered without spiritual wisdom and diligence. Let us not suppose, then, that we dwell too long on this consideration, which is of so great importance to us, and yet so hidden, and which we are apt to be very insensible of; and yet our carefulness in this matter is one of the best evidences that we have of our sincerity. Let us not, then, be like a man that is sensible, and complains of a cut finger, but not of a decay of spirits tending unto death. There remains therefore, as unto this head of our discourse, the consideration of the charge of the mind in reference unto particular duties and sins; and in the consideration of it we shall do these two things: 1. Show what is required in the mind of a believer in reference unto particular duties. 2. Declare the way of the working of the deceit of sin, to draw it off from its attendance thereunto. The like also shall be done with respect unto particular sins, and their avoidance:--

1. For the right performance of any duty, it is not enough that the thing itself required be performed, but that it be universally squared and fitted unto the rule of it. Herein lies the great duty of the mind, -- namely, to attend unto the rule of duties, and to take care that all the concernments of them be ordered thereby. Our progress in obedience is our edification or building. Now, it is but a very little furtherance unto a building, that a man bring wood and stones, and heap them up together without order; they must be hewed and squared, and fitted by line and rule, if we intend to build. Nor is it unto any advantage unto our edification in faith and obedience that we multiply duties, if we heap them upon one another, if we order and dispose them not according to rule; and therefore doth God expressly reject a multitude of duties, when not universally suited unto the rule: Isa. i. 11, "To what purpose is the multitude of your sacrifices?" and, verse 14, "They are a trouble unto me; I am weary to bear them." And therefore all acceptable obedience is called a proceeding according unto "rule," Gal. vi. 16; it is a canonical or regular obedience. As letters in the alphabet heaped together signify nothing, unless they

are disposed into their proper order, no more do our duties without this disposal. That they be so is the great duty of the mind, and which with all diligence it is to attend unto: Eph. v. 15, "Walk circumspectly," exactly, accurately, that is, diligently, in all things; take heed to the rule of what you do. We walk in duties, but we walk circumspectly in this attention of the mind.

(1.) There are some special things which the rule directs unto that the mind is to attend in every duty. As, --

[1.] That, as to the matter of it, it be full and complete. Under the law no beast was allowed to be a sacrifice that had any member wanting, any defect of parts. Such were rejected, as well as those that were lame or blind. Duties must be complete as to the parts, the matter of them. There may be such a part of the price kept back as may make the tendering of all the residue unacceptable. Saul sparing Agag and the fattest of the cattle, rendered the destroying of all the rest useless. Thus, when men will give alms, or perform other services, but not unto the proportion that the rule requireth, and which the mind by diligent attention unto it might discover, the whole duty is vitiated.

[2.] As to the principle of it, -- namely, that it be done in faith, and therein by an actual derivation of strength from Christ, John xv. 5, without whom we can do nothing. It is not enough that the person be a believer, though that be necessary unto every good work, Eph. ii. 10, but also that faith be peculiarly acted in every duty that we do; for our whole obedience is the "obedience of faith," Rom. i. 5, -- that is, which the doctrine of faith requireth, and which the grace of faith beareth or bringeth forth. So Christ is expressly said to be "our life," Col. iii. 4, our spiritual life; that is, the spring, author, and cause of it. Now, as in life natural, no vital act can be performed but by the actual operation of the principle of life itself; so, in life spiritual, no spiritually-vital act, -- that is, no duty acceptable to God, -- can be performed but by the actual working of Christ, who is our life. And this is no other way derived unto us but by faith; whence saith the apostle, Gal. ii. 20, "Christ liveth in me: and the life which I now live in the flesh I live by the faith of the Son of God." Not only was Christ his life, a living principle unto him, but he led a life, -- that is, discharged vital actions in all duties of holiness and obedience, -- by the faith of the Son of God, or in him, deriving supplies of grace and strength from him thereby. This, therefore, ought a believer diligently to attend unto, -- namely, that everything he doth to God be done in the strength of Christ; which wherein it consisteth ought diligently to be inquired into by all who intend to walk with God.

[3.] In this respect unto rule, the manner of the performance of every duty is to be regarded. Now, there are two things in the manner of the performance of any duty which a believer, who is trusted with spiritual light, ought to attend unto:--

1st. That it be done in the way and by the means that God hath prescribed with respect unto the outward manner of its performance And this is especially to be regarded in duties of the worship of God, the matter and outward manner whereof do both equally fall under his command. If this be not regarded, the whole duty is vitiated. I speak not of them who suffer themselves to be deluded by the deceitfulness of sin, utterly to disregard the rule of the word in such things, and to worship God according to their own imaginations; but of them principally who, although they in general profess to do nothing but what God requires, and as he requires it, yet do not diligently attend to the rule, to make the authority of God to be the sole cause and reason both of what they do and of the manner of the performance of it. And this is the reason that God so often calls on his people to consider diligently and wisely, that they may do all according as he had commanded.

2dly. The affections of the heart and mind in duties belong to the performance of them in the inward manner. The prescriptions and commands of God for attendance hereunto are innumerable, and the want hereof renders every duty an abomination unto him. A sacrifice without a heart, without salt, without fire, of what value is it? No more are duties without spiritual affections. And herein is the mind to keep the charge of God, -- to see that the heart which he requires be tendered to him. And we find, also, that God requireth especial affections to accompany special duties: "He that giveth, with cheerfulness;" which, if they are not attended unto, the whole is lost.

[4.] The mind is to attend unto the ends of duties, and therein principally the glory of God in Christ. Several other ends will sin and self impose upon our duties: especially two it will press hard upon us with, -- first, Satisfaction of our convictions and consciences; secondly, The praise of men; for self-righteousness and ostentation are the main ends of men that are fallen off from God in all moral duties whatsoever. In their sins they endeavour for to satisfy their lusts; in their duties, their conviction and pride. These the mind of a believer is diligently to watch against, and to keep up in all a single eye to the glory of God, as that which answers the great and general rule of all our obedience: "Whatsoever ye do, do all to the glory of God." These and the like things, I say, which are commonly spoken unto, is the mind of a believer obliged to attend diligently and constantly unto, with respect unto all the particular duties of our walking before God. Here, then, lies no small part of the deceit of sin, -- namely, to draw the mind off from this watch, to bring an inadvertency upon it, that it shall not in these things keep the watch and charge of the Lord. And if it can do so, and thereby strip our duties of all their excellencies, which lie in these concernments of them, that the mind is to attend unto, it will not much trouble itself nor us about the duties themselves. And this it attempts several ways:--

1st. By persuading the mind to content itself with generals, and to take it off from attending unto things in particular instances. For example, it would persuade the soul to rest satisfied in a general aim of doing things to the glory of God, without considering how every particular duty may have that tendency. Thus Saul thought that he had fulfilled his own duty, and done the will of God, and sought his glory in his war against Amalek, when, for want of attendance to every particular duty in that service, he had dishonoured God, and ruined himself and his posterity. And men may persuade themselves that they have a general design for the glory of God, when they have no active principle in particular duties tending at all that way. But if, instead of fixing the mind by faith on the peculiar advancing the glory of God in a duty, the soul content itself with a general notion of doing so, the mind is already diverted and drawn off from its charge by the deceitfulness of sin. If a man be travelling in a journey, it is not only required of him that he bend his course that way, and so go on; but if he attend not unto every turning, and other occurrences in his way, he may wander and never come to his journey's end. And if we suppose that in general we aim at the glory of God, as we all profess to do, yet if we attend not unto it distinctly upon every duty that occurs in our way, we shall never attain the end aimed at. And he who satisfies himself with this general purpose, without acting it in every special duty, will not long retain that purpose neither. It doth the same work upon the mind, in reference unto the principle of our duties, as it doth unto the end. Their principle is, that they be done in faith, in the strength of Christ; but if men content themselves that they are believers, that they have faith, and do not labour in every particular duty to act faith, to lead their spiritual lives, in all the acts of them, by the faith of the Son of God, the mind is drawn off from its duty. It is particular actions wherein we express and exercise our faith and obedience; and what we are in them, that we are, and no more.

2dly. It draws off the mind from the duties before mentioned by insinuating a secret contentment into it from the duty itself performed, as to the matter of it. This is a fair discharge of a natural conscience. If the duty be performed, though as to the manner of its performance it come short almost in all things of the rule, conscience and conviction will be satisfied; as Saul, upon his expedition against Amalek, cries to Samuel, "Come in, thou blessed of the Lord; I have performed the commandment of the Lord." He satisfied himself, though he had not attended as he ought to the whole will of God in that matter. And thus was it with them, Isa. lviii. 3, "Wherefore have we fasted, say they, and thou regardest it not?" They had pleased themselves in the performance of their duties, and expected that God also should be pleased with them. But he shows them at large wherein they had failed, and that so far as to render what they had done an abomination; and the like charge he expresseth against them, chap. xlviii. 1, 2. This the deceitfulness of sin endeavours to draw the mind unto, namely, to take up in the performance of the duty itself. "Pray thou oughtst, and thou hast prayed; give alms thou oughtst, and thou hast given alms; quiet, then, thyself in what thou hast done, and go on to do the like." If it prevail herein the mind is discharged from farther attendance and watching unto duty, which leaves the soul on the borders of many evils; for, --

3dly. Hence customariness in all duties will quickly ensue, which is the height of sin's drawing off the mind from duty: for men's minds may be drawn from all duties, in the midst of the most abundant performance of them; for in and under them the mind may be subject unto an habitual diversion from its charge and watch unto the rule. What is done with such a frame is not done to God, Amos v. 25. None of their sacrifices were to God, although they professed that they were all so. But they attended not unto his worship in faith, and unto his glory, and he despised all their duties, See also Hos. x. 1. And this is the great reason why professors thrive so little under the performance of a multitude of duties:-- They attend not unto them in a due manner, their minds being drawn off from their circumspect watch; and so they have little or no communion with God in them, which is the end whereunto they are designed, and by which alone they become useful and profitable unto themselves. And in this manner are many duties of worship and obedience performed by a woful generation of hypocrites, formalists, and profane persons, without either life or light in themselves, or acceptation with God, their minds being wholly estranged from a due attendance unto what they do by the power and deceitfulness of sin.

2. As it is in respect of duties, so also it is in respect of sins. There are sundry things in and about every sin that the mind of a believer, by virtue of its office and duty, is obliged to attend diligently unto, for the preservation of the soul from it. Things they are which God hath appointed and sanctified, to give effectual rebukes and checks to the whole working of the law of sin, and such as, in the law of grace, under which we are, are exceedingly suited and fitted unto that purpose. And these the deceit of sin endeavours by all means to draw off the mind from a due consideration of and attendance unto. Some few of them we shall a little reflect upon:--

(1.) The first and most general is the sovereignty of God, the great lawgiver, by whom it is forbidden. This Joseph fixed on in his great temptation: Gen. xxxix. 9, "How can I do this great wickedness, and sin against God?" There was in it a great evil, a great ingratitude against man, which he pleads also and insists upon, verses 8, 9; but that which fixed his heart and resolution against it was the formality of it, that it was sin against God, by whom it was severely forbidden. So the apostle informs us that in our dealing in any thing that is against the law, our respect is still to be unto the Lawgiver and his sovereignty: James iv. 11, 12, "If thou judge the law, thou art not a doer of the law, but a judge. There is one lawgiver, who is able to save and to destroy." Consider this always: there is one lawgiver, holy, righteous, armed with sovereign power and authority; he is able to save and destroy. Hence sin is called a rebellion, a casting off his yoke, a despising of him, and that in his sovereignty as the great lawgiver; and this ought the mind always practically to attend unto, in all the lustings, actings, and suggestions of the law of sin, especially when advantaged by any suitable or vigorous temptation: "It is God that hath forbidden this thing; the great lawgiver, under whose absolute sovereignty I am, in dependence on whom I live, and by whom I am to be disposed of, as to my present and eternal condition." This Eve fixed on at the beginning of her temptation, "God hath said, Ye shall not eat of this tree," Gen. iii. 3; but she kept not her ground, she abode not by that consideration, but suffered her mind to be diverted from it by the subtlety of Satan, which was the entrance of her transgression: and so it is unto us all in our deviations from obedience.

(2.) The deceit of sin, of every sin, the punishment appointed unto it in the law, is another thing that the mind ought actually to attend unto, in reference unto every particular evil And the diversions from this, that the minds of men have been doctrinally and practically attended withal, have been an inlet into all manner of abominations. Job professeth another frame in himself, Job xxxi. 23, "Destruction from God was a terror to me, and by reason of his highness I could not endure." Many evils he had mentioned in the foregoing verses, and pleads his innocency from them, although they were such as, upon the account of his greatness and power, he could have committed easily without fear of danger from men. Here he gives the reason that prevailed with him so carefully to abstain from them, "Destruction from God was a terror to me, and by reason of his highness I could not endure." "I considered," saith he, "that God had appointed death and destruction' for the punishment of sin, and that such was his greatness, highness, and power, that he could inflict it unto the uttermost, in such a way as no creature is able to abide or to avoid." So the apostle directs believers always to consider what a "fearful thing it is to fall into the hands of the living God," Heb. x. 31; and that because he hath said, "Vengeance is mine, I will recompense," verse 30. He is a sin-avenging God, that will by no means acquit the guilty; as in the declaration of his gracious name, infinitely full of encouragements to poor sinners in Christ, he adds that in the close, that "he will by no means clear the guilty," Exod. xxxiv. 7, -- that he may keep upon the minds of them whom he pardoneth a due sense of the punishment that is due from his vindictive justice unto every sin. And so the apostle would have us mind that even "our God is a consuming fire," Heb. xii. 29; that is, that we should consider his holiness and vindictive justice, appointing unto sin a meet recompense of reward. And men's breaking through this consideration he reckons as the height of the aggravation of their sins: Rom. i. 32, "They knew that it is the judgment of God, that they which commit such things were worthy of death, yet continued to do them." What hope is there for such persons? There is, indeed, relief against this consideration for humbled believing souls in the blood of Christ; but this relief is not to take off the mind from it as it is appointed of God to be a restraint from sin. And both these considerations, even the sovereignty of God and the punishment of sin, are put together by our Saviour: Matt. x. 28, "Fear not them which kill the body, but are not able to kill the soul; but rather fear him which is able to destroy both soul and body in hell."

(3.) The consideration of all the love and kindness of God, against whom every sin is committed, is another thing that the mind ought diligently to attend unto; and this is a prevailing consideration, if rightly and graciously managed in the soul. This Moses presseth on the people: Deut. xxxii. 6, "Do ye thus requite the Lord, O foolish people and unwise? is not he thy Father that bought thee? hath he not made thee, and established thee?" -- "Is this a requital for eternal love, and all the fruits of it? for the love and care of a Father, of a Redeemer, that we have been made partakers of?" And it is the same consideration which the apostle manageth to this purpose, 2 Cor. vii. 1, "Having therefore these promises, dearly beloved, let us cleanse ourselves from all filthiness of the flesh and spirit, perfecting holiness in the fear of God." The receiving of the promises ought to be effectual, as to stir us up unto all holiness, so to work and effect an abstinence from all sin. And what promises are these? -- namely, that "God will be a Father unto us, and receive us," 2 Cor. vi. 17, 18; which compriseth the whole of all the love of God towards us here and to eternity. If there be any spiritual ingenuity in the soul, whilst, the mind is attentive to this consideration, there can be no prevailing attempt made upon it by the power of sin. Now, there are two parts of this consideration:--

[1.] That which is general in it, that which is common unto all believers. This is managed unto this purpose, 1 John iii. 1-3, "Behold, what manner of love the Father hath bestowed upon us, that we should be called the sons of God: therefore the world knoweth us not, because it knew him not. Beloved, now are we the sons of God, and it doth not yet appear what we shall be: but we know that, when he shall appear, we shall be like him; for we shall see him as he is. And every man that hath this hope in him purifieth himself, even as he is pure." "Consider," saith he, "the love of God, and the privileges that we enjoy by it: Behold, what manner of love the Father hath bestowed upon us, that we should be called the sons of God.' Adoption is an especial fruit of it, and how great a privilege is this! Such love it is, and such are the fruits of it, that the world knoweth nothing of the blessed condition which we obtain and enjoy thereby: The world knoweth us not.' Nay, it is such love, and so unspeakably blessed and glorious are the effects of it, that we ourselves are not able to comprehend them." What use, then, ought we to make of this contemplation of the excellent, unspeakable love of God? Why, saith he, "Every one that hath this hope purifieth himself." Every man who has been made partaker of this love, and thereupon a hope of the full enjoyment of the fruits of it, of being made like to God in glory, "purifieth himself," -- that is, in an abstinence from all and every sin, as in the following words is at large declared.

[2.] It is to be considered as to such peculiar mercies and fruits of love as every one's soul hath been made partaker of. There is no believer but, besides the love and mercy which he hath in common with all his brethren, hath also in the lot of his inheritance some enclosures, some especial mercies, wherein he hath a single propriety, he hath some joy which no stranger intermeddleth withal, Prov. xiv. 10, -- particular applications of covenant love and mercy to his soul. Now, these are all provisions laid in by God, that they may be borne in mind against an hour of temptation, -- that the consideration of them may preserve the soul from the attempts of sin. Their neglect is a high aggravation of our provocations. 1 Kings xi. 9, it is charged as the great evil of Solomon, that he had sinned against special mercies, especial intimations of love; he sinned after God had "appeared unto him twice." God required that he should have borne in mind that especial favour, and have made it an argument against sin; but he neglected it, and is burdened with this sore rebuke. And, indeed, all especial mercies, all especial tokens and pledges of love, are utterly lost and misspent upon us, if they are not improved unto this end. This, then, is another thing that it is the duty of the mind greatly to attend unto, and to oppose effectually unto every attempt that is made on the soul by the law of sin.

(4.) The considerations that arise from the blood and mediation of Christ are of the same importance. So the apostle declares, 2 Cor. v. 14, 15, "For the love of Christ constraineth us; because we thus judge, that if one died for all, then were all dead: and that he died for all, that they which live should not henceforth live unto themselves, but unto him which died for them, and rose again." There is a constraining efficacy in this consideration; it is great, forcible, effectual, if duly attended unto. But I must not here in particular insist upon these things; nor, --

(5.) Shall I speak of the inhabitation of the Spirit, -- the greatest privilege that we are made partakers of in this world. The due consideration how he is grieved by sin; how his dwelling-place is defiled thereby; how his comforts are forfeited, lost, despised by it, -- might also be insisted on: but the instances passed through are sufficient unto our purpose. Now, herein lies the duty of the mind in reference unto particular sins and temptations:-- It is diligently and carefully to attend unto these things; to dwell constantly upon the consideration of them; to have them in a continual readiness to oppose unto all the lustings, actings, warrings, attempts, and rage of sin.

In reference hereunto doth sin in an especial manner put forth and act its deceit. It labours by all means to draw off the mind from its due attendance unto these things, -- to deprive the soul of this great preservative and antidote against its poison. It endeavours to cause the soul to satisfy itself with general undigested notions about sin, that it may have nothing in particular to betake itself unto in its own defence against its attempts and temptations. And the ways whereby it doth this may be also briefly considered:--

[1.] It is from the deceit of sin that the mind is spiritually slothful, whereby it becomes negligent unto this duty. The principal discharge of its trust in this matter is expressed by watching; which is the great caution that the Lord Jesus gave unto his disciples in reference unto all their dangers from sin and Satan: Mark xiii. 37, "I say unto all, Watch;" that is, "Use your utmost diligence and circumspection, that you be not surprised and entangled with temptations." It is called also consideration: "Consider your ways," -- "Consider your latter end;" the want whereof God complains of in his people, Deut. xxxii. 29. Now, that which is contrary to these indispensable conditions of our preservation is spiritual slothfulness, as the apostle declares, Heb. vi. 11, 12, "And we desire that every one of you do show the same diligence to the full assurance of hope unto the end: that ye be not slothful." If we show not diligence, we are slothful, and in danger of coming short to inherit the promises. See 2 Pet. i. 5-11, "And beside this, giving all diligence, add to your faith virtue; to virtue knowledge," etc. "For if these things be in you, and abound, they make you that ye shall neither be barren nor unfruitful in the knowledge of our Lord Jesus Christ. But he that lacketh these things is blind, and cannot see afar off, and hath forgotten that he was purged from his old sins. Wherefore the rather, brethren, give diligence to make your calling and election sure: for if ye do these things ye shall never fall: for so an entrance shall be ministered unto you abundantly into the everlasting kingdom of our Lord and Saviour Jesus Christ," All this the mind is turned from, if once, by the deceit of sin, it be made slothful. Now, this sloth consists in four things:--

1st. Inadvertency. It doth not set itself to consider and attend unto its special concernments. The apostle, persuading the Hebrews with all earnestness to attend diligently, to consider carefully, that they may not be hardened by the deceitfulness of sin, gives this reason of their danger, that they were "dull of hearing," Heb. v. 11; that is, that they were slothful, and did not attend unto the things of their duty. A secret regardlessness is apt to creep upon the soul, and it doth not set itself to a diligent marking how things go with it, and what is continually incumbent on it.

2dly. An unwillingness to be stirred up unto its duty. Prov. xix. 24, "A slothful man hideth his hand in his bosom, and will not so much as bring it to his mouth again." There is an unwillingness in sloth to take any notice of warnings, calls, excitations, or stirrings up by the word, Spirit, judgments, any thing that God maketh use of to call the mind unto a due consideration of the condition of the soul. And this is a perfect evidence that the mind is made slothful by the deceit of sin, when especial calls and warnings, whether in a suitable word or a pressing judgment, cannot prevail with it to pull its hand out of its bosom; that is, to set about the special duties that it is called unto.

3dly. Weak and ineffectual attempts to recover itself unto its duty. Prov. xxvi. 14, "As the door turneth upon its hinges, so doth the slothful man upon his bed." In the turning of a door upon its hinges, there is some motion but no progress. It removes up and down, but is still in the place and posture that it was. So is it with the spiritually slothful man on his bed, or in his security. He makes some motions or faint endeavours towards a discharge of his duty, but goes not on. There where he was one day, there he is the next; yea, there where he was one year, he is the next. His endeavours are faint, cold, and evanid; he gets no ground by them, but is always beginning and never finishing his work.

4thly. Heartlessness upon the apprehensions of difficulties and discouragements. Prov. xxii. 13, "The slothful man saith, There is a lion without, I shall be slain in the streets." Every difficulty deters him from duty. He thinks it impossible for him to attain to that accuracy, exactness, and perfection which he is in this matter to press after; and therefore contents himself in his old coldness, negligence, rather than to run the hazard of a universal circumspection. Now, if the deceit of sin hath once drawn away the mind into this frame, it lays it open to every temptation and incursion of sin. The spouse in the Canticles seems to have been overtaken with this distemper, Cant. v. 2, 3; and this puts her on various excuses why she cannot attend unto the call of Christ, and apply herself unto her duty in walking with him.

[2.] It draws away the mind from its watch and duty in reference unto sin by surprisals. It falls in conjunction with some urging temptation, and surpriseth the mind into thoughts quite of another nature than those which it ought to insist upon in its own defence. So it seems to have been with Peter: his carnal fear closing with the temptation wherein Satan sought to winnow him, filled his mind with so many thoughts about his own imminent danger, that he could not take into consideration the love and warning of Christ, nor the evil whereunto his temptation led him, nor any thing that he ought to have insisted on for his preservation. And, therefore, upon a review of his folly in neglecting those thoughts of God and the love of Christ which, through the assistance of the Holy Ghost, might have kept him from his scandalous fall, he wept bitterly. And this is the common way of the working of the deceit of sin as unto particular evils:-- It lays hold on the mind suddenly with thoughtfulness about the present sin, possesseth it, takes it up; so that either it recovers not itself at all to the considerations mentioned, or if any thoughts of them be suggested, the mind is so prepossessed and filled that they take no impression on the soul or make no abode in it. Thus, doubtless, was David surprised in the entrance of his great sin. Sin and temptation did so possess and fill his mind with the present object of his lust, that he utterly forgot, as it were, those considerations which he had formerly made use of when he so diligently kept himself from his iniquity. Here, therefore, lies the great wisdom of the soul, in rejecting the very first motions of sin, because by parleys with them the mind may be drawn off from attending unto its preservatives, and so the whole rush into evil.

[3.] It draws away the mind by frequency and long continuance of its solicitations, making as it were at last a conquest of it. And this happens not without an open neglect of the soul, in want of stirring up itself to give an effectual rebuke, in the strength and by the grace of Christ, unto sin; which would have prevented its prevalency. But of this more shall be spoken afterwards.

And this is the first way whereby the law of sin acts its deceit against the soul:-- It draws off the mind from attendance unto its charge and office, both in respect of duty and sin. And so far as this is done, the person is said to be "drawn away" or drawn off. He is "tempted;" every man is tempted, when he is thus drawn away by his own lust, or the deceit of sin dwelling in him. And the whole effect of this working of the deceitfulness of sin may be reduced unto these three heads:--

1. The remission of a universally watchful frame of spirit unto every duty, and against all, even the most hidden and secret, actings of sin.

2. The omission of peculiar attending unto such duties as have an especial respect unto the weakening and ruin of the whole law of sin, and the obviating of its deceitfulness.

3. Spiritual sloth, as to a diligent regard unto all the especial concernments of duties and sins.

When these three things, with their branches mentioned, less or more, are brought about, in or upon the soul, or so far as they are so, so far a man is drawn off by his own lust or the deceit of sin.

There is no need of adding here any directions for the prevention of this evil; they have sufficiently been laid down in our passage through the consideration both of the duty of the mind, and of the deceit of sin.

Chapter XI

The working of sin by deceit to entangle the affections -- The ways whereby it is done -- Means of their prevention.

The second thing in the words of the apostle ascribed unto the deceitful working of sin is its enticing. A man is "drawn away and enticed." And this seems particularly to respect the affections, as drawing away doth the mind. The mind is drawn away from duty, and the affections are enticed unto sin. From the prevalency hereof a man is said to be "enticed," or entangled as with a bait: so the word imports; for there is an allusion in it unto the bait wherewith a fish is taken on the hook which holds him to his destruction. And concerning this effect of the deceit of sin, we shall briefly show two things: 1. What it is to be enticed, or to be entangled with the bait of sin, to have the affections tainted with an inclination thereunto; and when they are so. 2. What course sin takes, and what way it proceedeth in, thus to entice, ensnare, or entangle the soul:--

1. For the first, --

(1.) The affections are certainly entangled when they stir up frequent imaginations about the proposed object which this deceit of sin leadeth and enticeth towards. When sin prevails, and the affections are gone fully after it, it fills the imagination with it, possessing it with images, likenesses, appearances of it continually. Such persons "devise iniquity, and work evil upon their beds;" which they also "practice" when they are able, when "it is in the power of their hand," Micah ii. 1. As, in particular, Peter tells us that "they have eyes full of an adulteress, [3] and they cannot cease from sin," 2 Pet. ii. 14, -- that is, their imaginations are possessed with a continual representation of the object of their lusts. And it is so in part where the affections are in part entangled with sin, and begin to turn aside unto it. John tells us that the things that are "in the world" are "the lust of the flesh, the lust of the eyes, and the pride of life," 1 John ii. 16. The lust of the eyes is that which by them is conveyed unto the soul. Now, it is not the bodily sense of seeing, but the fixing of the imagination from that sense on such things, that is intended. And this is called the "eyes," because thereby things are constantly represented unto the mind and soul, as outward objects are unto the inward sense by the eyes. And oftentimes the outward sight of the eyes is the occasion of these imaginations. So Achan declares how sin prevailed with him, Joshua vii. 21. First, he saw the wedge of gold and Babylonish garment, and then he coveted them. He rolled them, the pleasures, the profit of them, in his imagination, and then fixed his heart upon the obtaining of them. Now, the heart may have a settled, fixed detestation of sin; but yet, if a man find that the imagination of the mind is frequently solicited by it and exercised about it, such a one may know that his affections are secretly enticed and entangled.

(2.) This entanglement is heightened when the imagination can prevail with the mind to lodge vain thoughts in it, with secret delight and complacency. This is termed by casuists, "Cogitatio morosa cum delectatione," -- an abiding thought with delight; which towards forbidden objects is in all cases actually sinful. And yet this may be when the consent of the will unto sin is not obtained, -- when the soul would not for the world do the thing, which yet thoughts begin to lodge in the mind about. This "lodging of vain thoughts" in the heart the prophet complains of as a thing greatly sinful, and to be abhorred, Jer. iv. 14. All these thoughts are messengers that carry sin to and fro between the imagination and the affections, and still increase it, inflaming the imagination, and more and more entangling the affections. Achan thinks upon the golden wedge, this makes him like it and love it; by loving of it his thoughts are infected, and return to the imagination of its worth and goodly show; and so by little and little the soul is inflamed unto sin. And here if the will parts with its sovereignty, sin is actually conceived.

(3.) Inclinations or readiness to attend unto extenuations of sin, or the reliefs that are tendered against sin when committed, manifest the affections to be entangled with it. We have showed, and shall yet farther evidence, that it is a great part of the deceit of sin, to tender lessening and extenuating thoughts of sin unto the mind. "Is it not a little one?" or, "There is mercy provided;" or, "It shall be in due time relinquished and given over," is its language in a deceived heart. Now, when there is a readiness in the soul to hearken and give entertainment unto such secret insinuations, arising from this deceit, in reference unto any sin or unapprovable course, it is an evidence that the affections are enticed. When the soul is willing, as it were, to be tempted, to be courted by sin, to hearken to its dalliances and solicitations, it hath lost of its conjugal affections unto Christ, and is entangled. This is "looking on the wine when it is red, when it giveth its colour in the cup, when it moveth itself aright," Prov. xxiii. 31; -- a pleasing contemplation on the invitations of sin, whose end the wise man gives us, verse 32. When the deceit of sin hath prevailed thus far on any person, then he is enticed or entangled. The will is not yet come to the actual conception of this or that sin by its consent, but the whole soul is in a near inclination thereunto. And many other instances I could give as tokens and evidences of this entanglement: these may suffice to manifest what we intend thereby.

2. Our next inquiry is, How, or by what means, the deceit of sin proceeds thus to entice and entangle the affections? And two or three of its baits are manifest herein:--

(1.) It makes use of its former prevalency upon the mind in drawing it off from its watch and circumspection. Says the wise man, Prov. i. 17, "Surely in vain is the net spread in the sight of any bird;" or "before the eyes of every thing that hath a wing," as in the original. If it hath eyes open to discern the snare, and a wing to carry it away, it will not be caught. And in vain should the deceit of sin spread its snares and nets for the entanglement of the soul, whilst the eyes of the mind are intent upon what it doth, and so stir up the wings of its will and affections to carry it away and avoid it. But if the eyes be put out or diverted, the wings are of very little use for escape; and, therefore, thin is one of the ways which is used by them who take birds or fowls in their nets. They have false lights or shows of things, to divert the sight of their prey; and when that is done, they take the season to cast their nets upon them. So doth the deceit of sin; it first draws off and diverts the mind by false reasonings and pretences, as hath been showed, and then casts its net upon the affections for their entanglement.

(2.) Taking advantage of such seasons, it proposeth sin as desirable, as exceeding satisfactory to the corrupt part of our affections. It gilds over the object by a thousand pretences, which it presents unto corrupt lustings. This is the laying of a bait, which the apostle in this verse evidently alludes unto. A bait is somewhat desirable and suitable, that is proposed to the hungry creature for its satisfaction; and it is by all artifices rendered desirable and suitable. Thus is sin presented by the help of the imagination unto the soul; that is, sinful and inordinate objects, which the affections cleave unto, are so presented. The apostle tells us that there are "pleasures of sin," Heb. xi. 25; which, unless they are despised, as they were by Moses, there is no escaping of sin itself. Hence they that live in sin are said to "live in pleasure," James v. 5. Now, this pleasure of sin consisteth in its suitableness to give satisfaction to the flesh, to lust, to corrupt affections. Hence is that caution, Rom. xiii. 14, "Make not provision for the flesh, to fulfil the lusts thereof;" that is, "Do not suffer your minds, thoughts, or affections to fix upon sinful objects, suited to give satisfaction to the lusts of the flesh, to nourish and cherish them thereby." To which purpose he speaks again, Gal. v. 16, "Fulfil ye not the lust of the flesh;" -- "Bring not in the pleasures of sin, to give them satisfaction." When men are under the power of sin, they are said to "fulfil the desires of the flesh and of the mind," Eph. ii. 3. Thus, therefore, the deceit of sin endeavours to entangle the affections by proposing unto them, through the assistance of the imagination, that suitableness which is in it to the satisfaction of its corrupt lusts, now set at some liberty by the inadvertency of the mind. It presents its "wine sparkling in the cup," the beauty of the adulteress, the riches of the world, unto sensual and covetous persons; and somewhat in the like kind, in some degrees, to believers themselves. When, therefore, I say, sin would entangle the soul, it prevails with the imagination to solicit the heart, by representing this false-painted beauty or pretended satisfactoriness of sin; and then if Satan, with any peculiar temptation, fall in to its assistance, it oftentimes inflames all the affections, and puts the whole soul into disorder.

(3.) It hides the danger that attends sin; it covers it as the hook is covered with the bait, or the net spread over with meat for the fowl to be taken. It is not, indeed, possible that sin should utterly deprive the soul of the knowledge of the danger of it. It cannot dispossess it of its notion or persuasion that "the wages of sin is death," and that it is the "judgment of God that they that commit sin are worthy of death." But this it will do, -- it will so take up and possess the mind and affections with the baits and desirableness of sin, that it shall divert them from an actual and practical contemplation of the danger of it. What Satan did in and by his first temptation, that sin doth ever since. At first Eve guards herself with calling to mind the danger of sin: "If we eat or touch it we shall die," Gen. iii. 3. But so soon as Satan had filled her mind with the beauty and usefulness of the fruit to make one wise, how quickly did she lay aside her practical prevalent consideration of the danger of eating it, the curse due unto it; or else relieves herself with a vain hope and pretence that it should not be, because the serpent told her so! So was David beguiled in his great transgression by the deceit of sin. His lust being pleased and satisfied, the consideration of the guilt and danger of his transgression was taken away; and therefore he is said to have "despised the Lord," 2 Sam. xii. 9, in that he considered not the evil that was in his heart, and the danger that attended it in the threatening or commination of the law. Now sin, when it presseth upon the soul to this purpose, will use a thousand wiles to hide from it the terror of the Lord, the end of transgressions, and especially of that peculiar folly which it solicits the mind unto. Hopes of pardon shall be used to hide it; and future repentance shall hide it; and present importunity of lust shall hide it; occasions and opportunities shall hide it; surprisals shall hide it; extenuation of sin shall hide it; balancing of duties against it shall hide it; fixing the imagination on present objects shall hide it;

desperate resolutions to venture the uttermost for the enjoyment of lust in its pleasures and profits shall hide it. A thousand wiles it hath, which cannot be recounted.

(4.) Having prevailed thus far, gilding over the pleasures of sin, hiding its end and demerit, it proceeds to raise perverse reasonings in the mind, to fix it upon the sin proposed, that it may be conceived and brought forth, the affections being already prevailed upon; of which we shall speak under the next head of its progress.

Here we may stay a little, as formerly, to give some few directions for the obviating of this woeful work of the deceitfulness of sin. Would we not be enticed or entangled? would we not be disposed to the conception of sin? would we be turned out of the road and way which goes down to death? -- let us take heed of our affections; which are of so great concernment in the whole course of our obedience, that they are commonly in the Scripture called by the name of the heart, as the principal thing which God requires in our walking before him. And this is not slightly to be attended unto. Prov. iv. 23, saith the wise man, "Keep thy heart with all diligence;" or, as in the original, "above" or "before all keepings;" -- "Before every watch, keep thy heart. You have many keepings that you watch unto: you watch to keep your lives, to keep your estates, to keep your reputations, to keep up your families; but," saith he, "above all these keepings, prefer that, attend to that of the heart, of your affections, that they be not entangled with sin." There is no safety without it. Save all other things and lose the heart, and all is lost, -- lost unto all eternity. You will say, then, "What shall we do, or how shall we observe this duty?"

1. Keep your affections as to their object.

(1.) In general. This advice the apostle gives in this very case, Colossians iii. His advice in the beginning of that chapter is to direct us unto the mortification of sin, which he expressly engageth in: Verse 5, "Mortify therefore your members which are upon the earth;" -- "Prevent the working and deceit of sin which wars in your members." To prepare us, to enable us hereunto, he gives us that great direction: Verse 2, "Set your affection on things above, not on things on the earth." Fix your affections upon heavenly things; this will enable you to mortify sin; fill them with the things that are above, let them be exercised with them, and so enjoy the chiefest place in them. They are above, blessed and suitable objects, meet for and answering unto our affections; -- God himself, in his beauty and glory; the Lord Jesus Christ, who is "altogether lovely, the chiefest of ten thousand;" grace and glory; the mysteries revealed in the gospel; the blessedness promised thereby. Were our affections filled, taken up, and possessed with these things, as it is our duty that they should be, -- it is our happiness when they are, -- what access could sin, with its painted poisons, with its sugared poisons, with its envenomed baits, have unto our souls? how should we loathe all its proposals, and say unto them, "Get ye hence as an abominable thing!" For what are the vain, transitory pleasures of sin, in comparison of the exceeding recompense of reward which is proposed unto us? Which argument the apostle presses, 2 Cor. iv. 17, 18.

(2.) As to the object of your affections, in an especial manner, let it be the cross of Christ, which hath exceeding efficacy towards the disappointment of the whole work of indwelling sin: Gal. vi. 14, "God forbid that I should glory, save in the cross of our Lord Jesus Christ, whereby the world is crucified unto me, and I unto the world." The cross of Christ he gloried and rejoiced in; this his heart was set upon; and these were the effects of it, -- it crucified the world unto him, made it a dead and undesirable thing. The baits and pleasures of sin are taken all of them out of the world, and the things that axe in the world, -- namely, "the lust of the flesh, the lust of the eyes, and the pride of life." These are the things that are in the world; from these doth sin take all its baits, whereby it enticeth and entangleth our souls. If the heart be filled with the cross of Christ, it casts death and undesirableness upon them all; it leaves nò seeming beauty, no appearing pleasure or comeliness, in them. Again, saith he, "It crucifieth me to the world; makes my heart, my affections, my desires, dead unto any of these things." It roots up corrupt lusts and affections, leaves no principle to go forth and make provision for the flesh, to fulfil the lusts thereof. Labour, therefore, to fill your hearts with the cross of Christ. Consider the sorrows he underwent, the curse he bore, the blood he shed, the cries he put forth, the love that was in all this to your souls, and the mystery of the grace of God therein. Meditate on the vileness, the demerit, and punishment of sin as represented in the cross, the blood, the death of Christ. Is Christ crucified for sin, and shall not our hearts be crucified with him unto sin? Shall we give entertainment unto that, or hearken unto its dalliances, which wounded, which pierced, which slew our dear Lord Jesus? God forbid! Fill your affections with the cross of Christ, that there may be no room for sin. The world once put him out of the house into a stable, when he came to save us; let him now turn the world out of doors, when he is come to sanctify us.

2. Look to the vigour of the affections towards heavenly things; if they are not constantly attended, excited, directed, and warned, they are apt to decay, and sin lies in wait to take every advantage against them. Many complaints we have in the Scripture of those who lost their first love, in suffering their affections to decay. And this should make us jealous over our own hearts, lest we also should be overtaken with the like backsliding frame. Wherefore be jealous over them; often strictly examine them and call them to account; supply unto them due considerations for their exciting and stirring up unto

duty.

Footnote:

3. Marginal reading in the authorized version. -- Ed.

Chapter XII

The conception of sin through its deceit -- Wherein it consisteth -- The consent of the will unto sin -- The nature thereof -- Ways and means whereby it is obtained -- Other advantages made use of by the deceit of sin -- Ignorance -- Error.

The third success of the deceit of sin in its progressive work is the conception of actual sin. When it hath drawn the mind off from its duty, and entangled the affections, it proceeds to conceive sin in order to the bringing of it forth: "Then when lust hath conceived, it bringeth forth sin." Now, the conception of sin, in order unto its perpetration, can be nothing but the consent of the will; for as without the consent of the will sin cannot be committed, so where the will hath consented unto it, there is nothing in the soul to hinder its actual accomplishment. God doth, indeed, by various ways and means, frustrate the bringing forth of these adulterate conceptions, causing them to melt away in the womb, or one way or other prove abortive, so that not the least part of that sin is committed which is willed or conceived; yet there is nothing in the soul itself that remains to give check unto it when once the will hath given its consent. Ofttimes, when a cloud is full of rain and ready to fall, a wind comes and drives it away; and when the will is ready to bring forth its sin, God diverts it by one wind or other: but yet the cloud was as full of rain as if it had fallen, and the soul as full of sin as if it had been committed.

This conceiving of lust or sin, then, is its prevalency in obtaining the consent of the will unto its solicitations. And hereby the soul is deflowered of its chastity towards God in Christ, as the apostle intimates, 2 Cor. xi. 2, 3. To clear up this matter we must observe, --

1. That the will is the principle, the next seat and cause, of obedience and disobedience. Moral actions are unto us or in us so far good or evil as they partake of the consent of the will. He spake truth of old who said, "Omne peccatum est adeo voluntarium, ut non sit peccatum nisi sit voluntarium;" -- "Every sin is so voluntary, that if it be not voluntary it is not sin." It is most true of actual sins. The formality of their iniquity ariseth from the acts of the will in them and concerning them, -- I mean, as to the persons that commit them; otherwise in itself the formal reason of sin is its aberration from the law of God.

2. There is a twofold consent of the will unto sin:--

(1.) That which is full, absolute, complete, and upon deliberation, -- a prevailing consent; the convictions of the mind being conquered, and no principle of grace in the will to weaken it. With this consent the soul goes into sin as a ship before the wind with all its sails displayed, without any check or stop. It rusheth into sin like the horse into the battle; men thereby, as the apostle speaks, "giving themselves over to sin with greediness," Eph. iv. 19. Thus Ahab's will was in the murdering of Naboth. He did it upon deliberation, by contrivance, with a full consent; the doing of it gave him such satisfaction as that it cured his malady or the distemper of his mind. This is that consent of the will which is acted in the finishing and completing of sin in unregenerate persons, and is not required to the single bringing forth of sin, whereof we speak.

(2.) There is a consent of the will which is attended with a secret renitency and volition of the contrary. Thus Peter's will was in the denying of his Master. His will was in it, or he had not done it. It was a voluntary action, that which he chose to do at that season. Sin had not been brought forth if it had not been thus conceived. But yet, at this very time, there was resident in his will a contrary principle of love to Christ, yea, and faith in him, which utterly failed not. The efficacy of it was intercepted, and its operations suspended actually, through the violent urging of the temptation that he was under; but yet it was in his will, and weakened his consent unto sin. Though it consented, it was not done with self-pleasing, which such full acts of the will do produce.

3. Although there may be a predominant consent in the will, which may suffice for the conception of particular sins, yet there cannot be an absolute, total, full consent of the will of a believer unto any sin; for, --

(1.) There is in his will a principle fixed on good, on all good: Rom. vii. 21, "He would do good." The principle of grace in the will inclines him to all good. And this, in general, is prevalent against the principle of sin, so that the will is denominated from thence. Grace hath the rule and dominion, and not sin, in the will of every believer. Now, that consent unto sin in the will which is contrary to the inclination and generally prevailing principle in the same will, is not, cannot be, total, absolute, and complete.

(2.) There is not only a general, ruling, prevailing principle in the will against sin, but there is also a secret reluctancy in it against its own act in consenting unto sin. It is true, the soul is not sensible sometimes of this reluctancy, because the present consent carries away the prevailing act of the will, and takes away the sense of the lusting of the Spirit, or reluctancy of the principle of grace in the will. But the general rule holdeth in all things at all times: Gal. v. 17, "The Spirit lusteth against the flesh." It doth so actually, though not always to the same degree, nor with the same success; and the prevalency of the contrary principle in this or that particular act doth not disprove it. It is so on the other side. There is no acting of grace in the will but sin lusts against it; although that lusting be not made sensible in the soul, because of the prevalency of the contrary acting of grace, yet it is enough to keep those actings from perfection in their kind. So is it in this renitency of grace against the acting of sin in the soul; though it be not sensible in its operations, yet it is enough to keep that act from being full and complete. And much of spiritual wisdom lies in discerning aright between the spiritual renitency of the principle of grace in the will against sin, and the rebukes that are given the soul by conscience upon conviction for sin.

4. Observe, that reiterated, repeated acts of the consent of the will unto sin may beget a disposition and inclinableness in it unto the like acts, that may bring the will unto a proneness and readiness to consent unto sin upon easy solicitations; which is a condition of soul dangerous, and greatly to be watched against.

5. This consent of the will, which we have thus described, may be considered two ways:-- (1.) As it is exercised about the circumstances, causes, means, and inducements unto sin. (2.) As it respects this or that actual sin.

In the first sense there is a virtual consent of the will unto sin in every inadvertency unto the prevention of it, in every neglect of duty that makes way for it, in every hearkening unto any temptation leading towards it; in a word, in all the diversions of the mind from its duty, and entanglements of the affections by sin, before mentioned: for where there is no act of the will, formally or virtually, there is no sin. But this is not that which we now speak of; but, in particular, the consent of the will unto this or that actual sin, so far as that either sin is committed, or is prevented by other ways and means not of our present consideration. And herein consists the conceiving of sin.

These things being supposed, that which in the next place we are to consider is, the way that the deceit of sin proceedeth in to procure the consent of the will, and so to conceive actual sin in the soul. To this purpose observe:--

1. That the will is a rational appetite, -- rational as guided by the mind, and an appetite as excited by the affections; and so in its operation or actings hath respect to both, is influenced by both.

2. It chooseth nothing, consents to nothing, but "sub ratione boni," -- as it hath an appearance of good, some present good. It cannot consent to any thing under the notion or apprehension of its being evil in any kind. Good is its natural and necessary object, and therefore whatever is proposed unto it for its consent must be proposed under an appearance of being either good in itself, or good at present unto the soul, or good so circumstantiate as it is; so that, --

3. We may see hence the reason why the conception of sin is here placed as a consequent of the mind's being drawn away and the affections being entangled. Both these have an influence into the consent of the will, and the conception of this or that actual sin thereby. Our way, therefore, here is made somewhat plain. We have seen at large how the mind is drawn away by the deceit of sin, and how the affections are entangled; -- that which remains is but the proper effect of these things; for the discovery whereof we must instance in some of the special deceits, corrupt and fallacious reasonings before mentioned, and then show their prevalency on the will to a consent unto sin:--

(1.) The will is imposed upon by that corrupt reasoning, that grace is exalted in a pardon, and that mercy is provided for sinners. This first, as hath been showed, deceives the mind, and that opens the way to the will's consent by removing a sight of evil, which the will hath an aversation unto. And this, in carnal hearts, prevails so far as to make them think that their liberty consists in being "servants of corruption," 2 Pet. ii. 19. And the poison of it doth oftentimes taint and vitiate the minds of believers themselves; whence we are so cautioned against it in the Scripture. To what, therefore, hath been spoken before, unto the use and abuse of the doctrine of the grace of the gospel, we shall add some few other considerations, and fix upon one place of Scripture that will give light unto it There is a twofold mystery of grace, -- of walking with God, and of coming unto God; and the great design of sin is to change the doctrine and mystery of grace in reference unto these things, and that by applying those considerations unto the one which are proper unto the other, whereby each part is hindered, and the influence of the doctrine of grace into them for their furtherance defeated. See 1 John ii. 1, 2: "These things write I unto you, that ye sin not. And if any man sin, we have an advocate with the Father, Jesus Christ the righteous: and he is the propitiation for our sins." Here is the whole design and use of the gospel briefly expressed. "These things," saith he, "I write unto you." What things were these? Those mentioned, chap. i. verse 2: "The life was manifested, and we have seen it, and bear witness, and show unto you that eternal life, which was with the Father, and was manifested unto us," -- that is, the things concerning the person and mediation of Christ; and, verse 7, that pardon, forgiveness, and expiation from sin is to be attained by the blood of Christ. But to what end and purpose doth he write these things to them? what do they teach, what do they tend unto? A universal abstinence from sin: "I write unto you," saith he, "that ye sin not." This is the proper, only, genuine end of the doctrine of the gospel. But to abstain from all sin is not our condition in this world: verse 8, "If we say that we have no sin, we deceive ourselves, and the truth is not in us." What, then, shall be done in this case? In supposition of sin, that we have sinned, is there no relief provided for our souls and consciences in the gospel? Yes; saith he, "If any man sin, we have an advocate with the Father, Jesus Christ the righteous: and he is the propitiation for our sins." There is full relief in the propitiation and intercession of Christ for us. This is the order and method of the doctrine of the gospel, and of the application of it to our own souls:-- first, to keep us from sin; and then to relieve us against sin. But here entereth the deceit of sin, and puts this "new wine into old bottles," whereby the bottles are broken, and the wine perisheth, as to our benefit by it. It changeth this method and order of the application of gospel truths. It takes up the last first, and that excludes the use of the first utterly. "If any man sin, there is pardon provided," is all the gospel that sin would willingly suffer to abide on the minds of men. When we would come to God by believing, it would be pressing the former part, of being free from sin; when the gospel proposeth the latter principally, or the pardon of sin, for our encouragement. When we are come to God, and should walk with him, it will have only the latter proposed, that there is pardon of sin; when the gospel principally proposeth the former, of keeping ourselves from sin, the grace of God bringing salvation having appeared unto us to that end and purpose.

Now, the mind being entangled with this deceit, drawn off from its watch by it, diverted from the true ends of the gospel, doth several ways impose upon the will to obtain its consent:--

[1.] By a sudden surprisal in case of temptation. Temptation is the representation of a thing as a present good, a particular good, which is a real evil, a general evil. Now, when a temptation, armed with opportunity and provocation, befalls the soul, the principle of grace in the will riseth up with a rejection and detestation of it. But on a sudden, the mind being deceived by sin, breaks in upon the will with a corrupt, fallacious reasoning from gospel grace and mercy, which first staggers, then abates the will's opposition, and then causeth it to east the scale by its consent on the side of temptation, presenting evil as a present good, and sin in the sight of God is conceived, though it be never committed. Thus is the seed of God sacrificed to Moloch, and the weapons of Christ abused to the service of the devil.

[2.] It doth it insensibly. It insinuates the poison of this corrupt reasoning by little and little, until it hath greatly prevailed. And as the whole effect of the doctrine of the gospel in holiness and obedience consists in the soul's being cast into the frame and mold of it, Rom. vi. 17; so the whole of the apostasy from the gospel is principally the casting of the soul into the mould of this false reasoning, that sin may be indulged unto upon the account of grace and pardon. Hereby is the soul gratified in sloth and negligence, and taken off from its care as to particular duties and avoidance of particular sins. It works the soul insensibly off from the mystery of the law of grace, -- to look for salvation as if we had never performed any duty, being, after we have done all, unprofitable servants, with a resting on sovereign mercy through the blood of Christ, and to attend unto duties with all diligence as if we looked for no mercy; that is, with no less care, though with more liberty and freedom. This the deceitfulness of sin endeavoureth by all means to work the soul from; and thereby debaucheth the will when its consent is required unto particular sins.

(2.) The deceived mind imposeth on the will, to obtain its consent unto sin, by proposing unto it the advantages that may accrue and arise thereby; which is one medium whereby itself also is drawn away. It renders that which is absolutely evil a present appearing good. So was it with Eve, Gen. 3. Laying aside all considerations of the law, covenant and threats of God, she all at once reflects upon the advantages, pleasures, and benefits which she should obtain by her sin, and reckons them up to solicit the consent of her will. "It is," saith she, "good for food, pleasant to the eyes, and to be desired to make one wise." What should she do, then, but eat it? Her will consented, and she did so accordingly. Pleas for obedience are laid out of the way, and only the pleasures of sin are taken under consideration. So saith Ahab, 1 Kings xxi.; "Naboth's vineyard is near my house, and I may make it a garden of herbs; therefore I must have it." These considerations a deceived mind imposed on his will, until it made him obstinate in the pursuit of his covetousness through perjury and murder, to the utter ruin of himself and his family. Thus is the guilt and tendency of sin hid under the covert of advantages and pleasures, and so is conceived or resolved on in the soul.

As the mind being withdrawn, so the affections being enticed and entangled do greatly further the conception of sin in the soul by the consent of the will; and they do it two ways:--

[1.] By some hasty impulse and surprisal, being themselves stirred up, incited, and drawn forth by some violent provocation or suitable temptation, they put the whole soul, as it were, into a combustion, and draw the will into a consent unto what they are provoked unto and entangled withal. So was the case of David in the matter of Nabal. A violent provocation from the extreme unworthy carriage of that foolish churl stirs him up to wrath and revenge, 1 Sam. xxv. 13. He resolves upon it to destroy a whole family, the innocent with the guilty, verses 33, 34. Self-revenge and murder were for the season conceived, resolved, consented unto, until God graciously took him off his entangled, provoked affections surprised his will to consent unto the conception of many bloody sins. The case was the same with Asa in his anger, when he smote the prophet; and with Peter in his fear, when he denied his Master. Let that soul which would take heed of conceiving sin take heed of entangled affections; for sin may be suddenly conceived, the prevalent consent of the will may be suddenly obtained; which gives the soul a fixed guilt, though the sin itself be never actually brought forth.

[2.] Enticed affections procure the consent of the will by frequent solicitations, whereby they get ground insensibly upon it, and enthrone themselves. Take an instance in the sons of Jacob, Gen. xxxvii. 4. They hate their brother, because their father loved him. Their affections being enticed, many new occasions fall out to entangle them farther, as his dreams and the like. This lay rankling in their hearts, and never ceased soliciting their wills until they resolved upon his death. The unlawfulness, the unnaturalness of the action, the grief of their aged father, the guilt of their own souls, are all laid aside. That hatred and envy that they had conceived against him ceased not until they had got the consent of their wills to his ruin. This gradual progress of the prevalency of corrupt affections to solicit the soul unto sin the wise man excellently describes, Prov. xxiii. 31-35. And this is the common way of sin's procedure in the destruction of souls which seem to have made some good engagements in the ways of God:-- When it hath entangled them with one temptation, and brought the will to some liking of it, that presently becomes another temptation, either to the neglect of some duty or to the refusal of more light; and commonly that whereby men fall off utterly from God is not that wherewith they are first entangled. And this may briefly suffice for the third progressive act of the deceit of sin. It obtains the will's consent unto its conception; and by this means are multitudes of sins conceived in the heart which very little less defile the soul, or cause it to contract very little less guilt, than if they were actually committed.

Unto what hath been spoken concerning the deceitfulness of indwelling sin in general, which greatly evidenceth its power and efficacy, I shall add, as a close of this discourse, one or two particular ways of its deceitful actings; consisting in advantages that it maketh use of, and means of relieving itself against that disquisition which is made after it by the word and Spirit for its ruin. One head only of each sort we shall here name:--

1. It makes great advantage of the darkness of the mind, to work out its design and intendments. The shades of a mind totally dark, -- that is, devoid utterly of saving grace, -- are the proper working-place of sin. Hence the effects of it are called the "works of darkness," Eph. v. 11, Rom. xiii. 12, as springing from thence. Sin works and brings forth by the help of it. The working of lust under the covert of a dark mind is, as it were, the upper region of hell; for it lies at the next door to it for filth, horror, and confusion. Now, there is a partial darkness abiding still in believers; they "know but in part," 1 Cor. xiii. 12. Though there be in them all a principle of saving light, -- the day-star is risen in their hearts, -- yet all the shades of darkness are not utterly expelled out of them in this life. And there are two parts, as it were, or principal effects of the remaining darkness that is in believers:--

(1.) Ignorance, or a nescience of the will of God, either "juris" or "facti" of the rule and law in general, or of the reference of the particular fact that lies before the mind unto the law.

(2.) Error and mistakes positively; taking that for truth which is falsehood, and that for light which is darkness. Now, of both of these doth the law of sin make great advantage for the exerting of its power in the soul.

(1.) Is there a remaining ignorance of any thing of the will of God? sin will be sure to make use of it, and improve it to the uttermost. Though Abimelech were not a believer, yet he was a person that had a moral integrity with him in his ways and actions; he declares himself to have had so in a solemn appeal to God, the searcher of all hearts, even in that wherein he miscarried, Gen. xx. 5. But being ignorant that fornication was a sin, or so great a sin as that it became not a morally honest man to defile himself with it, lust hurries him into that intention of evil in reference unto Sarah, as we have it there related. God complains that his people "perished for lack of knowledge," Hos. iv. 6. Being ignorant of the mind and will of God, they rushed into evil at every command of the law of sin. Be it as to any duty to be performed, or as to any sin to be committed, if there be in it darkness or ignorance of the mind about them, sin will not lose its advantage. Many a man, being ignorant of the duty incumbent on him for the instruction of his family, casting the whole weight of it upon the public teaching, is, by the deceitfulness of sin, brought into an habitual sloth and negligence of duty. So much ignorance of the will of God and duty, so much advantage is given to the law of sin. And hence we may see what is that true knowledge which with God is acceptable. How exactly doth many a poor soul, who is low as to notional knowledge, yet walk with God! It seems they know so much, as sin hath not on that account much advantage against them; when others, high in their notions, give advantage to their lusts, even by their ignorance, though they know it not.

(2.) Error is a worse part or effect of the mind's darkness, and gives great advantage to the law of sin. There is, indeed, ignorance in every error, but there is not error in all ignorance; and so they may be distinguished. I shall need to exemplify this but with one consideration, and that is of men who, being zealous for some error, do seek to suppress and persecute the truth. Indwelling sin desires no greater advantage. How will it every day, every hour, pour forth wrath, revilings, hard speeches; breathe revenge, murder, desolation, under the name perhaps of zeal! On this account we may see poor creatures pleasing themselves every day; as if they vaunted in their excellency, when they are foaming out their own shame. Under their real darkness and pretended zeal, sin sits securely, and fills pulpits, houses, prayers, streets, with as bitter fruits of envy, malice, wrath, hatred, evil surmises, false speakings, as full as they can hold. The common issue with such poor creatures is, the holy, blessed, meek Spirit of God withdraws from them, and leaves them visibly and openly to that evil, froward, wrathful, worldly spirit, which the law of sin hath cherished and heightened in them. Sin dwells not anywhere more secure than in such a frame. Thus, I say, it lays hold in particular of advantages to practice upon with its deceitfulness, and therein also to exert its power in the soul; whereof this single instance of its improving the darkness of the mind unto its own ends is a sufficient evidence.

2. It useth means of relieving itself against the pursuit that is made after it in the heart by the word and Spirit of grace. One also of its wiles, in the way of instance, I shall name in this kind, and that is the alleviation of its own guilt. It pleads for itself, that it is not so bad, so filthy, so fatal as is pretended; and this course of extenuation it proceeds in two ways:--

(1.) Absolutely. Many secret pleas it will have that the evil which it tends unto is not so pernicious as conscience is persuaded that it is; it may be ventured on without ruin. These considerations it will strongly urge when it is at work in a way of surprisal, when the soul hath no leisure or liberty to weigh its suggestions in the balance of the sanctuary; and not seldom is the will imposed on hereby, and advantages gotten to shift itself from under the sword of the Spirit:-- "It is not such but that it may be let alone, or suffered to die of itself, which probably within a while it will do; no need of that violence which in mortification is to be offered; it is time enough to deal with a matter of no greater importance hereafter;" with other pleas like those before mentioned.

(2.) Comparatively; and this is a large field for its deceit and subtlety to lurk in:-- "Though it is an evil indeed to be relinquished, and the soul is to be made watchful against it, yet it is not of that magnitude and degree as we may see in the lives of others, even saints of God, much less such as some saints of old have fallen into." By these and the like pretences, I say, it seeks to evade and keep its abode in the soul when pursued to destruction. And how little a portion of its deceitfulness is it that we have declared!

Chapter XIII

Several ways whereby the bringing forth of conceived sin is obstructed.

Before we proceed to the remaining evidences of the power and efficacy of the law of sin, we shall take occasion from what hath been delivered to divert unto one consideration that offers itself from that Scripture which was made the bottom and foundation of our discourse of the general deceitfulness of sin, namely, James i. 14. The apostle tells us that "lust conceiving bringeth forth sin;" seeming to intimate, that look what sin is conceived, that also is brought forth. Now, placing the conception of sin, as we have done, in the consent of the will unto it, and reckoning, as we ought, the bringing forth of sin to consist of its actual commission, we know that these do not necessarily follow one another. There is a world of sin conceived in the womb of the wills and hearts of men that is never brought forth. Our present business, then, shall be to inquire whence that comes to pass. I answer, then, --

1. That this is not so, is no thanks unto sin nor the law of it What it conceives, it would bring forth; and that it doth not is for the most part but a small abatement of its guilt. A determinate will of actual sinning is actual sin. There is nothing wanting on sin's part that every conceived sin is not actually accomplished. The obstacle and prevention lies on another hand.

2. There are two things that are necessary in the creature that hath conceived sin, for the bringing of it forth; -- first, Power; secondly, Continuance in the will of sinning until it be perpetrated and committed. Where these two are, actual sin will unavoidably ensue. It is evident, therefore, that that which hinders conceived sin from being brought forth must affect either the power or the will of the sinner. This must be from God. And he hath two ways of doing it: (1.) By his providence, whereby he obstructs the power of sinning. (2.) By his grace, whereby he diverts or changes the will of sinning. I do not mention these ways of God's dispensations thus distinctly, as though the one of them were always without the other; for there is much of grace in providential administrations, and much of the wisdom of providence seen in the dispensations of grace. But I place them in this distinction, because they appear most eminent therein; -- providence, in outward acts respecting the power of the creature; grace, common or special, in internal efficacy respecting his will. And we shall begin with the first:--

(1.) When sin is conceived, the Lord obstructs its production by his providence, in taking away or cutting short that power which is absolutely necessary for its bringing forth or accomplishment; as, --

[1.] Life is the foundation of all power, the principle of operation; when that ceaseth, all power ceaseth with it. Even God himself, to evince the everlasting stability of his own power, gives himself the title of "The living God." Now, he frequently obviates the power of executing sin actually by cutting short and taking away the lives of them that have conceived it. Thus he dealt with the army of Sennacherib, when, according as he had purposed, so he threatened that "the Lord should not deliver Jerusalem out of his hand," 2 Kings xviii. 35. God threatens to cut short his power, that he should not execute his intendment, chap. xix. 28; which he performs accordingly, by taking away the lives of his soldiers, verse 35, without whom it was impossible that his conceived sin should be brought forth. This providential dispensation in the obstruction of conceived sin, Moses excellently sets forth in the case of Pharaoh: Exod. xv. 9, 10, "The enemy said, I will pursue, I will overtake, I will divide the spoil; my lust shall be satisfied upon them; I will draw my sword, my hand shall destroy them. Thou didst blow with thy wind, the sea covered them: they sank as lead in the mighty waters." Sin's conception is fully expressed, and as full a prevention is annexed unto it. In like manner he dealt with the companies of fifties and their captains, who came to apprehend Elijah, 2 Kings i. 9-12. Fire came down from heaven and consumed them, when they were ready to have taken him. And sundry other instances of the like nature might be recorded. That which is of universal concernment we have in that great providential alteration which put a period to the lives of men. Men living hundreds of years had a long season to bring forth the sins they had conceived; thereupon the earth was filled with violence, injustice, and rapine, and "all flesh corrupted his way," Gen. vi. 12, 13. To prevent the like inundation of sin, God shortens the course of the pilgrimage of men in the earth, and reduces their lives to a much shorter measure. Besides this general law, God daily thus cuts off persons who had conceived much mischief and violence in their hearts, and prevents the execution of it: "Blood-thirsty and deceitful men do not live out half their days." They have yet much work to do, might they have but space given them to execute the bloody and sinful purposes of their minds. The psalmist tells us, Ps. cxlvi. 4, "In the day that the breath of man goeth forth, his thoughts perish:" he had many contrivances about sin, but now they are all cut off. So also, Eccles. viii. 12, 13, "Though a sinner do evil a hundred times, and his days be prolonged, yet surely I know that it shall be well with them that fear God, which fear before him: but it shall not be well with the wicked, neither shall he prolong his days, which are as a shadow; because he feareth not before God." How long soever a wicked man lives, yet he dies judicially, and shall not abide to do the evil he had conceived.

But now, seeing we have granted that even believers themselves may conceive sin through the power and the deceitfulness of it, it may be inquired whether God ever thus obviates its production and accomplishment in them, by cutting off and taking away their lives, so as that they shall not be able to perform it. I answer, --

1st. That God doth not judicially cut off and take away the life of any of his for this end and purpose, that he may thereby prevent the execution or bringing forth of any particular sin that he had conceived, and which, without that taking away, he would have perpetrated; for, --

(1st.) This is directly contrary to the very declared end of the patience of God towards them, 2 Pet. iii. 9. This is the very end of the long-suffering of God towards believers, that before they depart hence they may come to the sense, acknowledgment, and repentance of every known sin. This is the constant and unchangeable rule of God's patience in the covenant of grace; which is so far from being in them an encouragement unto sin, that it is a motive to universal watchfulness against it, -- of the same nature with all gospel grace, and of mercy in the blood of Christ. Now, this dispensation whereof we speak would lie in a direct contradiction unto it.

(2dly.) This also flows from the former, that whereas conceived sin contains the whole nature of it, as our Saviour at large declares, Matt. v.; and to be cut off under the guilt of it, to prevent its farther progress, argues a continuance in the purpose of it without repentance, it cannot be but they must perish for ever who are so judicially cut off. But God deals not so with his; he casts not off the people whom he did foreknow. And thence David prays for the patience of God before mentioned, that it might not be so with him: Ps. xxxix. 13, "O spare me, that I may recover strength, before I go hence, and be no more." But yet, --

2dly. There are some cases wherein God may and doth take away the lives of his own, to prevent the guilt that otherwise they would be involved in; as, --

(1st.) In the coming of some great temptation and trial upon the world. God knowing that such and such of his would not be able to withstand it and hold out against it, but would dishonour him and defile themselves, he may, and doubtless often doth, take them out of the world, to take them out of the way of it: Isa. lvii. 1, "The righteous is taken away from the evil to come;" not only the evil of punishment and judgment, but the evil of temptations and trials, which oftentimes proves much the worse of the two. Thus a captain in war will call off a soldier from his watch and guard, when he knows that he is not able, through some infirmity, to bear the stress and force of the enemy that is coming upon him.

(2dly.) In case of their engagement into any way not acceptable to him, through ignorance or not knowing of his mind and will. This seems to have been the case of Josiah. And, doubtless, the Lord doth oftentimes thus proceed with his. When any of his own are engaged in ways that please him not, through the darkness and ignorance of their minds, that they may not proceed to farther evil or mischief, he calls them off from their station and employment and takes them to himself, where they shall err and mistake no more. But, in ordinary cases, God hath other ways of diverting his own from sin than by killing of them, as we shall see afterward.

[2.] God providentially hinders the bringing forth of conceived sin, by taking away and cutting short the power of them that had conceived it, so that, though their lives continue, they shall not have that power without which it is impossible for them to execute what they had intended, or to bring forth what they had conceived. Hereof also we have sundry instances. This was the case with the builders of Babel, Gen. xi. Whatever it were in particular that they aimed at, it was in the pursuit of a design of apostasy from God. One thing requisite to the accomplishing of what they aimed at was the oneness of their language; so God says, verse 6, "They have all one language; and this they begin to do: and now nothing will be restrained from them, that they have imagined to do." In an ordinary way they will accomplish their wicked design. What course doth God now take to obviate their conceived sin? Doth he bring a flood upon them to destroy them, as in the old world some time before? Doth he send his angel to cut them off, like the army of Sennacherib afterward? Doth he by any means take away their lives? No; their lives are continued, but he "confounds their language," so that they cannot go on with their work, verse 7, -- takes away that wherein their power consisted. In like manner did he proceed with the Sodomites, Gen. xix. 11. They were engaged in, and set upon the pursuit of, their filthy lusts. God smites them with blindness, so that they could not find the door, where they thought to have used violence for the compassing of their ends. Their lives were continued, and their will of sinning; but their power is cut short and abridged. His dealing with Jeroboam, 1 Kings xiii. 4, was of the same nature. He stretched out his hand to lay hold of the prophet, and it withered and became useless. And this is an eminent way of the effectual acting of God's providence in the world, for the stopping of that inundation of sin which would overflow all the earth were every womb of it opened. He cuts men short of their moral power, whereby they should effect it. Many a wretch that hath conceived mischief against the church of God hath by this means been divested of his power, whereby he thought to accomplish it. Some have their bodies smitten with diseases, that they can no more serve their lusts, nor accompany them in the perpetrating of folly; some are deprived of the instruments whereby they would work. There hath been, for many days, sin enough conceived to root out the generation of the righteous from the face of the earth, had men strength and ability to their will, did not God cut off and shorten their power and the days of their prevalency. Ps. lxiv. 6, "They search out iniquities; they accomplish a diligent search: both the inward thought of every one of them, and the heart, is deep." All things are in a readiness; the design is well laid, their counsels are deep and secret; what now shall hinder them from doing whatever they have imagined to do? Verses 7, 8, "But God shall shoot at them with an arrow; suddenly shall they be wounded. So they shall make their own tongue to fall upon themselves." God meets with them, brings them down, that they shall not be able to accomplish their design. And this way of God's preventing sin seems to be, at least ordinarily, peculiar to the men of the world; God deals thus with them every day, and leaves them to pine away in their sins. They go all their days big with the iniquity they have conceived, and are greatly burdened that they cannot be delivered of it. The prophet tells us that "they practice iniquity that they had conceived, because it is in the power of their hand," Micah ii. 1. If they have power for it, they will accomplish it: Ezek. xxii. 6, "To their power they shed blood." This is the measure of their sinning, even their power. They do, many of them, no more evil, they commit no more sin, than they can. Their whole restraint lies in being cut short in power, in one kind or another. Their bodies will not serve them for their contrived uncleannesses, nor their hands for their revenge and rapine, nor their instruments for persecution; but they go burdened with conceived sin, and are disquieted and tortured by it all their days. And hence they become in themselves, as well as unto others, "a troubled sea, that cannot rest," Isa. lvii. 20.

It may be, also, in some cases, under some violent temptations, or in mistakes, God may thus obviate the accomplishment of conceived sin in his own. And there seems to be an instance of it in his dealing with Jehoshaphat, who had designed, against the mind of God, to join in affinity with Ahab, and to send his ships with him to Tarshish; but God breaks his ships by a wind, that he could not accomplish what he had designed. But in God's dealing with his in this way, there is a difference from the same dispensation towards others; for, --

1st. It is so only in cases of extraordinary temptation. When, through the violence of temptation and craft of Satan, they are hurried from under the conduct of the law of grace, God one way or other takes away their power, or may do so, that they shall not be able to execute what they had designed. But this is an ordinary way of dealing with wicked men. This hook of God is upon them in the whole course of their lives; and they struggle with it, being "as a wild bull in a net," Isa. li. 20. God's net is upon them, and they are filled with fury that they cannot do all the wickedness that they would.

2dly. God doth it not to leave them to wrestle with sin, and to attempt other ways of its accomplishment, upon the failure of that which they were engaged in; but by their disappointment awakens them to think of their condition and what they are doing, and so consumes sin in the womb by the ways that shall afterward be insisted on. Some men's deprivation of power for the committing of conceived, contrived sin hath been sanctified to the changing of their hearts from all dalliances with that or other sins.

[3.] God providentially hinders the bringing forth of conceived sin by opposing an external hindering power unto sinners. He leaves them their lives, and leaves them power to do what they intend; only he raiseth up an opposite power to coerce, forbid, and restrain them. An instance hereof we have, 1 Sam. xiv. 45. Saul had sworn that Jonathan should be put to death; and, as far as appears, went on resolutely to have slain him. God stirs up the spirit of the people; they oppose themselves to the wrath and fury of Saul, and Jonathan is delivered. So also, 2 Chron. xxvi. 16-20, when king Uzziah would have in his own person offered incense, contrary to the law, eighty men of the priests resisted him, and drove him out of the temple. And to this head are to be referred all the assistances which God stirreth up for deliverance of his people against the fury of persecutors. He raiseth up saviours or deliverers on mount Zion, "to judge the mount of Edom." So, Rev. xii. 16, the dragon, and those acting under him, spirited by him, were in a furious endeavour for the destruction of the church; God stirs up the earth to her assistance, even men of the world not engaged with others in the design of Satan; and by their opposition hinders them from the execution of their designed rage. Of this nature seems to be that dealing of God with his own people, Hos. ii. 6, 7. They were in the pursuit of their iniquities, following after their lovers; God leaves them for a while to act in the folly of their spirits; but he sets a hedge and a wall before them, that they shall not be able to fulfil their designs and lusts.

[4.] God obviates the accomplishment of conceived sin by removing or taking away the objects on whom, or about whom, the sin conceived was to be committed. Acts xii. 1-11 yields us a signal instance of this issue of providence. When the day was coming wherein Herod thought to have slain Peter, who was shut up in prison, God sends and takes him away from their rage and lying in wait. So also was our

Saviour himself taken away from the murderous rage of the Jews before his hour was come, John viii. 59, John x. 39. Both primitive and latter times are full of stories to this purpose. Prison doors have been opened, and poor creatures appointed to die have been frequently rescued from the jaws of death. In the world itself, amongst the men thereof, adulterers and adulteresses, the sin of the one is often hindered and stifled by the taking away of the other. So wings were given to the woman to carry her into the wilderness, and to disappoint the world in the execution of their rage, Rev. xii. 14.

[5.] God doth this by some eminent diversions of the thoughts of men who had conceived sin. Gen. xxxvii. 24, the brethren of Joseph cast him into a pit, with an intent to famish him there. Whilst they were, as it seems, pleasing themselves with what they had done, God orders a company of merchants to come by, and diverts their thoughts with that new object from the killing to the selling of their brother, verses 25-27; and how far therein they were subservient to the infinitely wise counsel of God we know. Thus, also, when Saul was in the pursuit of David, and was even ready to prevail against him to his destruction, God stirs up the Philistines to invade the land, which both diverted his thoughts and drew the course of his actings another way, 1 Sam. xxiii. 27.

And these are some of the ways whereby God is pleased to hinder the bringing forth of conceived sin, by opposing himself and his providence to the power of the sinning creature. And we may a little, in our passage, take a brief view of the great advantages to faith and the church of God which may be found in this matter; as, --

1st. This may give us a little insight into the ever-to-be-adored providence of God, by these and the like ways in great variety obstructing the breaking forth of sin in the world. It is he who makes those dams, and shuts up those flood-gates of corrupted nature, that it shall not break forth in a deluge of filthy abominations, to overwhelm the creation with confusion and disorder. As it was of old, so it is at this day: "Every thought and imagination of the heart of man is evil, and that continually." That all the earth is not in all places filled with violence, as it was of old, is merely from the mighty hand of God working effectually for the obstructing of sin. From hence alone it is that the highways, streets, and fields are not all filled with violence, blood, rapine, uncleanness, and every villany that the heart of man can conceive. Oh, the infinite beauty of divine wisdom and providence in the government of the world! for the conservation of it asks daily no less power and wisdom than the first making of it did require.

2dly. If we will look to our own concernments, they will in a special manner enforce us to adore the wisdom and efficacy of the providence of God in stopping the progress of conceived sin. That we are at peace in our houses, at rest in our beds, that we have any quiet in our enjoyments, is from hence alone. Whose person would not be defiled or destroyed, -- whose habitation would not be ruined, -- whose blood almost would not be shed, -- if wicked men had power to perpetrate all their conceived sin? It may be the ruin of some of us hath been conceived a thousand times. We are beholding to this providence of obstructing sin for our lives, our families, our estates, our liberties, for whatsoever is or may be dear unto us; for may we not say sometimes, with the psalmist, Ps. lvii. 4 "My soul is among lions: and I lie even among them that are set on fire, even the sons of men, whose teeth are spears and arrows, and their tongue a sharp sword." And how is the deliverance of men contrived from such persons? Ps. lviii. 6, "God breaks their teeth in their mouths, even the great teeth of the young lions." He keeps this fire from burning, or quencheth it when it is ready to break out into a flame. He breaks their spears and arrows, so that sometimes we are not so much as wounded by them. Some he cuts off and destroys; some he cuts short in their power; some he deprives of the instruments whereby alone they can work; some he prevents of their desired opportunities, or diverts by other objects for their lusts; and oftentimes causeth them to spend them among themselves, one upon another. We may say, therefore, with the psalmist, Ps. civ. 24, "O Lord, how manifold are thy works! in wisdom hast thou made them all: the earth is full of thy riches;" and with the prophet, Hos. xiv. 9, "Who is wise, and he shall understand these things? prudent, and he shall know them? all the ways of the Lord are right, and the just shall walk in them: but the transgressors shall fall therein."

3dly. If these and the like are the ways whereby God obviates the bringing forth of conceived sin in wicked men, we may learn hence how miserable their condition is, and in what perpetual torment, for the most part, they spend their days. They "are like a troubled sea," saith the Lord, "that cannot rest." As they endeavour that others may have no peace, so it is certain that themselves have not any; the principle of sin is not impaired nor weakened in them, the will of sinning is not taken away. They have a womb of sin, that is able to conceive monsters every moment. Yea, for the most part, they are forging and framing folly all the day long. One lust or other they are contriving how to satisfy. They are either devouring by malice and revenge, or vitiating by uncleanness, or trampling on by ambition, or swallowing down by covetousness, all that stand before them. Many of their follies and mischiefs they bring to the very birth, and are in pain to be delivered; but God every day fills them with disappointment, and shuts up the womb of sin. Some are filled with hatred of God's people all their days, and never once have an opportunity to exercise it. So David describes them, Ps. lix. 6, "They return at evening: they make a noise like a dog, and go round about the city." They go up and down and "belch out with their mouth: swords are in their lips," verse 7, and yet are not able to accomplish their designs. What tortures do such poor creatures live in! Envy, malice, wrath, revenge, devour their hearts by not getting vent. And when God hath exercised the other acts of his wise providence in cutting short their power, or opposing, a greater power to them, when nothing else will do, he cuts them off in their sins, and to the grave they go, full of purposes of iniquity. Others are no less hurried and diverted by the power of other lusts which they are not able to satisfy. This is the sore travail they are exercised with all their days:-- If they accomplish their designs they are more wicked and hellish than before; and if they do not, they are filled with vexation and discontentment. This is the portion of them who know not the Lord nor the power of his grace. Envy not their condition. Notwithstanding their outward, glittering show, their hearts are full of anxiety, trouble, and sorrow.

4thly. Do we see sometimes the flood-gates of men's lusts and rage set open against the church and interest of it, and doth prevalency attend them, and power is for a season on their side? Let not the saints of God despond. He hath unspeakably various and effectual ways for the stifling of their conceptions, to give them dry breasts and a miscarrying womb. He can stop their fury when he pleaseth. "Surely," saith the psalmist, "the wrath of man shall praise thee: the remainder of wrath shalt thou restrain," Ps. lxxvi. 10. When so much of their wrath is let out as shall exalt his praise, he can, when he pleaseth, set up a power greater than the combined strength of all sinning creatures, and restrain the remainder of the wrath that they had conceived. "He shall cut off the spirit of princes: he is terrible to the kings of the earth," verse 12. Some he will cut off and destroy, some he will terrify and affright, and prevent the rage of all. He can knock them on the head, or break out their teeth, or chain up their wrath; and who can oppose him

5thly. Those who have received benefit by any of the ways mentioned may know to whom they owe their preservation, and not look on it as a common thing. When you have conceived sin, hath God weakened your power for sin, or denied you opportunity, or taken away the object of your lusts, or diverted your thoughts by new providences? -- know assuredly that you have received mercy thereby. Though God deal not these providences always in a subserviency to the covenant of grace, yet there is always mercy in them, always a call in them to consider the author of them. Had not God thus dealt with you, it may be this day you had been a terror to yourselves, a shame to your relations, and under the punishment due to some notorious sins which you had conceived. Besides, there is commonly an additional guilt in sin brought forth, above what is in the mere conception of it. It may be others would have been ruined by it here, or drawn into a partnership in sin by it, and so have been eternally ruined by it, all which are prevented by these providences; and eternity will witness that there is a singularity of mercy in them. Do not look, then, on any such things as common accidents; the hand of God is in them all, and that a merciful hand if not despised. If it be, yet God doth good to others by it: the world is the better; and you are not so wicked as you would be.

6thly. We may also see hence the great use of magistracy in the world, that great appointment of God. Amongst other things, it is peculiarly subservient to this holy providence, in obstructing the bringing forth of conceived sin, -- namely, by the terror of him that bears the sword. God fixes that on the hearts of evil men, which he expresseth, Rom. xiii. 4, "If thou do that which is evil, be afraid; for he beareth not the sword in vain: for he is the minister of God, a revenger to execute wrath on them that do evil." God fixes this on the hearts of men, and by the dread and terror of it closeth the womb of sin, that it shall not bring forth. When there was no king in Israel, none to put to rebuke, and none of whom evil men were afraid, there was woful work and havoc amongst the children of men made in the world, as we may see in the last chapters of the book of Judges. The greatest mercies and blessings that in this world we are made partakers of, next to them of the gospel and covenant of grace, come to us through this channel and conduit. And, indeed, this whereof we have been speaking is the proper work of magistracy, -- namely, to be subservient to the providence of God in obstructing the bringing forth of conceived sin.

These, then, are some of the ways whereby God providentially prevents the bringing forth of sin, by opposing obstacles to the power of the sinner. And [yet] by them sin is not consumed, but shut up in the womb. Men are not burdened for it, but with it; not laden in their hearts and consciences with its guilt, but perplexed with its power, which they are not able to exert and satisfy.

(2.) The way, that yet remains for consideration, whereby God obviates the production of conceived sin is his working on the will of the sinner, so making sin to consume away in the womb.

There are two ways in general whereby God thus prevents the bringing forth of conceived sin by working on the will of the sinner; and they are, -- [1.] By restraining grace; [2.] By renewing grace. He doth it sometimes the one way, sometimes the other. The first of these is common to regenerate and unregenerate persons, the latter peculiar to believers; and God doth it variously as to particulars by them both. We shall begin with the first of them:--

[1.] God doth this, in the way of restraining grace, by some arrow of particular conviction, fixed in the heart and conscience of the sinner, in reference unto the particular sin which he had conceived. This staggers and changes the mind as to the particular intended, causeth the hands to hang down and the weapons of lust to fall out of them. Hereby conceived sin proves abortive. How God doth this work, --

by what immediate touches, strokes, blows, rebukes of his Spirit, -- by what reasonings, arguments, and commotions of men's own consciences, -- is not for us thoroughly to find out It is done, as was said, in unspeakable variety, and the works of God are past finding out. But as to what light may be given unto it from Scripture instances, after we have manifested the general way of God's procedure, it shall be insisted on.

Thus, then, God dealt in the case of Esau and Jacob. Esau had long conceived his brother's death; he comforted himself with the thoughts of it, and resolutions about it, Gen. xxvii. 41, as is the manner of profligate sinners. Upon his first opportunity he comes forth to execute his intended rage, and Jacob concludes that he would "smite the mother with the children," Gen. xxxii. 11. An opportunity is presented unto this wicked and profane person to bring forth that sin that had lain in his heart now twenty years; he hath full power in his hand to perform his purpose. In the midst of this posture of things, God comes in upon his heart with some secret and effectual working of his Spirit and power, changeth him from his purpose, causeth his conceived sin to melt away, that he falls upon the neck of him with embraces whom he thought to have slain.

Of the same nature, though the way of it was peculiar, was his dealing with Laban the Syrian, in reference to the same Jacob, Gen. xxxi. 24. By a dream, a vision in the night, God hinders him from so much as speaking roughly to him. It was with him as in Micah ii. 1:-- he had devised evil on his bed; and when he thought to have practiced it in the morning, God interposed in a dream, and hides sin from him, as he speaks, Job xxxiii. 15-17. To the same purpose is that of the psalmist concerning the people of. God: Ps. cvi. 46, "He made them to be pitied of all those that carried them captives." Men usually deal in rigor with those whom they have taken captive in war. It was the way of old to rule captives with force and cruelty. Here God turns and changes their hearts, not in general unto himself, but to this particular of respect to his people. And this way in general doth God every day prevent the bringing forth of a world of sin. He sharpens arrows of conviction upon the spirits of men as to the particular that they are engaged in. Their hearts are not changed as to sin, but their minds are altered as to this or that sin. They break, it may be, the vessel they had fashioned, and go to work upon some other. Now, that we may a little see into the ways whereby God doth accomplish this work, we must premise the ensuing considerations:--

1st. That the general medium wherein the matter of restraining grace doth consist, whereby God thus prevents the bringing forth of sin, doth lie in certain arguments and reasonings presented to the mind of the sinner, whereby he is induced to desert his purpose, to change and alter his mind, as to the sin he had conceived. Reasons against it are presented unto him, which prevail upon him to relinquish his design and give over his purpose. This is the general way of the working of restraining grace, -- it is by arguments and reasonings rising up against the perpetration of conceived sin.

2dly. That no arguments or reasonings, as such, materially considered, are sufficient to stop or hinder any purpose of sinning, or to cause conceived sin to prove abortive, if the sinner have power and opportunity to bring it forth. They are not in themselves, and on their own account, restraining grace; for if they were, the administration and communication of grace, as grace, were left unto every man who is able to give advice against sin. Nothing is nor can be called grace, though common, and such as may perish, but with respect unto its peculiar relation to God. God, by the power of his Spirit, making arguments and reasons effectual and prevailing, turns that to be grace (I mean of this kind) which in itself and in its own nature was bare reason. And that efficacy of the Spirit which the Lord puts forth in these persuasions and motives is that which we call restraining grace. These things being premised, we shall now consider some of the arguments which we find that he hath made use of to this end and purpose:--

(1st.) God stops many men in their ways, upon the conception of sin, by an argument taken from the difficulty, if not impossibility, of doing that they aim at. They have a mind unto it, but God sets a hedge and a wall before them, that they shall judge it to be so hard and difficult to accomplish what they intend, that it is better for them to let it alone and give over. Thus Herod would have put John Baptist to death upon the first provocation, but he feared the multitude, because they accounted him as a prophet, Matt. xiv. 5. He had conceived his murder, and was free for the execution of it. God raised this consideration in his heart, "If I kill him, the people will tumultuate; he hath a great party amongst them, and sedition will arise that may cost me my life or kingdom." He feared the multitude, and durst not execute the wickedness he had conceived, because of the difficulty he foresaw he should be entangled withal. And God made the argument effectual for the season; for otherwise we know that men will venture the utmost hazards for the satisfaction of their lusts, as he also did afterward. The Pharisees were in the very same state and condition. Matt. xxi. 26, they would fain have decried the ministry of John, but durst not for fear of the people; and, verse 46 of the same chapter, by the same argument were they deterred from killing our Saviour, who had highly provoked them by a parable setting out their deserved and approaching destruction. They durst not do it for fear of a tumult among the people, seeing they looked on him as a prophet. Thus God overawes the hearts of innumerable persons in the world every day, and causeth them to desist from attempting to bring forth the sins which they had conceived.

Difficulties they shall be sure to meet withal, yea, it is likely, if they should attempt it, it would prove impossible for them to accomplish. We owe much of our quiet in this world unto the efficacy given to this consideration in the hearts of men by the Holy Ghost; adulteries, rapines, murders, are obviated and stifled by it. Men would engage into them daily, but that they judge it impossible for them to fulfil what they aim at.

(2dly.) God doth it by an argument taken "ab incommodo," -- from the inconveniences, evils, and troubles that will befall men in the pursuit of sin. If they follow it, this or that inconvenience will ensue, -- this trouble, this evil, temporal or eternal. And this argument, as managed by the Spirit of God, is the great engine in his hand whereby he casts up banks and gives bounds to the lusts of men, that they break not out to the confusion of all that order and beauty which yet remains in the works of his hands. Paul gives us the general import of this argument, Rom. ii. 14, 15, "For when the Gentiles, which have not the law, do by nature the things contained in the law, these, having not the law, are a law unto themselves: which show the work of the law written in their hearts, their conscience also bearing witness, and their thoughts the mean while accusing or else excusing one another." If any men in the world may be thought to be given up to pursue and fulfil all the sins that their lusts can conceive, it is those that have not the law, to whom the written law of God doth not denounce the evil that attends it. "But though they have it not," saith the apostle, "they show forth the work of it; they do many things which it requireth, and forbear or abstain from many things that it forbiddeth, and so show forth its work and efficacy." But whence is it that they so do? Why, their thoughts accuse or excuse them. It is from the consideration and arguings that they have within themselves about sin and its consequents, which prevail upon them to abstain from many things that their hearts would carry them out unto; for conscience is a man's prejudging of himself with respect unto the future judgment of God. Thus Felix was staggered in his pursuit of sin, when he trembled at Paul's preaching of righteousness and judgment to come, Acts xxiv. 25. So Job tells us that the consideration of punishment from God hath a strong influence on the minds of men to keep them from sin, Job xxxi. 1-3. How the Lord makes use of that consideration, even towards his own, when they have broken the cords of his love and cast off the rule of his grace for a season, I have before declared.

(3dly.) God doth this same work by making effectual an argument "ab inutili," -- from the unprofitableness of the thing that men are engaged in. By this were the brethren of Joseph stayed from slaying him: Gen. xxxvii. 26, 27, "What profit is it," say they, "if we slay our brother, and conceal his blood?" -- "We shall get nothing by it; it will bring in no advantage or satisfaction unto us." And the heads of this way of God's obstructing conceived sin, or the springs of these kinds of arguments, are so many and various that it is impossible to insist particularly upon them. There is nothing present or to come, nothing belonging to this life or another, nothing desirable or undesirable, nothing good or evil, but, at one time or another, an argument may be taken from it for the obstructing of sin.

(4thly.) God accomplisheth this work by arguments taken "ab honesto," -- from what is good and honest, what is comely, praiseworthy, and acceptable unto himself. This is the great road wherein he walks with the saints under their temptations, or in their conceptions of sin. He recovers effectually upon their minds a consideration of all those springs and motives to obedience which are discovered and proposed in the gospel, some at one time, some at another. He minds them of his own love, mercy, and kindness, -- his eternal love, with the fruits of it, whereof themselves have been made partakers; he minds them of the blood of his Son, his cross, sufferings, tremendous undertaking in the work of mediation, and the concernment of his heart, love, honour, name, in their obedience; minds them of the love of the Spirit, with all his consolations, which they have been made partakers of, and privileges wherewith by him they have been intrusted; minds them of the gospel, the glory and beauty of it, as it is revealed unto their souls; minds them of the excellency and comeliness of obedience, -- of their performance of that duty they owe to God, -- of that peace, quietness, and serenity of mind that they have enjoyed therein. On the other side, he minds them of being a provocation by sin unto the eyes of his glory, saying in their hearts, "Do not that abominable thing which my soul hateth;" minds them of their wounding the Lord Jesus Christ, and putting him to shame, -- of their grieving the Holy Spirit, whereby they are sealed to the day of redemption, -- of their defiling his dwelling-place; minds them of the reproach, dishonour, scandal, which they bring on the gospel and the profession thereof; minds them of the terrors, darkness, wounds, want of peace, that they may bring upon their own souls. From these and the like considerations doth God put a stop to the law of sin in the heart, that it shall not go on to bring forth the evil which it hath conceived. I could give instances in argument of all these several kinds recorded in the Scripture, but it would be too long a work for us, who are now engaged in a design of another nature; but one or two examples may be mentioned. Joseph resists his first temptation on one of these accounts: Gen. xxxix. 9, "How can I do this great wickedness, and sin against God?" The evil of sinning against God, his God, that consideration alone detains him from the least inclination to his temptation. "It is sin against God, to whom I owe all obedience, the God of my life and of all my mercies. I will not do it." The argument wherewith Abigail prevailed on David, 1 Sam. xxv. 31, to withhold him from self-revenge and murder, was of the same nature; and he acknowledgeth that it was from the Lord, verse 32. I shall add no more; for all the Scripture motives which we have to duty, made effectual by grace, are instances of this way of God's procedure.

Sometimes, I confess, God secretly works the hearts of men by his own finger, without the use and means of such arguments as those insisted on, to stop the progress of sin. So he tells Abimelech, Gen. xx. 6, "I have withheld thee from sinning against me." Now, this could not be done by any of the arguments which we have insisted on, because Abimelech knew not that the thing he intended was sin; and therefore he pleads, that in the "integrity of his heart and innocency of his hands" he did it, verse 5. God turned about his will and thoughts, that he should not accomplish his intention; but by what ways or means is not revealed. Nor is it evident what course he took in the change of Esau's heart, when he came out against his brother to destroy him, Gen. xxxiii. 4. Whether he stirred up in him a fresh spring of natural affection, or caused him to consider what grief by this means he should bring to his aged father, who loved him so tenderly; or whether, being now grown great and wealthy, he more and more despised the matter of difference between him and his brother, and so utterly slighted it, is not known. It may be God did it by an immediate, powerful act of his Spirit upon his heart, without any actual intervening of these or any of the like considerations. Now, though the things mentioned are in themselves at other times feeble and weak, yet when they are managed by the Spirit of God to such an end and purpose, they certainly become effectual, and are the matter of his preventing grace.

[2.] God prevents the bringing forth of conceived sin by real spiritual saving grace, and that either in the first conversion of sinners or in the following supplies of it:--

1st. This is one part of the mystery of his grace and love. He meets men sometimes, in their highest resolutions for sin, with the highest efficacy of his grace. Hereby he manifests the power of his own grace, and gives the soul a farther experience of the law of sin, when it takes such a farewell of it as to be changed in the midst of its resolutions to serve the lusts thereof. By this he melts down the lusts of men, causeth them to wither at the root, that they shall no more strive to bring forth what they have conceived, but be filled with shame and sorrow at their conception. An example and instance of this proceeding of God, for the use and instruction of all generations, we have in Paul. His heart was full of wickedness, blasphemy, and persecution; his conception of them was come unto rage and madness, and a full purpose of exercising them all to the utmost: so the story relates it, Acts 9; so himself declares the state to have been with him, Acts xxvi. 9-12, 1 Tim. i. 13. In the midst of all this violent pursuit of sin, a voice from heaven shuts up the womb and dries the breasts of it, and he cries, "Lord, what wilt thou have me to do?" Acts ix. 6. The same person seems to intimate that this is the way of God's procedure with others, even to meet them with his converting grace in the height of their sin and folly, 1 Tim. i. 16: for he himself, he says, was a pattern of God's dealing with others; as he dealt with him, so also would he do with some such-like sinners: "For this cause I obtained mercy, that in me first Jesus Christ might show forth all long-suffering, for a pattern to them which should hereafter believe on him to life everlasting." And we have not a few examples of it in our own days. Sundry persons on set purpose going to this or that place to deride and scoff at the dispensation of the word, have been met withal in the very place wherein they designed to serve their lusts and Satan, and have been cast down at the foot of God. This way of God's dealing with sinners is at large set forth, Job xxxiii. 15-18. Dionysius the Areopagite is another instance of this work of God's grace and love. Paul is dragged either by him or before him, to plead for his life, as "a setter forth of strange gods," which at Athens was death by the law. In the midst of this frame of spirit God meets with him by converting grace, sin withers in the womb, and he cleaves to Paul and his doctrine, Acts xvii. 18-34. The like dispensation towards Israel we have, Hos. xi. 7-10. But there is no need to insist on more instances of this observation. God is pleased to leave no generation unconvinced of this truth, if they do but attend to their own experiences and the examples of this work of his mercy amongst them. Every day, one or other is taken in the fullness of the purpose of his heart to go on in sin, in this or that sin, and is stopped in his course by the power of converting grace.

2dly. God doth it by the same grace in the renewed communications of it; that is, by special assisting grace. This is the common way of his dealing with believers in this case. That they also, through the deceitfulness of sin, may be carried on to the conceiving of this or that sin, was before declared. God puts a stop to their progress, or rather to the prevalency of the law of sin in them, and that by giving in unto them special assistances needful for their preservation and deliverance. As David says of himself, Ps. lxxiii. 2, "His feet were almost gone, his steps had well-nigh slipped," -- he was at the very brink of unbelieving, despairing thoughts and conclusions about God's providence in the government of the world, from whence he was recovered, as he afterwards declares, -- so is it with many a believer; he is oftentimes at the very brink, at the very door of some folly or iniquity, when God puts in by the efficacy of actually assisting grace, and recovers them to an obediential frame of heart again. And this is a peculiar work of Christ, wherein he manifests and exerts his faithfulness towards his own: Heb. ii. 18, "He is able to succour them that are tempted." It is not an absolute power, but a power clothed with mercy, that is intended, -- such a power as is put forth from a sense of the suffering of poor believers under their temptations. And how doth he exercise this merciful ability towards us? Heb. iv.

16, he gives forth, and we find in him, "grace to help in time of need," -- seasonable help and assistance for our deliverance, when we are ready to be overpowered by sin and temptation. When lust hath conceived, and is ready to bring forth, -- when the soul lies at the brink of some iniquity, -- he gives in seasonable help, relief, deliverance, and safety. Here lies a great part of the care and faithfulness of Christ towards his poor saints. He will not suffer them to be worried with the power of sin, nor to be carried out unto ways that shall dishonour the gospel, or fill them with shame and reproach, and so render them useless in the world; but he steps in with the saving relief and assistance of his grace, stops the course of sin, and makes them in himself more than conquerors. And this assistance lies under the promise, 1 Cor. x. 13, "There hath no temptation taken you but such as is common to man: but God is faithful, who will not suffer you to be tempted above that ye are able; but will with the temptation also make a way to escape, that ye may be able to bear it." Temptation shall try us, -- it is for our good; many holy ends doth the Lord compass and bring about by it. But when we are tried to the utmost of our ability, so that one assault more would overbear us, a way of escape is provided. And as this may be done several ways, as I have elsewhere declared, so this we are now upon is one of the most eminent, -- namely, by supplies of grace to enable the soul to bear up, resist, and conquer. And when once God begins to deal in this way of love with a soul, he will not cease to add one supply after another, until the whole work of his grace and faithfulness be accomplished; an example hereof we have, Isa. lvii. 17, 18. Poor sinners there are so far captivated to the power of their lusts that the first and second dealings of God with them are not effectual for their delivery, but he will not give them over; he is in the pursuit of a design of love towards them, and so ceaseth not until they are recovered. These are the general heads of the second way whereby God hinders the bringing forth of conceived sin, -- namely, by working on the will of the sinner. He doth it either by common convictions or special grace, so that of their own accord they shall let go the purpose and will of sinning that they are risen up unto. And this is no mean way of his providing for his own glory and the honour of his gospel in the world, whose professors would stain the whole beauty of it were they left to themselves to bring forth all the evil that is conceived in their hearts.

3dly. Besides these general ways, there is one yet more special, that at once worketh both upon the power and will of the sinner, and this is the way of afflictions, concerning which one word shall close this discourse. Afflictions, I say, work by both these ways in reference unto conceived sin. They work providentially on the power of the creature. When a man hath conceived a sin, and is in full purpose of the pursuit of it, God oftentimes sends a sickness and abates his strength, or a loss cuts him short in his plenty, and so takes him off from the pursuit of his lusts, though it may be his heart is not weaned from them. His power is weakened, and he cannot do the evil he would. In this sense it belongs to the first way of God's obviating the production of sin Great afflictions work sometimes not from their own nature, immediately and directly, but from the gracious purpose and intendment of him that sends them. He insinuates into the dispensation of them that of grace and power, of love and kindness, which shall effectually take off the heart and mind from sin: Ps. cxix. 67, "Before I was afflicted I went astray, but now have I kept thy word." And in this way, because of the predominancy of renewing and assisting grace, they belong unto the latter means, of preventing sin.

And these are some of the ways whereby it pleaseth God to put a stop to the progress of sin, both in believers and unbelievers, which at present we shall instance in; and if we would endeavour farther to search out his ways unto perfection, yet we must still conclude that it is but a little portion which we know of him.

Chapter XIV

The power of sin farther demonstrated by the effects it hath had in the lives of professors -- First, in actual sins -- Secondly, in habitual declensions.

We are now to proceed unto other evidences of that sad truth which we are in the demonstration of. But the main of our work being passed through, I shall be more brief in the management of the arguments that do remain.

That, then, which in the next place may be fixed upon, is the demonstration which this law of sin hath in all ages given of its power and efficacy, by the woful fruits that it hath brought forth, even in believers themselves. Now, these are of two sorts:-- 1. The great actual eruptions of sin in their lives; 2. Their habitual declensions from the frames, state, and condition of obedience and communion with God, which they had obtained; -- both which, by the rule of James, before unfolded, are to be laid to the account of this law of sin, and belong unto the fourth head of its progress, and are both of them convincing evidences of its power and efficacy.

1. Consider the fearful eruptions of actual sin that have been in the lives of believers, and we shall find our position evidenced. Should I go through at large with this consideration, I must recount all the sad and scandalous failings of the saints that are left on record in the holy Scripture; but the particulars of them are known to all, so that I shall not need to mention them, nor the many aggravations that in their circumstances they are attended with. Only some few things tending to the rendering of our present consideration of them useful may be remarked; as, --

(1.) They are most of them in the lives of men that were not of the lowest form or ordinary sort of believers, but of men that had a peculiar eminency in them on the account of their walking with God in their generation. Such were Noah, Lot, David, Hezekiah, and others. They were not men of an ordinary size, but higher than their brethren, by the shoulders and upwards, in profession, yea, in real holiness. And surely that must needs be of a mighty efficacy that could hurry such giants in the ways of God into such abominable sins as they fell into. An ordinary engine could never have turned them out of the course of their obedience. It was a poison that no athletic constitution of spiritual health, no antidote, could withstand.

(2.) And these very men fell not into their great sins at the beginning of their profession, when they had had but little experience of the goodness of God, of the sweetness and pleasantness of obedience, of the power and craft of sin, of its impulsions, solicitations, and surprisals; but after a long course of walking with God, and acquaintance with all these things, together with innumerable motives unto watchfulness. Noah, according to the lives of men in those days of the world, had walked uprightly with God some hundreds of years before he was so surprised as he was, Gen. ix. Righteous Lot seems to have been towards the end of his days ere he defiled himself with the abominations recorded. David, in a short life, had as much experience of grace and sin, and as much close, spiritual communion with God, as ever had any of the sons of men, before he was cast to the ground by this law of sin. So was it with Hezekiah in his degree, which was none of the meanest. Now, to set upon such persons, so well acquainted with its power and deceit, so armed and provided against it, that had been conquerors over it for so many years, and to prevail against them, it argues a power and efficacy too mighty for every thing but the Spirit of the Almighty to withstand. Who can look to have a greater stock of inherent grace than those men had; to have more experience of God and the excellency of his ways, the sweetness of his love and of communion with him, than they had? who hath either better furniture to oppose sin withal, or more obligation so to do, than they? and yet we see how fearfully they were prevailed against.

(3.) As if God had permitted their falls on set purpose, that we might learn to be wary of this powerful enemy, they all of them fell out when they had newly received great and stupendous mercies from the hand of God, that ought to have been strong obligations unto diligence and watchfulness in close obedience. Noah was but newly come forth of that world of waters, wherein he saw the ungodly world perishing for their sins, and himself preserved by that astonishable miracle which all ages must admire. Whilst the world's desolation was an hourly remembrancer unto him of his strange preservation by the immediate care and hand of God, he falls into drunkenness. Lot had newly seen that which every one that thinks on cannot but tremble, lie saw, as one speaks, "hell coming out of heaven" upon unclean sinners; the greatest evidence, except the cross of Christ, that God ever gave in his providence of the judgment to come. He saw himself and children delivered by the special care and miraculous hand of God; and yet, whilst these strange mercies were fresh upon him, he fell into drunkenness and incest. David was delivered out of all his troubles, and had the necks of his enemies given him round about, and he makes use of his peace from a world of trials and troubles to contrive murder and adultery. Immediately it was after Hezekiah's great and miraculous deliverance that he falls into his carnal pride and boasting. I say, their falls in such seasons seem to be permitted on set purpose to instruct us all in the truth that we have in hand; so that no persons, in no seasons, with what furniture of grace soever, can promise themselves security from its prevalency any other ways than by keeping close constantly to Him who hath supplies to give out that are above its reach and efficacy. Methinks this should make us look about us. Are we better than Noah, who had that testimony from God, that he was "a perfect man in his generations," and "walked with God?" Are we better than Lot, whose "righteous soul was vexed with the evil deeds of ungodly men," and is therefore commended by the Holy Ghost? Are we more holy, wise, and watchful than David, who obtained this testimony, that he was "a man after God's own heart?" or better than Hezekiah, who appealed to God himself, that he had served him uprightly, with a perfect heart? And yet what prevalency this law of sin wrought in and over them we see. And there is no end of the like examples. They are all set up as buoys to discover unto us the sands, the shelves, the rocks, whereupon they made their shipwreck, to their hazard, danger, loss, yea, and would have done to their ruin, had not God been pleased in his faithfulness graciously to prevent it. And this is the first part of this evidence of the power of sin from its effects.

2. It manifests its power in the habitual declensions from zeal and holiness, from the frames, state, and condition of obedience and communion with God whereunto they had attained, which are found in many believers. Promises of growth and improvement are many and precious, the means excellent and effectual, the benefits great and unspeakable; yet it often falls out, that instead hereof decays and declensions are found upon professors, yea, in and upon many of the saints of God. Now, whereas this must needs principally and chiefly be from the strength and efficacy of indwelling sin, and is therefore a great evidence thereof, I shall first evince the observation itself to be true, -- namely, that some of the saints themselves do oftentimes so decline from that growth and improvement in faith, grace, and holiness which might justly be expected from them, -- and then show that the cause of this evil lies in that that we are treating of. And that it is the cause of total apostasy in unsound professors shall be after declared. But this is a greater work which we have in hand. The prevailing upon true believers unto a sinful declension and gradual apostasy, requires a putting forth of more strength and efficacy than the prevailing upon unsound professors unto total apostasy; as the wind which will blow down a dead tree that hath no root to the ground will scarcely shake or bow a living, well-rooted tree. But this it will do. There is mention made in the Scripture of "the first ways of David," and they are commended above his latter, 2 Chron. xvii. 3. The last ways even of David were tainted with the power of indwelling sin. Though we have mention only of the actual eruption of sin, yet that uncleanness and pride which was working in him in his numbering of the people were certainly rooted in a declension from his first frame. Those rushes did not grow without mire. David would not have clone so in his younger days, when he followed God in the wilderness of temptations and trials, full of faith, love, humility, brokenness of heart, zeal, tender affection unto all the ordinances of God; all which were eminent in him. But his strength is impaired by the efficacy and deceitfulness of sin, his locks cut, and he becomes a prey to vile lusts and temptations. We have a notable instance in most of the churches that our Saviour awakens to the consideration of their condition in the Revelation. We may single out one of them. Many good things were there in the church of Ephesus, Rev. ii. 2, 3, for which it is greatly commended; but yet it is charged with a decay, a declension, a gradual falling off and apostasy: Verses 4, 5, "Thou hast left thy first love. Remember therefore from whence thou art fallen, and repent, and do the first works." There was a decay, both inward, in the frame of heart, as to faith and love, and outward, as to obedience and works, in comparison of what they had formerly, by the testimony of Christ himself. The same also might be showed concerning the rest of those churches, only one or two of them excepted. Five of them are charged with decays and declensions. Hence there is mention in the Scripture of the "kindness of youth," of the "love of espousals," with great commendation, Jer. ii. 2, 3; of our "first faith," 1 Tim. v. 12; of "the beginning of our confidence," Heb. iii. 14. And cautions are given that we "lose not the things that we have wrought," 2 John 8. But what need we look back or search for instances to confirm the truth of this observation? An habitual declension from first engagements unto God, from first attainments of communion with God, from first strictness in duties of obedience, is ordinary and common amongst professors.

Might we to this purpose take a general view of the professors in these nations, -- among whom the lot of the best of us will be found, in part or in whole, in somewhat or in all, to fall, -- we might be plentifully convinced of the truth of this observation:--

(1.) Is their zeal for God as warm, living, vigorous, effectual, solicitous, as it was in their first giving themselves unto God? or rather, is there not a common, slight, selfish frame of spirit in the room of it come upon most professors? Iniquity hath abounded, and their love hath waxed cold. Was it not of old a burden to their spirits to hear the name, and ways, and worship of God blasphemed and profaned? Could they not have said, with the psalmist, Ps. cxix. 136, "Rivers of waters run down mine eyes, because men keep not thy law?" Were not their souls solicitous about the interest of Christ in the world, like Eli's about the ark? Did they not contend earnestly for the faith once delivered to the saints, and every parcel of it, especially wherein the grace of God and the glory of the gospel was especially concerned? Did they not labour to judge and condemn the world by a holy and separate conversation? And do now the generality of professors abide in this frame? Have they grown, and made improvement in it? or is there not a coldness and indifference grown upon the spirits of many in this thing? yea, do not many despise all these things, and look upon their own former zeal as folly? May we not see many, who have formerly been of esteem in ways of profession, become daily a scorn and reproach through their miscarriages, and that justly, to the men of the world? Is it not with them as it was of old with the daughters of Zion, Isa. iii. 24, when God judged them for their sins and wantonness? Hath not the world and self utterly ruined their profession? and are they not regardless of the things wherein they have formerly declared a singular concermnent? yea, are not some come, partly on one pretence, partly on another, to an open enmity unto, and hatred of, the ways of God? They please them no more, but are evil in their eyes. But not to mention such open apostates any farther, whose hypocrisy the Lord Jesus Christ will shortly judge, how is it with the best? Are not almost all men grown cold and slack as to these things? are they not less concerned in them than formerly? are they not grown weary, selfish in their religion; and so things be indifferent well at home, scarce care how they go abroad in the world? at least, do they not prefer their ease, credit, safety, secular advantages before these things? -- a frame that Christ abhors, and declares that those in whom it prevails are none of his. Some, indeed, seem to retain a good zeal for truth; but wherein they make the fairest appearance, therein will they be found to be most abominable. They cry out against errors, -- not for truth, but for party's and interest's sake. Let a man be on their party and promote their interest, be he never so corrupt in his judgment, he is embraced, and, it may be, admired. This is not zeal for God, but for a man's self. It is not, "The zeal of thine house hath eaten me up," but, "Master, forbid them, because they follow not with us." Better it were, doubtless, for men never to pretend unto any zeal at all than to substitute such wrathful selfishness in the room of it.

(2.) Is men's delight in the ordinances and worship of God the same as in former days? do they find the same sweetness and relish in them as they have done of old? How precious hath the word been to them formerly! What joy and delight have they had in attendance thereon! How would they have run and gone to have been made partakers of it, where it was dispensed in its power and purity, in the evidence and demonstration of the Spirit! Did they not call the Sabbath their delight, and was not the approach of it a real joy unto their souls? Did they not long after the converse and corn-mullion of saints, and could they not undergo manifold perils for the attainment of it? And doth this frame still abide upon them? Are there not decays and declensions to be found amongst them? May it not be said, "Grey hairs are here and there upon them, and they perceive it not?" Yea, are not men ready to say with them of old, "What a weariness is it!" Mal. i. 13. It is even a burden and a weariness to be tied up to the observation of all these ordinances. What need we be at all so strict in the observation of the Sabbath? What need we hear so often? What need this distinction in hearing? Insensibly a great disrespect, yea, even a contempt of the pleasant and excellent ways of Christ and his gospel is fallen upon many professors.

(3.) May not the same conviction be farther carried on by an inquiry into the universal course of obedience and the performance of duties that men have been engaged in? Is there the same conscientious tenderness of sinning abiding in many as was in days of old, the same exact performance of private duties, the same love to the brethren, the same readiness for the cross, the same humility of mind and spirit, the same self-denial? The steam of men's lusts, wherewith the air is tainted, will not suffer us so to say.

We need, then, go no farther than this wretched generation wherein we live, to evince the truth of the observation laid down as the foundation of the instance insisted on. The Lord give repentance before it be too late!

Now, all these declensions, all these decays, that are found in some professors, they all proceed from this root and cause; -- they are all the product of indwelling sin, and all evince the exceeding power and efficacy of it: for the proof whereof I shall not need to go farther than the general rule which out of James we have already considered, -- namely, that lust or indwelling sin is the cause of all actual sin and all habitual declensions in believers. This is that which the apostle intends in that place to teach and declare. I shall, therefore, handle these two things, and show, -- 1. That this doth evince a great efficacy and power in sin; 2. Declare the ways and means whereby it brings forth or brings about this cursed effect; -- all in design of our general end, in calling upon and cautioning believers to avoid it, to oppose it.

1. It appears to be a work of great power and efficacy from the provision that is made against it, which it prevails over. There is in the covenant of grace plentiful provision made, not only for the

preventing of declensions and decays in believers, but also for their continual carrying on towards perfection; as, --

(1.) The word itself and all the ordinances of the gospel are appointed and given unto us for this end, Eph. iv. 11-15. That which is the end of giving gospel officers to the church is the end also of giving all the ordinances to be administered by them; for they are given "for the work of the ministry," -- that is, for the administration of the ordinances of the gospel. Now, what is or what are these ends? They are all for the preventing of decays and declensions in the saints, all for the carrying them on to perfection; so it is said, verse 12. In general, it is for the "perfecting of the saints," carrying on the work of grace in them, and the work of holiness and obedience by them; or for the edifying of the body of Christ, their building up in an increase of faith and love, even of every true member of the mystical body. But how far are they appointed thus to carry them on, thus to build them up? Hath it bounds fixed to its work? Doth it carry them so far, and then leave them? "No," saith the apostle, verse 13. The dispensation of the word of the gospel, and the ordinances thereof, is designed for our help, assistance, and furtherance, until the whole work of faith and obedience is consummate. It is appointed to perfect and complete that faith, knowledge, and growth in grace and holiness, which is allotted unto us in this world. But what and if oppositions and temptations do lie in the way, Satan and his instruments working with great subtlety and deceit? Why, verse 14, these ordinances are designed for our safeguarding and deliverance from all their attempts and assaults, that so being preserved in the use of them, or "speaking the truth in love, we may grow up unto him in all things who is the head, even Christ Jesus." This is, in general, the use of all gospel ordinances, the chief and main end for which they were given and appointed of God, -- namely, to preserve believers from all decays of faith and obedience, and to carry them on still towards perfection. These are means which God, the good husbandman, makes use of to cause the vine to thrive and bring forth fruit. And I could also manifest the same to be the especial end of them distinctly. Briefly, the word is milk and strong meat, for the nourishing and strengthening of all sorts and all degrees of believers. It hath both seed and water in it, and manuring with it, to make them fruitful The ordinance of the supper is appointed on purpose for the strengthening of our faith, in the remembrance of the death of the Lord, and the exercise of love one towards another. The communion of saints is for the edifying each other in faith, love, and obedience.

(2.) There is that which adds weight to this consideration. God suffers us not to be unmindful of this assistance he hath afforded us, but is continually calling upon us to make use of the means appointed for the attaining of the end proposed. He shows them unto us, as the angel showed the water-spring to Hagar. Commands, exhortations, promises, threatenings, are multiplied to this purpose; see them summed up, Heb. ii. 1. He is continually saying to us, "Why will ye die? why will ye wither and decay? Come to the pastures provided for you, and your souls shall live." If we see a lamb run from the fold into the wilderness, we wonder not if it be torn and rent of wild beasts. If we see a sheep leaving its green pastures and watercourses, to abide in dry barren heaths, we count it no marvel, nor inquire farther, if we see him lean and ready to perish; but if we find lambs wounded in the fold, we wonder at the boldness and rage of the beasts of prey that durst set upon them there. If we see sheep pining in full pastures, we judge them to be diseased and unsound. It is indeed no marvel that poor creatures who forsake their own mercies, and run away from the pasture and fold of Christ in his ordinances, are rent and torn with divers lusts, and do pine away with hunger and famine; but to see men living under and enjoying all the means of spiritual thriving, yet to decay, not to be fat and flourishing, but rather daily to pine and wither, this argues some secret powerful distemper, whose poisonous and noxious qualities hinder the virtue and efficacy of the means they enjoy. This is indwelling sin. So wonderfully powerful, so effectually poisonous it is, that it can bring leanness on the souls of men in the midst of all precious means of growth and flourishing. It may well make us tremble, to see men living under and in the use of the means of the gospel, preaching, praying, administration of sacraments, and yet grow colder every day than others in zeal for God, more selfish and worldly, even habitually to decline as to the degrees of holiness which they had attained unto.

(3.) Together with the dispensation of the outward means of spiritual growth or improvement, there are also supplies of grace continually afforded the saints from their head, Christ. He is the head of all the saints; and he is a living head, and so a living head as that he tells us that "because he liveth we shall live also," John xiv. 19. He communicates of spiritual life to all that are His. In him is the fountain of our life; which is therefore said to be "hid with him in God," Col. iii. 3. And this life he gives unto his saints by quickening of them by his Spirit, Rom. viii. 11; and he continues it unto them by the supplies of living grace which he communicates unto them. From these two, his quickening of us, and continually giving out supplies of life unto us, he is said to live in us: Gal. ii. 20, "I live; yet not I, but Christ liveth in me;" -- "The spiritual life which I have is not mine own; not from myself was it educed, not by myself is it maintained, but it is merely and solely the work of Christ: so that it is not I that live, but he lives in me, the whole of my life being from him alone." Neither doth this living head communicate only a bare life unto believers, that they should merely live and no more, a poor, weak, dying life, as it were; but he gives out sufficiently to afford them a strong, vigorous, thriving, flourishing life, John x. 10. He comes not only that his sheep "may have life," but that "they may have it more abundantly;" that is, in a plentiful manner, so as that they may flourish, be fat and fruitful. Thus is it with the whole body of Christ, and every member thereof, Eph. iv. 15, 16, whereby it "grows up into him in all things, which is the head, even Christ: from whom the whole body fitly joined together and compacted by that which every joint supplieth, according to the effectual working in the measure of every part, maketh increase of the body unto the edifying of itself in love." The end of all communications of grace and supplies of life from this living and blessed head, is the increase of the whole body and every member of it, and the edifying of itself in love. His treasures of grace are unsearchable; his stores inexhaustible; his life, the fountain of ours, full and eternal; his heart bounteous and large; his hand open and liberal: so that there is no doubt but that he communicates supplies of grace for their increase in holiness abundantly unto all his saints. Whence, then, is it that they do not all flourish and thrive accordingly? As you may see it oftentimes in a natural body, so is it here. Though the seat and rise of the blood and spirits in head and heart be excellently good and sound, yet there may be a withering member in the body; somewhat intercepts the influences of life unto it, so that though the heart and head do perform their orifice, in giving of supplies no less to that than they do to any other member, yet all the effect produced is merely to keep it from utter perishing, -- it grows weak and decays every day. The withering and decaying of any member in Christ's mystical body is not for the want of his communication of grace for an abundant life, but from the powerful interception that is made of the efficacy of it, by the interposition and opposition of indwelling sin. Hence it is that where lust grows strong, a great deal of grace will but keep the soul alive, and not give it any eminency in fruitfulness at all. Oftentimes Christ gives very much grace where not many of its effects do appear. It spends its strength and power in withstanding the continual assaults of violent corruptions and lusts, so that it cannot put forth its proper virtue towards farther fruitfulness. As a virtuous medicine, that is fit both to check vicious and noxious humours, and to comfort, refresh, and strengthen nature, if the evil humour be strong and greatly prevailing, spends its whole strength and virtue in the subduing and correcting of it, contributing much less to the relief of nature than otherwise it would do, if it met not with such opposition; so is it with the eye-salve and the healing grace which we have abundantly from the wings of the Sun of Righteousness. It is forced oftentimes to put forth its virtue to oppose and contend against, and in any measure subdue, prevailing lusts and corruptions. That the soul receiveth not that strengthening unto duties and fruitfulness which otherwise it might receive by it is from hence. How sound, healthy, and flourishing, how fruitful and exemplary in holiness, might many a soul be by and with that grace which is continually communicated to it from Christ, which now, by reason of the power of indwelling sin, is only not dead, but weak, withering, and useless! And this, if any thing, is a notable evidence of the efficacy of indwelling sin, that it is able to give such a stop and check to the mighty and effectual power of grace, so that notwithstanding the blessed and continual supplies that we receive from our Head, yet many believers do decline and decay, and that habitually, as to what they had attained unto, their last ways not answering their first. This makes the vineyard in the "very fruitful hill" to bring forth so many wild grapes; this makes so many trees barren in fertile fields.

(4.) Besides the continual supplies of grace that constantly, according to the tenure of the covenant, are communicated unto believers, which keeps them that they thirst no more as to a total indigence, there is, moreover, a readiness in the Lord Christ to yield peculiar succour to the souls of his, according as their occasions shall require. The apostle tells us that he is "a merciful High Priest," and "able" (that is, ready, prepared, and willing) "to succour them that are tempted," Heb. ii. 18; and we are on that account invited to "come with boldness to the throne of grace, that we may obtain mercy, and find grace to help in time of need," -- that is, grace sufficient, seasonable, suitable unto any especial trial or temptation that we may be exercised withal. Our merciful High Priest is ready to give out this especial seasonable grace over and above those constant communications of supplies of the Spirit which we mentioned before. Besides the never-failing springs of ordinary covenant grace, he hath also peculiar refreshing showers for times of drought; and this is exceedingly to the advantage of the saints for their preservation and growth in grace; and there may very many more of the like nature be added. But now, I say, notwithstanding all these, and the residue of the like importance, such is the power and efficacy of indwelling sin, so great its deceitfulness and restlessness, so many its wiles and temptations, it often falls out that many of them for whose growth and improvement all this provision is made do yet, as was showed, go back and decline, even as to their course of walking with God. Samson's strength fully evidenced itself when he brake seven new withes and seven new cords, wherewith he was bound, as burning tow and as thread. The noxious humour in the body, which is so stubborn as that no use of the most sovereign remedies can prevail against it, ought to be regarded. Such is this indwelling sin if not watched over. It breaks all the cords made to bind it; it blunts the instruments appointed to root it up; it resists all healing medicines, though never so sovereign; and is therefore assuredly of exceeding efficacy. Besides, believers have innumerable obligations upon them, from the love, the command of God, to grow in grace, to press forward towards perfection, as they have abundant means provided for them so to do. Their doing so is a matter of the greatest advantage, profit, sweetness, contentment unto them in the world. It is the burden, the trouble of their souls, that they do not so do, that they are not more holy, more zealous, useful, fruitful; they desire it above life itself. They know it is their duty to watch against this enemy, to fight against it, to pray against it; and so they do. They more desire his destruction than the enjoyment of all this world and all that it can afford. And yet, notwithstanding all this, such is the subtlety, and fraud, and violence, and fury, and urgency, and importunity of this adversary, that it frequently prevails to bring them into the woful condition mentioned. Hence it is with believers sometimes as it is with men in some places at sea. They have a good and fair gale of wind, it may be, all night long; they ply their tackling, attend diligently their business, and, it may be, take great contentment to consider how they proceed in their voyage. In the morning, or after a season, coming to measure what way they have made, and what progress they have had, they find that they axe much backward of what they were, instead of getting one step forward. Falling into a swift tide or current against them, it hath frustrated all their labours, and rendered the wind in their sails almost useless; somewhat thereby they have borne up against the stream, but have made no progress. So is it with believers. They have a good gale of supplies of the Spirit from above; they attend duties diligently, pray constantly, hear attentively, and omit nothing that may carry them on their voyage towards eternity; but after a while, coming seriously to consider, by the examination of their hearts and ways, what progress they have made, they find that all their assistance and duties have not been able to bear them up against some strong tide or current of indwelling sin. It hath kept them, indeed, that they have not been driven and split on rocks and shelves, -- it hath preserved them from gross, scandalous sins: but yet they have lost in their spiritual frame, or gone backwards, and are entangled under many woful decays; which is a notable evidence of the life of sin, about which we are treating. Now, because the end of our discovering this power of sin is, that we may be careful to obviate and prevent it in its operation; and, because of all the effects that it produceth, there is none more dangerous or pernicious than that we have last insisted on, -- namely, that it prevails upon many professors unto an habitual declension from their former ways and attainments, notwithstanding all the sweetness and excellency which their souls have found in them; -- I shall, as was said, in the next place, consider by what ways and means, and through what assistance, it usually prevails in this kind, that we may the better be instructed to watch against it.

Chapter XV

Decays in degrees of grace caused by indwelling sin -- The ways of its prevalency to this purpose.

2. The ways and means whereby indwelling sin prevaileth on believers unto habitual declensions and decays as to degrees of grace and holiness is that now which comes under consideration; and they are many:--

(1.) Upon the first conversion and calling of sinners unto God and Christ, they have usually many fresh springs breaking forth in their souls and refreshing showers coming upon them, which bear them up to a high rate of faith, love, holiness, fruitfulness, and obedience; as upon a land-flood, when many lesser streams run into a river, it swells over its bounds, and rolls on with a more than ordinary fulness. Now, if these springs be not kept open, if they prevail not for the continuance of these showers, they must needs decay and go backwards. We shall name one or two of them:--

[1.] They have a fresh, vigorous sense of pardoning mercy. According as this is in the soul, so will its love and delight in God, so will its obedience be; as, I say, is the sense of gospel pardon, so will be the life of gospel love. Luke vii. 47, "I say unto thee," saith our Saviour of the poor woman, "Her sins, which were many, are forgiven; for she loved much: but to whom little is forgiven, the same loveth little." Her great love was an evidence of great forgiveness, and her great sense of it: for our Saviour is not rendering a reason of her forgiveness, as though it were for her love; but of her love, that it was because of her forgiveness. Having in the foregoing parable, from verse 40 and onwards, convinced the Pharisee with whom he had to do that he to whom most was forgiven would love most, as verse 43, he thence gives an account of the great love of the woman, springing from the sense she had of the great forgiveness which she had so freely received. Thus sinners at their first conversion are very sensible of great forgiveness; "Of whom I am chief," lies next their heart. This greatly subdues their hearts and spirits unto all in God, and quickens them unto all obedience, even that such poor cursed sinners as they were should so freely be delivered and pardoned. The love of God and of Christ in their forgiveness highly conquers and constrains them to make it their business to live unto God.

[2.] The fresh taste they have had of spiritual things keeps up such a savour and relish of them in their souls, as that worldly contentments, whereby men are drawn off from close walking with God, are rendered sapless and undesirable unto them. Having tasted of the wine of the gospel, they desire no other, for they say, "This is best." So was it with the apostles, upon that option offered them as to a departure from Christ, upon the apostasy of many false professors: "Will ye also go away?" John vi. 67. They answer by Peter, "Lord, to whom shall we go? thou hast the words of eternal life," verse 68. They had such a fresh savour and relish of the doctrine of the gospel and the grace of Christ upon their souls, that they can entertain no thoughts of declining from it. As a man that hath been long kept in a dungeon, if brought forth on a sudden into the light of the sun, finds so much pleasure and contentment in it, in the beauties of the old creation, that he thinks he can never be weary of it, nor shall ever be contented on any account to be under darkness again; so is it with souls when first translated into the marvellous light of Christ, to behold the beauties of the new creation. They see a new glory in him, that hath quite sullied the desirableness of all earthly diversions. And they see a new guilt and filth in sin, that gives them an utter abhorrency of its old delights and pleasures; and so of other things.

Now, whilst these and the like springs are kept open in the souls of converted sinners, they constrain them to a vigorous, active holiness. They can never do enough for God; so that oftentimes their zeal as saints suffers them not to escape without some blots on their prudence as men, as might be instanced in many of the martyrs of old.

This, then, is the first, at least one way whereby indwelling sin prepares men for decays and declensions in grace and obedience, -- it endeavours to stop or taint these springs. And there are several ways whereby it brings this to pass:--

1st. It works by sloth and negligence. It prevails in the soul to a neglect of stirring up continual thoughts of or about the things that so powerfully influence it unto strict and fruitful obedience. If care be not taken, if diligence and watchfulness be not used, and all means that are appointed of God to keep a quick and living sense of them upon the soul, they will dry up and decay; and, consequently, that obedience that should spring from them will do so also. Isaac digged wells, but the Philistines stopped them, and his flocks had no benefit by them. Let the heart never so little disuse itself to gracious, soul-affecting thoughts of the love of God, the cross of Christ, the greatness and excellency of gospel mercy, the beauties of holiness, they will quickly be as much estranged to a man as he can be to them. He that shuts his eyes for a season in the sun, when he opens them again can see nothing at all. And so much as a man loseth of faith towards these things, so much will they lose of power towards him. They can do little or nothing upon him because of his unbelief, which formerly were so exceedingly effectual towards him. So was it with the spouse in the Canticles, chap. v. 2; Christ calls unto her, verse 1, with a marvellous loving and gracious invitation unto communion with himself. She who had formerly been ravished at the first hearing of that joyful sound, being now under the power of sloth and carnal ease, returns a sorry excusing answer to his call, which ended in her own signal loss and sorrow. Indwelling sin, I say, prevailing by spiritual sloth upon the souls of men unto an inadvertency of the motions of God's Spirit in their former apprehensions of divine love, and a negligence of stirring up continual thoughts of faith about it, a decay grows insensibly upon the whole soul. Thus God oft complains that his people had "forgotten him;" that is, grew unmindful of his love and grace, -- which was the beginning of their apostasy.

2dly. By unframing the soul, so that it shall have formal, weary, powerless thoughts of those things which should prevail with it unto diligence in thankful obedience. The apostle cautions us that in dealing with God we should use reverence and godly fear, because of his purity, holiness, and majesty, Heb. xii. 28, 29. And this is that which the Lord himself spake in the destruction of Nadab and Abihu, "I will be sanctified in them that come nigh me," Lev. x. 3. He will be dealt withal in an awful, holy, reverent manner. So are we to deal with all the things of God wherein or whereby we have communion with him. The soul is to have a great reverence of God in them. When men begin to take them into slight or common thoughts, not using and improving them unto the utmost for the ends whereunto they are appointed, they lose all their beauty, and glory, and power towards them. When we have any thing to do wherein faith or love towards God is to be exercised, we must do it with all our hearts, with all our minds, strength, and souls; not slightly and perfunctorily, which God abhors. He doth not only require that we bear his love and grace in remembrance, but that, as much as in us lieth, we do it according to the worth and excellency of them. It was the sin of Hezekiah that he "rendered not again according to the benefits done to him," 2 Chron. xxxii. 25. So, whilst we consider gospel truths, the uttermost endeavour of the soul ought to be, that we may be "changed into the same image" or likeness, 2 Cor. iii. 18; that is, that they may have their full power and effect upon us. Otherwise, James tells us what our "beholding the glory of the Lord in a glass," there mentioned by the apostle, -- that is, reading or hearing the mind of God in Christ revealed in the gospel, -- comes unto: James i. 23, 24, "It is but like unto a man beholding his natural face in a glass: for he beholdeth himself, and goeth away, and straightway forgetteth what manner of man he was." It makes no impression upon him, begets no idea or image of his likeness in his imagination; because he doth it only slightly, and with a transient look. So is it with men that will indeed think of gospel truths but in a slight manner, without endeavouring, with all their hearts, minds, and strength, to have them ingrafted upon their souls, and all the effects of them produced in them. Now, this is the way of sinners in their first engagements unto God. They never think of pardoning mercy, but they labour to affect their whole souls with it, and do stir up themselves unto suitable affections and returns of constant obedience. They think not of the excellency of Christ and spiritual things, now newly discovered unto them in a saving light, but they press with all their might after a farther, a fuller enjoyment of them. This keeps them humble and holy, this makes them thankful and fruitful. But now, if the utmost diligence and carefulness be not used to improve and grow in this wisdom, to keep up this frame, indwelling sin, working by the vanity of the minds of men, will insensibly bring them to content themselves with slight and rare thoughts of these things, without a diligent, sedulous endeavour to give them their due improvement upon the soul. As men decay herein, so will they assuredly decay and decline in the power of holiness and close walking with God. The springs being stopped or tainted, the streams will not run so swiftly, at least not so sweetly, as formerly. Some, by this means, under an uninterrupted profession, insensibly wither almost into nothing. They talk of religion and spiritual things as much as ever they did in their lives, and perform duties with as much constancy as ever they did; but yet they have poor, lean, starving souls, as to any real and effectual communion with God. By the power and subtlety of indwelling sin they have grown formal, and learned to deal about spiritual things in an overly manner; whereby they have lost all their life, vigour, savour, and efficacy towards them. Be always serious in spiritual things if ever you intend to be bettered by them.

3dly. Indwelling sin oftentimes prevails to the stopping of these springs of gospel obedience, by false and foolish opinions corrupting the simplicity of the gospel. False opinions are the work of the flesh. From the vanity and darkness of the minds of men, with a mixture more or less of corrupt affections, do they mostly proceed. The apostle was jealous over his Corinthians in this matter. He was afraid lest their minds "should by any means be corrupted from the simplicity that is in Christ," 2 Cor. xi. 2, 3; which he knew would be attended by a decay and declension in faith, love, and obedience. And thus matters in this case often fall out. We have seen some who, after they have received a sweet taste of the love of God in Christ, of the excellency of pardoning mercy, and have walked humbly with God for many years in the faith and apprehension of the truth, have, by the corruption of their minds from the simplicity that is in Christ, by false and foolish opinions, despised all their own experiences, and rejected all the efficacy of truth, as to the furtherance of their obedience. Hence John cautions the elect lady and her children to take heed they were not seduced, lest they should "lose the things that they had wrought," 2 Epist. verse 8; -- lest they should themselves cast away all their former obedience as lost, and a thing of no value. We have innumerable instances hereof in the days wherein we live. How many are there who, not many years since, put an unspeakable value on the pardon of sin in the blood of Christ, -- who delighted in gospel discoveries of spiritual things, and walked in obedience to God on the account of them, -- who, being beguiled and turned aside from the truth as it is in Jesus, do despise these springs of their own former obedience! And as this is done grossly and openly in some, so there are more secret and more plausible insinuations of corrupt opinions tainting the springs and fountains of gospel obedience, and, through the vanity of men's minds, which is a principal part of indwelling sin, getting ground upon them. Such are all those that tend to the extenuation of special grace in its freedom and efficacy, and the advancement of the wills or the endeavours of men in their spiritual power and ability. They are works of the flesh; and howsoever some may pretend a usefulness in them to the promotion of holiness, they will be found to taint the springs of true evangelical obedience, insensibly to turn the heart from God, and to bring the whole soul into a spiritual decay.

And this is one way whereby indwelling sin produceth this pernicious effect of drawing men off from the power, purity, and fruitfulness attending their first conversion and engagements unto God, bringing them into habitual declension, at least as unto degrees, of their holiness and -- grace. There is not any thing we ought to be more watchful against, if we intend effectually to deal with this powerful and subtle enemy. It is no small part of the wisdom of faith, to observe whether gospel truths continue to have the same savour unto and efficacy upon the soul as formerly they have had; and whether an endeavour be maintained to improve them continually as at the first. A commandment that is always practiced is always new, as John speaks of that of love. And he that really improves gospel truths, though he hears them a thousand times, they will be always new and fresh unto him, because they put him on newness of practice; when to another, that grows common under them, they are burdensome and common unto him, and he even loathes the manna that he is so accustomed unto.

(2.) Indwelling sin doth this by taking men off from their watch against the returns of Satan. When our Lord Christ comes first to take possession of any soul for himself, he binds that strong man and spoils his goods; he deprives him of all his power, dominion, and interest. Satan being thus dispossessed and frustrated in his hopes and expectations, leaves the soul, as finding it newly mortified to his baits. So he left our Saviour upon his first fruitless attempts. But it is said he left him only "for a season," Luke iv. 13. He intended to return again, as he should see his advantage. So is it with believers also. Being cast out from his interest in them, he leaves them for a season, at least comparatively he doth so. Freed from his assaults and perplexing temptations, they proceed vigorously in the course of their obedience, and so flourish in the ways of God. But this holds not; Satan returns again, and if the soul stands not continually upon his guard against him, he will quickly get such advantages as shall put a notable interruption upon his fruitfulness and obedience. Hence some, after they have spent some time, it may be some years, in cheerful, exemplary walking with God, have, upon Satan's return, consumed all their latter days in wrestling with perplexing temptations, wherewith he hath entangled them. Others have plainly fallen under the power of his assaults. It is like a man who, having for a while lived usefully amongst his neighbours, done good and communicated according to his ability, distributing to the poor, and helping all around about him, at length, falling into the hands of vexatious, wrangling, oppressive men, he is forced to spend his whole time and revenue in defending himself against them at law, and so becomes useless in the place where he lives. So is it with many a believer: after he hath walked in a fruitful course of obedience, to the glory of God and edification of the church of Christ, being afresh set upon, by the return of Satan in one way or other, he hath enough to do all the remainder of his life to keep himself alive; in the meantime, as to many graces, wofully decaying and going backward, Now, this also, though Satan hath a hand in it, is from indwelling sin; I mean, the success is so which Satan doth obtain in his undertaking. This encourageth him, maketh way for his return, and gives entrance to his temptations You know how it is with them out of whom he is cast only by gospel conviction; after he hath wandered and waited a while, he saith he will return to his house from whence he was ejected. And what is the issue? Carnal lusts have prevailed over the man's convictions, and made his soul fit to entertain returning devils. It is so as to the measure of prevalency that Satan obtains against believers, upon advantages administered unto him, by sin's disposing the soul unto an obnoxiousness to his temptations.

Now, the way and means whereby indwelling sin doth give advantage to Satan for his return are all those which dispose them toward a declension, which shall afterward be mentioned. Satan is a diligent, watchful, and crafty adversary; he will neglect no opportunity, no advantage that is offered unto him. Wherein, then, soever our spiritual strength is impaired by sin, or which way soever our lusts press, Satan falls in with that weakness and presseth towards that ruin; so that all the actings of the law of sin are subservient to this end of Satan. I shall therefore only at present mention one or two that seem principally to invite Satan to attempt a return:--

[1.] It entangleth the soul in the things of the world, all which axe so many purveyors for Satan. When Pharaoh had let the people go, he heard after a while that they were entangled in the wilderness, and supposeth that he shall therefore now overtake them and destroy them. This stirs him up to pursue after them. Satan finding those whom he hath been cast out from entangled in the things of the world, by which he is sure to find an easy access unto them, is encouraged to attempt upon them afresh, as the spider to come down upon the strongest fly that is entangled in his web; for he comes by his temptations only to impel them unto that whereunto by their own lusts they axe inclined, by adding poison to their lusts, and painting to the objects of them. And oftentimes by this advantage he gets so in upon the souls of men, that they are never well free of him more whilst they live. And as men's diversions increase from the world, so do their entanglements from Satan. When they have more to do in the world than they can well manage, they shall have more to do from Satan than they can well withstand. When men are made spiritually faint, by dealing in and with the world, Satan sets on them, as Amalek did on the faint and weak of the people that came out of Egypt.

[2.] It produceth this effect by making the soul negligent, and taking it off from its watch. We have before showed at large that it is one main part of the effectual deceitfulness of indwelling sin to make the soul inadvertent, to turn it off from the diligent, watchful attendance unto its duty which is required. Now, there is not any thing in reference whereunto diligence and watchfulness are more strictly enjoined than the returning assaults of Satan: 1 Pet. v. 8, "Be sober, be vigilant." And why so? "Because of your adversary the devil." Unless you are exceeding watchful, at one time or other he will surprise you; and all the injunctions of our blessed Saviour to watch axe still with reference unto him and his temptations. Now, when the soul is made careless and inadvertent, forgetting what an enemy it hath to deal withal, or is lifted up with the successes it hath newly obtained against him, then is Satan's time to attempt a re-entrance of his old habitation; which if he cannot obtain, yet he makes their lives uncomfortable to themselves and unfruitful to others, in weakening their root and withering their fruit through his poisonous temptations. He comes down upon our duties of obedience as the fowls upon Abraham's sacrifice; so that if we watch not, as he did, to drive them away (for by resistance he is overcome and put to flight), he will devour them.

[3.] Indwelling sin takes advantage to put forth its efficacy and deceit to withdraw men from their primitive zeal and holiness, from their first faith, love, and works, by the evil examples of professors amongst whom they live. When men first engage into the ways of God, they have a reverent esteem of those whom they believe to have been made partakers of that mercy before themselves; these they love and honour, as it is their duty. But after a while they find many of them walking in many things unevenly, crookedly, and not unlike the men of the world. Here sin is not wanting to its advantage. Insensibly it prevails with men to a compliance with them. "This way, this course of walking, doth well enough with others; why may it not do so with us also?" Such is the inward thought of many, that works effectually in them. And so, through the craft of sin, the generation of professors corrupt one another. As a stream arising from a clear spring or a fountain, whilst it runs in its own peculiar channel and keeps its water unmixed, preserves its purity and cleanness, but when it falls in its course with other streams that are turbid and foul, though running the same way with it, it becomes muddy and discoloured also; so is it in this case. Believers come forth from the spring of the new birth with some purity and cleanness; this for a while they keep in the course of their private walking with God: but now, when they come sometimes to fall into society with others, whose profession flows and runs the same way with theirs, even towards heaven, but yet are muddied and sullied with sin and the world, they are often corrupted with them and by them, and so decline from their first purity, faith, and holiness. Now, lest this may have been the case of any who shall read this discourse, I shall add some few cautions that are necessary to preserve men from this infection:--

1st. In the body of professors there is a great number of hypocrites. Though we cannot say of this or that man that he is so, yet that some there are is most certain. Our Saviour hath told us that it will be so to the end of the world. All that have oil in their lamps have it not in their vessels. Let men take heed how they give themselves up unto a conformity to the professors they meet withal, lest, instead of saints and the best of men, they sometimes propose for their example hypocrites, which are the worst; and when they think they are like unto them who bear the image of God, they conform themselves unto those who bear the image of Satan.

2dly. You know not what may be the present temptation of those whose ways you observe. It may be they are under some peculiar desertion from God, and so are withering for a season, until he send them some refreshing showers from above. It may be they are entangled with some special corruptions, which is their burden, that you know not of; and for any voluntarily to fall into such a frame as others are cast into by the power of their temptations, or to think that will suffice in them which they see to suffice in others whose distempers they know not, is folly and presumption. He that knows such or such a person to be a living man and of a healthy constitution, if he sees him go crawling up and down about his affairs, feeble and weak, sometimes falling, sometimes standing, and making small progress in any thing, will he think it sufficient for himself to do so also? will he not inquire whether the person he sees have not lately fallen into some distemper or sickness that hath weakened him and brought him into that condition? Assuredly he will so do. Take heed, Christians; many of the professors with whom ye do converse are sick and wounded, -- the wounds of some of them do stink and are corrupt because of their folly. If you have any spiritual health, do not think their weak and uneven walking will be accepted at your hands; much less think it will be well for you to become sick and to be wounded also.

3dly. Remember that of many of the best Christians, the worst only is known and seen. Many who keep up precious communion with God do yet oftentimes, by their natural tempers of freedom or passion, not carry so glorious appearances as others who perhaps come short of them in grace and the power of godliness. In respect of their outward conversation it may seem they are scarcely saved, when in respect of their faith and love they may be eminent. They may, as the King's daughter, be all glorious within, though their clothes be not always of wrought gold. Take heed, then, that you be not infected with their worst, when ye are not able, it may be, to imitate them in their best. But to return.

[4.] Sin doth this work by cherishing some secret particular lust in the heart. This the soul contends against faintly. It contends against it upon the account of sincerity; it cannot but do so: but it doth not make thorough work, vigorously to mortify it by the strength and power of grace. Now, where it is thus with a soul, an habitual declension as to holiness will assuredly ensue. David shows us how, in his first days, he kept his heart close unto God: Ps. xviii. 23, "I was upright before him, and I kept myself from mine iniquity." His great care was lest any one lust should prevail in him or upon him, that might be called his iniquity in a peculiar manner. The same course steered Paul also, 1 Cor. ix. 27. He was in danger to be lifted up by his spiritual revelations and enjoyments. This makes him "keep his body in subjection," that no carnal reasonings or vain imagination might take place in him. But where indwelling sin hath provoked, irritated, and given strength unto a special lust, it proves assuredly a principal means of a general declension; for as an infirmity and weakness in any one vital part will make the whole body consumptive, so will the weakness in any one grace, which a perplexing lust brings with it, make the soul. It every way weakens spiritual strength. It weakens confidence in God in faith and prayer. The knees will be feeble and the hands will hang down in dealing with God, where a galling and unmortified lust lies in the heart. It will take such hold upon the soul that it shall not be "able to look up," Ps. xl. 12. It darkens the mind by innumerable foolish imaginations, which it stirs up to make provision for itself. It galls the conscience with those spots and stains which in and by its actings it brings upon the soul. It contends in the will for rule and dominion. An active, stirring corruption would have the commanding power in the soul, and it is ever and anon ready to take the throne. It disturbs the thoughts, and sometimes will even frighten the soul from dealing with it by meditation, lest, corrupt affections being entangled by it, grace loses ground instead of prevailing. It breaks out oftentimes into scandalous sins, as it did in David and Hezekiah, and loads the sinner with sorrow and discouragement. By these and the like means it becomes to the soul like a moth in a garment, to eat up and devour the strongest threads of it, so that though the whole hang loose together, it is easily torn to pieces. Though the soul with whom it is thus do for a season keep up a fair profession, yet his strength is secretly devoured, and every temptation tears and rends his conscience at pleasure. It becomes with such men as it is with some who have for many years been of a sound, strong, athletic constitution. Some secret, hectical distemper seizeth on them. For a season they take no notice of it, or, if they do, they think they shall do well enough with it, and easily shake it off when they have a little leisure to attend to it; but for the present, they think, as Samson with his locks cut, they will do as at other times. Sometimes, it may be, they complain that they are not well, they know not what aileth them, and it may be rise violently in an opposition to their distemper; but after a while struggling in vain, the vigour of their spirits and strength failing them, they are forced to yield to the power of a consumption. And now all they can do is little enough to keep them alive. It is so with men brought into spiritual decay by any secret perplexing corruption. It may be they have had a vigorous principle of obedience and holiness. Indwelling sin watching its opportunities, by some temptation or other hath kindled and inflamed some particular lust in them -- For a while, it may be, they take little notice of it. Sometimes they complain, but think they will do as in former times, until, being insensibly weakened in their spiritual strength, they have work enough to do in keeping alive what remains and is ready to die, Hos. v. 13. I shall not add any thing here as to the prevention and obviating this advantage of indwelling sin, having elsewhere treated of it peculiarly and apart.

[5.] It works by negligence of private communion with God in prayer and meditation. I have showed before how indwelling sin puts forth its deceitfulness in diverting the soul from watchfulness in and unto these duties. Here, if it prevails, it will not fail to produce an habitual declension in the whole course of obedience. All neglect of private duties is principled by a weariness of God, as he complaineth, Isa. xliii. 22, "Thou hast not called upon me, thou hast been weary of me." Neglect of invocation proceeds from weariness; and where there is weariness, there will be withdrawing from that whereof we are weary. Now, God alone being the fountain and spring of spiritual life, if there be a weariness of him and withdrawing from him, it is impossible but that there will a decay in the life ensue. Indeed, what men are in these duties (I mean as to faith and love in them), that they are, and no more. Here lies the root of their obedience; and if this fail, all fruit will quickly fail. You may sometimes see a tree flourishing with leaves and fruit, goodly and pleasant. After a while the leaves begin to decay, the fruit to wither, the whole to droop. Search, and you shall find the root, whereby it should draw in moisture and fatness from the earth to supply the body and branches with sap and juice for growth and fruit, hath received a wound, is some way perished, and doth not perform its duty, so that though the branches are flourishing a while with what they had received, their sustenance being intercepted they must decay. So it is here. These duties of private communion with God are the means of receiving supplies of spiritual strength from him, -- of sap and fatness from Christ, the vine and olive. Whilst they do so, the conversation and course of obedience flourisheth and is fruitful, -- all outward duties are cheerfully and regularly performed; but if there be a wound, a defect, a failing, in that which should first take in the spiritual radical moisture, that should be communicated unto the whole, the rest may for a season maintain their station and appearance, but after a while profession will wither, fruits will decay, and the whole be ready to die. Hence our Saviour lets us know, Matt. vi. 6, what a man is in secret, in these private duties, that he is in the eyes of God, and no more; and one reason amongst others is, because they have a more vigorous acting of unmixed grace than any other duties whatever. In all or most particular duties, besides the influence that they may have from carnal respects, which are many, and the ways of their insinuation subtile and imperceptible, there is an alloy of gifts, which sometimes even devours the pure gold of grace, which should be the chief and principal in them. In these there is immediate intercourse between God and that which is of himself in the soul. If once sin, by its deceits and treacheries, prevail to take off the soul from diligent attendance unto communion with God and constancy in these duties, it will not fail to effect a declining in the whole of a man's obedience. It hath made its entrance, and will assuredly make good its progress.

[6.] Growing in notions of truth without answerable practice is another thing that indwelling sin makes use of to bring the souls of believers unto a decay. The apostle tell us that "knowledge puffeth up," 1 Cor. viii. 1. If it be alone, not improved in practice, it swells men beyond a due proportion; like a man that hath a dropsy, we are not to expect that he hath strength to his bigness; like trees that are continually running up a head, which keeps them from bearing fruit. When once men have attained to this, that they can entertain and receive evangelical truths in a new and more glorious light or more clear discovery than formerly, or new manifestations of truth which they knew not before, and please themselves in so doing, without diligent endeavours to have the power of those truths and notions upon their hearts, and their souls made conformable unto them, they generally learn so to dispose of all truths formerly known, which were sometimes inlaid in their hearts with more efficacy and power. This hath proved, if not the ruin, yet the great impairing of many in these days of light wherein we live. By this means, from humble, close walking, many have withered into an empty, barren, talking profession. All things almost have in a short season become alike unto them; -- have they been true or false, so they might be debating of them and disputing about them, all is well. This is food for sin; it hatcheth, increaseth it, and is increased by it. A notable way it is for the vanity that is in the mind to exert itself without a rebuke from conscience. Whilst men are talking, and writing, and studying about religion, and hearing preaching, it may be, with great delight, as those in Ezek. xxxiii. 32, conscience, unless thoroughly awake and circumspect, and furnished with spiritual wisdom and care, will be very well pacified, and enter no rebukes or pleas against the way that the soul is in. But yet all this may be nothing but the acting of that natural vanity which lies in the mind, and is a principal part of the sin we treat of. And generally this is so when men content themselves, as was said, with the notions of truth, without labouring after an experience of the power of them in their hearts, and the bringing forth the fruit of them in their lives, on which a decay must needs ensue.

[7.] Growth in carnal wisdom is another help to sin in producing this sad effect. "Thy wisdom and thy knowledge," saith the prophet, "it hath perverted thee," Isa. xlvii. 10. So much as carnal wisdom increaseth, so much faith decays. The proper work of it is to teach a man to trust to and in himself; of faith, to trust wholly in another. So it labours to destroy the whole work of faith, by causing the soul to return into a deceiving fullness of its own. We have woful examples of the prevalency of this principle of declension in the days wherein we live. How many a poor, humble, broken-hearted creature, who followed after God in simplicity and integrity of spirit, have we seen, through the observation of the ways and walkings of others, and closing with the temptations to craft and subtlety which opportunities in the world have administered unto them, come to be dipped in a worldly, carnal frame, and utterly to wither in their profession! Many are so sullied hereby that they are not known to be the men they were.

[8.] Some great sin lying long in the heart and conscience unrepented of, or not repented of as it ought, and as the matter requires, furthers indwelling sin in this work. The great turn of the life of David, whence his first ways carried the reputation, was in the harbouring his great sin in his conscience without suitable repentance. It was otherwise, we know, with Peter, and he had another issue. A great sin will certainly give a great turn to the life of a professor. If it be well cured in the blood of Christ, with that humiliation which the gospel requires, it often proves a means of more watchfulness, fruitfulness, humility, and contentation, than ever before the soul obtained. If it be neglected, it certainly hardens the heart, weakens spiritual strength, enfeebles the soul, discouraging it unto all communion with God, and is a notable principle of a general decay. So David complains, Ps. xxxviii. 5, "My wounds stink and are corrupt because of my foolishness." His present distemper was not so much from his sin as his folly, -- not so much from the wounds he had received as from his neglect to make a timely application for their cure. It is like a broken bone, which, being well set, leaves the place stronger than before; if otherwise, makes the man a cripple all his days. These things we do but briefly name, and sundry other advantages of the like nature that sin makes use of to produce this effect might also be instanced in; but these may suffice unto our present purpose. Whatever it useth, itself is still the principle; and this is no small demonstration of its efficacy and power.

Chapter XVI

The strength of indwelling sin manifested from its power and effects in persons unregenerate.

It is of the power and efficacy of indwelling sin, as it remains in several degrees in believers, that we are treating. Now, I have elsewhere showed that the nature and all the natural properties of it do still remain in them; though, therefore, we cannot prove directly what is the strength of sin in them, from what its power is in those in whom it is only checked and not at all weakened, yet may we, from an observation thereof, caution believers of the real power of that mortal enemy with whom they have to do.

If the plague do violently rage in one city, destroying multitudes, and there be in another an infection of the same bind, which yet arises not unto that height and fury there, by reason of the correction that it meets withal from a better air and remedies used; yet a man may demonstrate unto the inhabitants the force and danger of that infection got in among them by the effects that it hath and doth produce among others, who have not the benefit of the preventives and preservatives which they enjoy; which will both teach them to value the means of their preservation, and be the more watchful against the power of the infection that is among them. It is so in this case. Believers may be taught what is the power and efficacy of that plague of sin which is in and among them by the effects the same plague produceth in and among others, who have not those corrections of its poison and those preservatives from death which the Lord Jesus Christ hath furnished them withal.

Having, then, fixed on the demonstration of the power of sin from the effects it doth produce, and having given a double instance hereof in believers themselves, I shall now farther evidence the same truth or pursue the same evidence of it, by showing somewhat of the power that it acteth in them who are unregenerate, and so have not the remedies against it which believers are furnished withal.

I shall not handle the whole power of sin in unregenerate persons, which is a very large field, and not the business I have in hand; but only, by some few instances of its effects in them, intimate, as I said, unto believers what they have to deal withal:--

1. It appears in the violence it offers to the nature of men, compelling them unto sins fully contrary to all the principles of the reasonable nature wherewith they are endued from God. Every creature of God hath in its creation a law of operation implanted in it, which is the rule of all that proceedeth from it, of all that it doth of its own accord. So the fire ascends upwards, bodies that are weighty and heavy descend, the water flows; each according to the principles of their nature, which give them the law of their operation. That which hinders them in their operation is force and violence; as that which hinders a stone from descending or the fire from going upwards. That which forceth them to move contrary to the law of their nature, as a stone to go upwards or the fire to descend, is in its kind the greatest violence, of which the degrees are endless. Now, that which should take a great millstone and fling it upwards into the air, all would acknowledge to be a matter of wonderful force, power, and efficacy.

Man, also, hath his law of operation and working concreated with him. And this may be considered two ways; -- either, first, as it is common to him with other creatures; or as peculiar, with reference unto that special end for which he was made. Some things are, I say, in this law of nature common to man with other creatures; as to nourish their young, to live quietly with them of the same kind and race with them, -- to seek and follow after that which is good for them in that state and condition wherein they are created. These are things which all brute living creatures have in the law of their nature, as man also hath.

But, now, besides these things, man being created in an especial manner to give glory to God by rational and moral obedience, and so to obtain a reward in the enjoyment of him, there are many things in the law of his creation that are peculiar to him, -- as to love God above all, to seek the enjoyment of him as his chiefest good and last end, to inquire after his mind and will and to yield obedience and the like; all which are part of the law of his nature.

Now, these things are not distinguished so, as though a man might perform the actions of the law of his nature, which are common to him with other creatures, merely from the principles of his nature, as they do; but the law of his dependence upon God, and doing all things in obedience unto him, passeth on them all also. He can never be considered as a mere creature, but as a creature made for the glory of God by rational, moral obedience, -- rational, because by him chosen, and performed with reason; and moral, because regulated by a law whereunto reason doth attend.

For instance, it is common to man with other creatures to take care for the nourishing of his children, of the young, helpless ones that receive their being by him. There is implanted in him, in the principles of his nature, concreated with them, a love and care for them; so is it with other living creatures. Now, let other creatures answer this instinct and inclination, and be not hardened against them like the foolish ostrich, into whom God hath not implanted this natural wisdom, Job xxxix. 16, 17, they fully answer the law of their creation. With man it is not so. It is not enough for him to answer the instinct and secret impulse and inclination of his nature and kind, as in the nourishing of his children; but he must do it also in subjection to God, and obey him therein, and do it unto his glory, -- the law of moral obedience passing over all his whole being and all his operations. But in these things lie, as it were, the whole of a man, namely, in the things which are implanted in his nature as a creature, common to him with all other living creatures, seconded by the command or will of God, as he is a creature capable of yielding moral obedience and doing all things for his glory.

That, then, which shall drive and compel a man to transgress this law of his nature, -- which is not only as to throw millstones upward, to drive beasts from taking care of their young, to take from cattle of the same kind the herding of themselves in quietness, but, moreover, to cast off, what lies in him, his fundamental dependence on God as a creature made to yield him obedience, -- must needs be esteemed of great force and efficacy.

Now, this is frequently done by indwelling sin in persons unregenerate. Let us take some few instances:--

(1.) There is nothing that is more deeply inlaid in the principles of the natures of all living creatures, and so of man himself, than a love unto and a care for the preservation and nourishing of their young. Many brute creatures will die for them; some feed them with their own flesh and blood; all deprive themselves of that food which nature directs them to as their best, to impart it to them, and act in their behalf to the utmost of their power.

Now, such is the efficacy, power, and force of indwelling sin in man, -- an infection that the nature of other creatures knows nothing of, -- that in many it prevails to stop this fountain, to beat back the stream of natural affections, to root up the principles of the law of nature, and to drive them unto a neglect, a destruction of the fruit of their own loins. Paul tells us of the old Gentiles that they were αστοργοι, Rom. i. 31, "without natural affection." That which he aims at is that barbarous custom among the Romans, who ofttimes, to spare the trouble in the education of their children, and to be at liberty to satisfy their lusts, destroyed their own children from the womb; so far did the strength of sin prevail to obliterate the law of nature, and to repel the force and power of it.

Examples of this nature are common in all nations; amongst ourselves, of women murdering their own children, through the deceitful reasoning of sin. And herein sin turns the strong current of nature, darkens all the light of God in the soul, controls all natural principles, influenced with the power of the command and will of God. But yet this evil hath, through the efficacy of sin, received a fearful aggravation. Men have not only slain but cruelly sacrificed their children to satisfy their lusts. The apostle reckons idolatry, and so, consequently, all superstition, among the works of the flesh, Gal. v. 20; that is, the fruit and product of indwelling sin. Now, from hence it is that men have offered that horrid and unspeakable violence to the law of nature mentioned. So the psalmist tells us, Ps. cvi. 37, 38. The same is again mentioned, Ezek. xvi. 20, 21, and in sundry other places. The whole manner of that abomination I have elsewhere declared. [4] For the present it may suffice to intimate that they took their children and burnt them to ashes in a soft fire; the wicked priests that assisted in the sacrifice affording them this relief, that they made a noise and clamour that the vile wretches might not hear the woeful moans and cries of the poor, dying, tormented infants. I suppose in this case we need no farther evidence. Naturalists can give no rational account, they can only admire the secret force of that little fish which, they say, will stop a ship in full sail in the midst of the sea; and we must acknowledge that it is beyond our power to give an account of that secret force and unsearchable deceit that is in that inbred traitor, sin, that can not only stop the course of nature, when all the sails of it, that carry it forward, are so filled as they are in that of affections to children, but also drive it backward with such a violence and force as to cause men so to deal with their own children as a good man would not be hired with any reward to deal with his dog. And it may not be to the disadvantage of the best to know and consider that they carry that about them and in them which in others hath produced these effects.

(2.) The like may be spoken of all other sins against the prime dictates of the law of nature, that mankind is or hath been stained and defamed withal, -- murder of parents and children, of wives and husbands, sodomy, incest, and the like enormities; in all which sin prevails in men against the whole law of their being and dependence upon God.

What [why?] should I reckon up the murders of Cain and Abel, the treason of Judas, with their aggravations; or remind the filth and villany of Nero, in whom sin seemed to design an instance of what it could debase the nature of man unto? In a word, all the studied, premeditated perjuries; all the designed, bloody revenges; all the filth and uncleanness; all the enmity to God and his ways that is in the world, -- is fruit growing from this root alone.

2. It evidences its efficacy in keeping men off from believing under the dispensation of the gospel. This evidence must be a little farther cleared:--

(1.) Under the dispensation of the gospel, there are but few that do believe. So the preachers of it complain, Isa. liii. 1, "Who hath believed our report?" which the apostle interprets of the paucity of believers, John xii. 38. Our Saviour, Christ himself, tells us that "many are called," -- the word is preached unto many, -- "but few are chosen." And so the church complains of its number, Micah vii. 1. Few there be who enter the narrow gate; daily experience confirms this woful observation. How many villages, parishes, yea, towns, may we go unto where the gospel, it may be, hath been preached many years, and perhaps scarce meet a true believer in them, and one who shows forth the death of Christ in his conversation! In the best places, and most eminent for profession, are not such persons like the berries after the shaking of an olive-tree, -- two or three in the top of the utmost boughs, and four or five in the highest branches?

(2.) There is proposed to men in the preaching of the gospel, as motives unto believing, every thing in conjunction that severally prevails with men to do whatever else they do in their lives. Whatever any one doth with consideration, he doth it either because it is reasonable and good for him so to do, or profitable and advantageous, or pleasant, or, lastly, necessary for the avoidance of evil; whatever, I say, men do with consideration, whether it be good or evil, whether it be in the works of this life or in things that lead to another, they do it from one or other of the reasons or motives mentioned. And, God knows, ofttimes they are very poor and mean in their kind that men are prevailed upon by. How often will men, for a very little pleasure, a very little profit, be induced to do that which shall embitter their lives and damn their souls; and what industry will they use to avoid that which they apprehend evil or grievous to them! And any one of these is enough to oil the wheels of men's utmost endeavours, and set men at work to the purpose.

But now all these things centre in the proposal of the gospel and the command of believing; and every one of them in a kind that the whole world can propose nothing like unto it:--

[1.] It is the most reasonable thing that can be proposed to the understanding of a man, that he who, through his own default, hath lost that way of bringing glory to God and saving his own soul (for which ends he was made) that he was first placed in, should accept of and embrace that other blessed, easy, safe, excellent way for the attaining of the ends mentioned, which God, in infinite grace, love, mercy, wisdom, and righteousness, hath found out, and doth propose unto him. And, --

[2.] It is the profitablest thing that a man can possibly be invited unto, if there be any profit or benefit, any advantage, in the forgiveness of sins, in the love and favour of God, in a blessed immortality, in eternal glory. And, --

[3.] It is most pleasant also. Surely it is a pleasant thing to be brought out of darkness into light, -- out of a dungeon unto a throne, -- from captivity and slavery to Satan and cursed lusts, to the glorious liberty of the children of God, with a thousand heavenly sweetnesses not now to be mentioned. And, --

[4.] It is surely necessary, and that not only from the command of God, who hath the supreme authority over us, but also indispensably so for the avoidance of eternal ruin of body and soul, Mark xvi. 16. It is constantly proposed under these terms: "Believe, or you perish under the weight of the wrath of the great God, and that for evermore."

But now, notwithstanding that all these considerations are preached unto men, and pressed upon them in the name of the great God from day to day, from one year to another, yet, as was before observed, very few there are who set their hearts unto them, so as to embrace that which they lead unto. Tell men ten thousand times that this is wisdom, yea, riches, -- that all their profit lies in it, -- that they will assuredly and eternally perish, and that, it may be, within a few hours, if they receive not the gospel; assure them that it is their only interest and concernment; let them know that God himself speaks all this unto them; -- yet all is one, they regard it not, set not their hearts unto it, but, as it were, plainly say, "We will have nothing to do with these things." They will rather perish in their lusts than accept of mercy.

(3.) It is indwelling sin that both disenableth men unto and hinders them from believing, and that alone. Blindness of mind, stubbornness of the will, sensuality of the affections, all concur to keep poor perishing souls at a distance from Christ. Men are made blind by sin, and cannot see his excellencies; obstinate, and will not lay hold of his righteousness; senseless, and take no notice of their own eternal concernments.

Now, certainly that which can prevail with men wise, and sober, and prudent in other things, to neglect and despise the love of God, the blood of Christ, the eternal welfare of their own souls, upon weak and worthless pretences, must be acknowledged to have an astonishable force and efficacy accompanying it.

Whose heart, who hath once heard of the ways of God, can but bleed to see poor souls eternally perishing under a thousand gracious invitations to accept of mercy and pardon in the blood of Christ? And can we but be astonished at the power of that principle from whence it is that they run headlong to their own destruction? And yet all this befalls them from the power and deceit of sin that dwelleth in them.

3. It is evident in their total apostasies. Many men not really converted are much wrought upon by the word. The apostle tells us that they do "clean escape from them that live in error," 2 Pet. ii. 18. They separate themselves from idolatry and false worship, owning and professing the truth: and they also escape the "pollutions of the world," verse 20; that is, "the corruption that is in the world through lust," as he expresseth it, chap. i. 4, -- those filthy, corrupt, and unclean ways which the men of the world, in the pursuit of their lusts, do walk and live in. These they escape from, in the amendment of their lives and ordering of their conversation according to the convictions which they have from the word; for so he tells us, that all this is brought about "through the knowledge of the Lord and Saviour Jesus Christ," -- that is, by the preaching of the gospel. They are so far wrought upon as to forsake all ways of false worship, to profess the truth, to reform their lives, and to walk answerable to the convictions that are upon them.

By this means do they gain the reputation of professors: "They have a name to live," Rev. iii. 1, and are made "partakers" of some or all of those privileges of the gospel that are numbered by the apostle, Heb. vi. 4, 5.

It is not my present business to show how far or wherein a man may be effectually wrought upon by the word, and yet not be really wrought over to close with Christ, or what may be the utmost bounds and limits of a common work of grace upon unregenerate men. It is on all hands confessed that it may be carried on so far that it is very difficult to discern between its effects and productions and those of that grace which is special and saving.

But now, notwithstanding all this, we see many of these daily fall off from God, utterly and wickedly; some into debauchery and uncleanness, some to worldliness and covetousness, some to be persecutors of the saints, -- all to the perdition of their own souls. How this comes about the apostle declares in that place mentioned. "They are," saith he, "entangled again." To entice and entangle, as I have showed before from James i. 14, 15, is the proper work of indwelling sin; it is that alone which entangles the soul, as the apostle speaks, 2 Pet. ii. 18, 20. They are allured from their whole profession into cursed apostasy through the lusts of the flesh.

It prevails upon them, through its deceit and power, to an utter relinquishment of their profession and their whole engagement unto God. And this several ways evinces the greatness of its strength and efficacy:--

(1.) In that it giveth stop or control unto that exceeding greatness of power which is put forth in the word in their conviction and reformation. We see it by experience that men are not easily wrought upon by the word; the most of men can live under the dispensation of it all the days of their lives, and continue as senseless and stupid as the seats they sit upon, or the flint in the rock of stone. Mighty difficulties and prejudices must be conquered, great strokes must be given to the conscience, before this can be brought about. It is as the stopping of a river in his course, and turning his streams another way; the hindering of a stone in his falling downwards; or the turning away of the wild ass, when furiously set to pursue his way, as the prophet speaks, Jer. ii. 24. To turn men from their corrupt ways, sins, and pleasures; to make them pray, fast, hear, and do many things contrary to the principle of flesh, which is secretly predominant in them, willingly and gladly; to cause them to profess Christ and the gospel, it may be under some trials and reproaches; to give them light to see into sundry mysteries, and gifts for the discharge of sundry duties; to make dead, blind, senseless men to walk, and talk, and do all the outward offices and duties of living and healthy men, with the like attendancies of conviction and reformation, are the effects and products of mighty power and strength. Indeed, the power that the Holy Ghost puts forth by the word, in the staggering and conviction of sinners, in the wakening of their consciences, the enlightening of their minds, the changing of their affections, the awing of their hearts, the reforming of their lives and compelling them to duties, is inexpressible.

But now unto all these is there check and control given by indwelling sin. It prevails against this whole work of the Spirit by the word, with all the advantages of providential dispensations, in afflictions and mercies, wherewith it is attended. When sin is once enraged, all these things become but like the withes and cords wherewith Samson was bound before his head was shaven. Cry but to it, "The Philistines are upon thee; there is a subtle, a suitable temptation; now show thy strength and efficacy," -- all these things become like tow that has smelt the fire; conscience is stifled, reputation in the church of God despised, light supplanted, the impressions of the word cast off, convictions digested, heaven and hell are despised: sin makes its way through all, and utterly turns the soul from the good and right ways of God. Sometimes it doth this subtilely, by imperceptible degrees, taking off all force of former impressions from the Spirit by the word, sullying conscience by degrees, hardening the heart, and making sensual the affections by various workings, that the poor backslider in heart scarce knows what he is doing, until he be come to the very bottom of all impiety, profaneness, and enmity against God. Sometimes, falling in conjunction with some vigorous temptation, it suddenly and at once plunges the soul into a course of alienation from God and the profession of his ways.

(2.) It takes them off from those hopes of heaven which, upon their convictions, obedience, and temporary faith or believing, they had attained. There is a general hope of heaven, or at least of the escaping of hell, of an untroublesome immortality, in the most sottish and stupid souls in the world, who, either by tradition or instruction from the word, are persuaded that there is another state of things to come after this life; but it is, in unconvinced, unenlightened persons, a dull, senseless, unaffecting thing, that hath no other hold upon them nor power in them but only to keep them free from the trouble and perplexity of contrary thoughts and apprehensions. The matter is otherwise with them who by the word are so wrought upon as we have before declared; their hope of heaven and a blessed immortality is ofttimes accompanied with great joys and exultations, and is a relief unto them under and against the worst of their fears and trials. It is such as they would not part withal for all the world; and upon all occasions they retreat in their minds unto it for comfort and relief.

Now, all this by the power of sin are they prevailed withal to forego. Let heaven go if it will, a blessed immortality with the enjoyment of God himself, sin must be served, and provision made to fulfil the lusts thereof.

If a man, in the things of this world, had such a hope of a large inheritance, of a kingdom, as wherein he is satisfied that it will not fail him, but that in the issue he shall surely enjoy it, and lead a happy and a glorious life in the possession of it many days; if one should go to him and tell him, "It is true, the kingdom you look for is an ample and honourable dominion, full of all good things desirable, and you may attain it; but come, cast away all hopes and expectations of it, and come join with me in the service and slavery of such or such an oppressing tyrant;" -- you will easily grant he must have some strange bewitching power with him, that should prevail with a man in his wits to follow his advice. Yet thus it is, and much more so, in the case we have in hand. Sin itself cannot deny but that the kingdom of heaven, which the soul is in hope and expectation of, is glorious and excellent, nor doth it go about to convince him that his thoughts of it are vain and such as will deceive him, but plainly prevails with him to cast away his hopes, to despise his kingdom that he was in expectation of, and that upon no other motive but that he may serve some worldly, cruel, or filthy and sensual lust. Certainly, here lies a secret efficacy, whose depths cannot be fathomed.

(3.) The apostle manifests the power of the entanglements of sin in and upon apostates, in that it turns them off from the way of righteousness after they have known it, 2 Pet. ii. 21. It will be found at the last day an evil thing and a bitter that men live all their days in the service of sin, self, and the world, refusing to make any trial of the ways of God, whereunto they are invited. Though they have no experience of their excellency, beauty, pleasantness, safety; yet, having evidence brought unto them from God himself that they are so, the refusal of them will, I say, be bitterness in the latter end. But their condition is yet far worse, who, as the apostle speaks, "having known the way of righteousness," are by the power of indwelling sin "turned aside from the holy commandment." To leave God for the devil, after a man hath made some trial of him and his service, -- heaven for hell, after a man hath had some cheering, refreshing thoughts of it, -- the fellowship of the saints for an ale-house or a brothel-house, after a man hath been admitted unto their communion, and tasted of the pleasantness of it; to leave walking in pure, clear, straight paths, to wallow in mire, draughts and filth; -- this will be for a lamentation: yet this doth sin prevail upon apostates unto; and that against all their light, conviction, experiences, professions, engagements, or whatever may be strong upon them to keep them up to the known ways of righteousness.

(4.) It evinces its strength in them by prevailing with them unto a total renunciation of God as revealed in Christ, and the power of all gospel truth, -- in the sin against the Holy Ghost. I do not now precisely determine what is the sin against the Holy Ghost, nor wherein it doth consist. There are different apprehensions of it. All agree in this, that by it an end is put to all dealings between God and man in a way of grace. It is a sin unto death. And this doth the hardness and blindness of many men's hearts bring them to; they are by them at length set out of the reach of mercy. They choose to have no more to do with God; and God swears that they shall never enter into his rest: so sin brings forth death. A man by it is brought to renounce the end for which he was made, wilfully to reject the means of his coming to the enjoyment of God, to provoke him to his face, and so to perish in his rebellion.

I have not mentioned these things as though I hoped by them to set out to the full the power of indwelling sin in unregenerate men; only by a few instances I thought to give a glimpse of it. He that would have a fuller view of it had need only to open his eyes, to take a little view of that wickedness which reigneth, yea, rageth all the world over. Let him consider the prevailing flood of the things mentioned by Paul to be "the fruits of the flesh," Gal. v. 19-21, -- that is, among the sons of men, in all places, nations, cities, towns, parishes; and then let him add thereunto but this one consideration, that the world, which is full of the steam, filth, and blood of these abominations, as to their outward actings of them, is a pleasant garden, a paradise, compared to the heart of man, wherein they are all conceived, and hourly millions of more vile abominations, which, being stifled in the womb by some of the ways before insisted on, they are never able to bring forth to light; -- let a man, I say, using the law for his light and rule, take this course, and if he have any spiritual discerning, he may quickly attain satisfaction in this matter.

And I showed in the entrance of this discourse how this consideration doth fully confirm the truth proposed.

Footnote:

4. See his work entitled, "A Dissertation on Divine Justice," chap. iv., vol. x.

Chapter XVII

The strength of sin evidenced from its resistance unto the power of the law.

The measure of the strength of any person or defenced city may be well taken from the opposition that they are able to withstand and not be prevailed against. If we hear of a city that has endured a long siege from a potent enemy, and yet is not taken or conquered, whose walls have endured great batteries and are not demolished, though we have never seen the place, yet we conclude it strong, if not impregnable.

And this consideration will also evidence the power and strength of indwelling sin. It is able to hold out, and not only to live, but also to secure its reign and dominion, against very strong opposition that is made to it.

I shall instance only in the opposition that is made unto it by the law, which is ofttimes great and terrible, always fruitless; all its assaults are borne by it, and it is not prevailed against. There are sundry things wherein the law opposeth itself to sin, and the power of it; as, --

1. It discovers it. Sin in the soul is like a secret hectical distemper in the body, -- its being unknown and unperceived is one great means of its prevalency; or as traitors in a civil state, -- whilst they lie hid, they vigorously carry on their design. The greatest part of men in the world know nothing of this sickness, yea, death of their souls. Though they have been taught somewhat of the doctrine of it, yet they know nothing of its power. They know it not so as to deal with it as their mortal enemy; as a man, whatever he be told, cannot be said to know that he hath a hectical fever, if he love his life, and set not himself to stop its progress.

This, then, the law doth, -- it discovers this enemy; it convinceth the soul that there is such a traitor harbouring in its bosom: Rom. vii. 7, "I had not known sin, but by the law: for I had not known lust, except the law had said, Thou shalt not covet." "I had not known it;" that is, fully, clearly, distinctly. Conscience will somewhat tumultuate about it; but a man cannot know it clearly and distinctly from thence. It gives a man such a sight of it as the blind man had in the gospel upon the first touch of his eyes: "He saw men like trees walking," -- obscurely, confusedly. But when the law comes, that gives the soul a distinct sight of this indwelling sin. Again, "I had not known it;" that is, the depths of it, the root, the habitual inclination of my nature to sin, which is here called "lust," as it is in James i. 14. "I had not known it," or not known it to be sin, "but by the law." This, then, the law doth, -- it draws out this traitor from secret lurking places, the intimate recedes of the soul. A man, when the law comes, is no more ignorant of his enemy. If he will now perish by him, it is openly and knowingly; he cannot but say that the law warned him of him, discovered him unto him, yea, and raised a concourse about him in the soul of various affections, as an officer doth that discovers a thief or robber, calling out for assistance to apprehend him.

2. The law not only discovers sin, but discovers it to be a very bad inmate, dangerous, yea, pernicious to the soul: Rom. vii. 13, "Was then that which is good," -- that is, the law, -- "made death unto me? God forbid. But sin, that it might appear sin, working death in me by that which is good; that sin by the commandment might become exceeding sinful." There are many things in this verse wherein we are not at present concerned: that which I only aim at is the manifestation of sin by the law, -- it appears to be sin; and the manifestation of it in its own colours, -- it appears to be exceeding sinful. The law gives the soul to know the filth and guilt of this indwelling sin, -- how great they are, how vile it is, what an abomination, what an enmity to God, how hated of him. The soul shall never more look upon it as a small matter, what thoughts soever it had of it before, whereby it is greatly surprised.

As a man that finds himself somewhat distempered, sending for a physician of skill, when he comes requires his judgment of his distemper; he, considering his condition, tells him, "Alas! I am sorry for you; the case is far otherwise with you than you imagine: your disease is mortal, and it hath proceeded so far, pressing upon your spirits and infecting the whole mass of your blood, that I doubt, unless most effectual remedies be used, you will live but a very few hours." So it is in this case. A man may have some trouble in his mind and conscience about indwelling sin; he finds all not so well as it should be with him, more from the effects of sin and its continual eruptions than the nature of it, which he hopes to wrestle withal. But now, when the law comes, that lets the soul know that its disease is deadly and mortal, that it is exceeding sinful, as being the root and cause of all his alienation from God;

and thus also the law proceeds against it.

3. The law judgeth the person, or lets the sinner plainly know what he is to expect upon the account of this sin. This is the law's proper work; its discovering property is but preparative to its judging. The law is itself when it is in the throne. Here it minceth not the matter with sinners, as we use to do one with another, but tells him plainly, "?Thou' art the man' in whom this exceeding sinful sin doth dwell, and you must answer for the guilt of it." And this, methinks, if any thing, should rouse up a man to set himself in opposition to it, yea, utterly to destroy it. The law lets him know that upon the account of this sin he is obnoxious to the curse and wrath of the great God against him; yea, pronounceth the sentence of everlasting condemnation upon him upon that account. "Abide in this state and perish," is its language. It leaves not the soul without this warning in this world, and will leave it without excuse on that account in the world to come.

4. The law so follows on its sentence, that it disquiets and affrights the soul, and suffers it not to enjoy the least rest or quietness in harbouring its sinful inmate. Whenever the soul hath indulged to its commands, made provision for it, immediately the law flies upon it with the wrath and terror of the Lord, makes it quake and tremble. It shall have no rest, but is like a poor beast that hath a deadly arrow sticking in its sides, that makes it restless wherever it is and whatever it doth.

5. The law stays not here, but also it slays the soul, Rom. vii. 9; that is, by its conviction of the nature, power, and desert of this indwelling sin, it deprives him in whom it is of all that life of self-righteousness and hope which formerly he sustained himself withal, -- it leaves him as a poor, dead, helpless, hopeless creature; and all this in the pursuit of that opposition that it makes against this sin. May we not now expect that the power of it will be quelled and its strength broken, -- that it will die away before these strokes of the law of God? But the truth is, such is its power and strength, that it is quite otherwise. Like him whom the poets feign to be born of the earth, when one thought to slay him by casting him on the ground, by every fall he recovered new strength, and was more vigorous than formerly; so is it with all the falls and repulses that are given to indwelling sin by the law: for, --

(1.) It is not conquered. A conquest infers two things in respect of the conquered, -- first, loss of dominion; and, secondly, loss of strength. Whenever any one is conquered he is despoiled of both these; he loses both his authority and his power. So the strong man armed, being prevailed against, he is bound and his goods are spoiled. But now neither of these befalls indwelling sin by the assaults of the law. It loseth not one jot of its dominion nor strength by all the blows that are given unto it. The law cannot do this thing, Rom. viii. 3; it cannot deprive sin of its power and dominion, for he that "is under the law is also under sin;" -- that is, whatever power the law gets upon the conscience of a man, so that he fear to sin, lest the sentence and curse of it should befall him, yet sin still reigns and rules in his heart. Therefore saith the apostle, Rom. vi. 14, "Sin shall not have dominion over you: for ye are not under the law, but under grace;" intimating plainly, that though a person be in never so much subjection to the authority of the law, yet that will not exempt and acquit him from the dominion of sin. Yea, the law, by all its work upon the soul, instead of freeing and acquitting it from the reign of sin and bondage unto it, doth accidentally greatly increase its misery and bondage, as the sentence of the judge on the bench against a malefactor adds to his misery. The soul is under the dominion of sin, and, it may be, abides in its woful condition in much security, fearing neither sin nor judgment. The law setting upon him in this condition, by all the ways fore mentioned, brings him into great trouble and perplexity, fear and terror, but delivers him not at all. So that it is with the soul as it was with the Israelites when Moses had delivered his message unto Pharaoh; they were so far from getting liberty by it that their bondage was increased, and "they found that they were in a very evil case," Exod. v. 19. Yea, and we shall see that sin doth like Pharaoh; finding its rule disturbed, it grows more outrageously oppressive, and doubles the bondage of their souls. This is not, then, the work of the law, to destroy sin, or deprive it of that dominion which it hath by nature. Nor doth it, by all these strokes of the law, lose any thing of its strength; it continues both its authority and its force; it is neither destroyed nor weakened; yea, --

(2.) It is so far from being conquered that it is only enraged. The whole work of the law doth only provoke and enrage sin, and cause it, as it hath opportunity, to put out its strength with more power, and vigour, and force than formerly. This the apostle shows at large, Rom. vii. 9-13.

But you will say, "Do we not see it by experience, that many are wrought upon by the preaching of the law to a relinquishment of many sins and amendment of their lives, and to a great contending against the eruptions of those other corruptions which they cannot yet mortify? And it cannot be denied but that great is the power and efficacy of the law when preached and applied to the conscience in a due manner." I answer, --

[1.] It is acknowledged that very great and effectual is the power of the law of God. Great are the effects that are wrought by it, and it shall surely accomplish every end for which of God it is appointed. But yet the subduing of sin is none of its work, -- it is not designed of God unto that purpose; and therefore it is no dishonour if it cannot do that which is not its proper work, Rom. viii. 3.

[2.] Whatever effects it have upon some yet we see that in the most, such is the power and prevalency of sin, that it takes no impression at all upon them. May you not see everywhere men living many years in congregations where the law is powerfully preached, and applied unto the consciences as to all the ends and purposes for which the Lord is pleased to make use of it, and not once be moved by it, -- that receive no more impression from the stroke of it than blows with a straw would give to an adamant? They are neither convinced by it, nor terrified, nor awed, nor instructed; but continue deaf, ignorant, senseless, secure, as if they had never been told of the guilt of sin or terror of the Lord. Such as these are congregations full of, who proclaim the triumphing power of sin over the dispensation of the law.

[3.] When any of the effects mentioned are wrought, it is not from the power of the letter of the law, but from the actual efficacy of the Spirit of God putting forth his virtue and power for that end and purpose; and we deny not but that the Spirit of the Lord is able to restrain and quell the power of lust when he pleaseth, and some ways whereby he is pleased so to do we have formerly considered. But, --

[4.] Notwithstanding all that may be observed of the power of the law upon the souls of men, yet it is most evident that lust is not conquered, not subdued, nor mortified by it; for, --

1st. Though the course of sin may be repelled for a season by the dispensation of the law, yet the spring and fountain of it is not dried up thereby. Though it withdraws and hides itself for a season, it is, as I have elsewhere showed, but to shift out of a storm, and then to return again. As a traveller, in his way meeting with a violent storm of thunder and rain, immediately turns out of his way to some house or tree for his shelter, but yet this causeth him not to give over his journey, -- so soon as the storm is over he returns to his way and progress again; so it is with men in bondage unto sin. They are in a course of pursuing their lusts; the law meets with them in a storm of thunder and lightning from heaven, terrifies and hinders them in their way. This turns them for a season out of their course; they will run to prayer or amendment of life, for some shelter from the storm of wrath which is feared coming upon their consciences. But is their course stopped? are their principles altered? Not at all; so soon as the storm is over, [so] that they begin to wear out that sense and the terror that was upon them, they return to their former course in the service of sin again. This was the state with Pharaoh once and again.

2dly. In such seasons sin is not conquered, but diverted. When it seems to fall under the power of the law, indeed it is only turned into a new channel; it is not dried up. If you go and set a dam against the streams of a river, so that you suffer no water to pass in the old course and channel, but it breaks out another way, and turns all its streams in a new course, you will not say you have dried up that river, though some that come and look into the old channel may think, perhaps, that the waters are utterly gone. So is it in this case. The streams of sin, it may be, run in open sensuality and profaneness, in drunkenness and viciousness; the preaching of the law sets a dam against these courses, -- conscience is terrified, and the man dares not walk in the ways wherein he hath been formerly engaged. His companions in sin, not finding him in his old ways, begin to laugh at him, as one that is converted and growing precise; professors themselves begin to be persuaded that the work of God is upon his heart, because they see his old streams dried up: but if there have been only a work of the law upon him, there is a dam put to his course, but the spring of sin is not dried up, only the streams of it are turned another way. It may be the man is fallen upon other more secret or more spiritual sins; or if he be beat from them also, the whole strength of lust and sin will take up its residence in self-righteousness, and pour out thereby as filthy streams as in any other way whatever. So that notwithstanding the whole work of the law upon the souls of men, indwelling sin will keep alive in them still: which is another evidence of its great power and strength.

I shall yet touch upon some other evidences of the same truth that I have under consideration; but I shall be brief in them.

1. In the next place, then, the great endeavours of men ignorant of the righteousness of Christ, for the subduing and mortifying of sin, which are all fruitless, do evidence the great strength and power of it.

Men who have no strength against sin may yet be made sensible of the strength of sin. The way whereby, for the most part, they come to that knowledge is by some previous sense that they have of the guilt of sin. This men have by the light of their consciences; they cannot avoid it. This is not a thing in their choice; whether they will or no, they cannot but know sin to be evil, and that such an evil that renders them obnoxious to the judgment of God. This galls the minds and consciences of some so far as that they are kept in awe, and dare not sin as they would. Being awed with a sense of the guilt of sin and the terror of the Lord, men begin to endeavour to abstain from sin, at least from such sins as they have been most terrified about. Whilst they have this design in hand, the strength and power of sin begins to discover itself unto them. They begin to find that there is something in them that is not in their own power; for, notwithstanding their resolutions and purposes, they sin still, and that so, or in such a manner, as that their consciences inform them that they must therefore perish eternally. This puts them on self-endeavours to suppress the eruption of sin, because they cannot be quiet unless so they do, nor have any rest or peace within. Now, being ignorant of that only way whereby sin is to be mortified, -- that is, by the Spirit of Christ, -- they fix on many ways in their own strength to suppress it, if not to slay it; as being ignorant of that only way whereby consciences burdened with the guilt of sin may be pacified, -- that is, by the blood of Christ, -- they endeavour, by many other ways, to accomplish that end in vain: for no man, by any self-endeavours, can obtain peace with God.

Some of the ways whereby they endeavour to suppress the power of sin, which casts them into an unquiet condition, and their insufficiency for that end, we must look into:--

(1.) They will promise and bind themselves by vows from those sins which they have been most liable unto, and so have been most perplexed withal. The psalmist shows this to be one great engine whereby false and hypocritical persons do endeavour to extricate and deliver themselves out of trouble and perplexity. They make promises to God, which he calls flattering him with the mouth, Ps. lxxviii. 36. So is it in this case. Being freshly galled with the guilt of any sin, that, by the power of their temptations, they, it may be, have frequently been overtaken in, they vow and promise that, at least for some such space of time as they will limit, they will not commit that sin again; and this course of proceeding is prescribed unto them by some who pretend to direct their consciences in this duty. Conscience of this now makes them watch over themselves as to the outward act of the sin that they are galled with; and so it hath one of these two effects, -- for either they do abstain from it for the time they have prefixed, or they do not. If they do not, as seldom they do, especially if it be a sin that hath a peculiar root in their nature and constitution, and is improved by custom into a habit, if any suitable temptation be presented unto them, their sin is increased, and therewith their terror, and they are wofully discouraged in making any opposition to sin; and therefore, for the most part, after one or two vain attempts, or more, it may be, knowing no other way to mortify sin but this of vowing against it, and keeping of that vow in their own strength, they give over all contests, and become wholly the servants of sin, being bounded only by outward considerations, without any serious endeavours for a recovery. Or, secondly, suppose that they have success in their resolutions, and do abstain from actual sins their appointed season, commonly one of these two things ensues, -- either they think that they have well discharged their duty, and so may a little now, at least for a season, indulge to their corruptions and lusts, and so are entangled again in the same snares of sin as formerly; or else they reckon that their vow and promise hath preserved them, and so sacrifice to their own net and drag, setting up a righteousness of their own against the grace of God, -- which is so far from weakening indwelling sin, that it strengthens it in the root and principle, that it may hereafter reign in the soul in security. Or, at the most, the best success that can be imagined unto this way of dealing with sin is but the restraining of some outward eruptions of it, which tends nothing to the weakening of its power; and therefore such persons, by all their endeavours, are very far from being freed from the inward toiling, burning, disquieting, perplexing power of sin. And this is the state of most men that are kept in bondage under the power of conviction. Hell, death, and the wrath of God, are continually presented unto their consciences; this makes them labour with all their strength against that in sin which most enrageth their consciences and most increaseth their fears, -- that is, the actual eruption of it: for, for the most part, while they are freed from that they are safe, though, in the meantime, sin lie tumultuating in and defiling of the heart continually. As with running sores, outward repelling medicines may skin them over, and hinder their corruption from coming forth, but the issue of them is, that they cause them to fester inwardly, and so prove, though it may be not so noisome and offensive as they were before, yet far more dangerous: so is it with this repelling of the power of corruption by men's vows and promises against it, -- external eruptions are, it may be, restrained for a season, but the inward root and principle is not weakened in the least. And most commonly this is the issue of this way:-- that sin, having gotten more strength, and being enraged by its restraint, breaks all its bounds, and captivates the soul unto all filthy abominations; which is the principle, as was before observed, of most of the visible apostasies which we have in the world, 2 Pet. ii. 19, 20.

The Holy Ghost compares sinners, because of the odious, fierce, poisonous nature of this indwelling sin, unto lions, bears, and asps, Isa. xi. 6-9. Now, this is the excellency of gospel grace, that it changes the nature and inward principles of these otherwise passionate and untamed beasts, making the wolf as the kid, the lion as the lamb, and the bear as the cow. When this is effected, they may safely be trusted in, -- "a little child may lead them." But these self-endeavours do not at all change the nature, but restrain their outward violence. He that takes a lion or a wolf and shuts him up from ravening, whilst yet his inward violence remains, may well expect that at one time or other they will break their bonds, and fall to their former ways of rapine and violence. However, shutting them up doth not, as we see, change their natures, but only restrain their rage from doing open spoil. So it is in this case: it is grace alone that changeth the heart and takes away that poison and fierceness that is in them by nature; men's self-endeavours do but coerce them as to some outward eruptions But, --

(2.) Beyond bare vows and promises, with some watchfulness to observe them in a rational use of ordinary means, men have put, and some do yet put, themselves on extraordinary ways of mortifying sin. This is the foundation of all that hath a show of wisdom and religion in the Papacy: their hours of prayer, lastings; their immuring and cloistering themselves; their pilgrimages, penances, and self-torturing discipline, -- spring all from this root. I shall not speak of the innumerable evils that have attended these self-invented ways of mortification, and how they all of them have been turned into means, occasions, and advantages of sinning; nor of the horrible hypocrisy which evidently cleaves unto the most of their observers; nor of that superstition which gives life to them all, being a thing riveted in the natures of some and their constitutions, fixed on others by inveterate prejudices, and the same by others taken up for secular advantages. But I will suppose the best that can be made of it, and it will be found to be a self-invented design of men ignorant of the righteousness of God, to give a check to this power of indwelling sin whereof we speak. And it is almost incredible what fearful self-macerations and horrible sufferings this design hath carried men out unto; and, undoubtedly, their blind zeal and superstition will rise in judgment and condemn the horrible sloth and negligence of the most of them to whom the Lord hath granted the saving light of the gospel. But what is the end of these things? The apostle, in brief, gives us an account, Rom. ix. 31, 32. They attain not the righteousness aimed at; they come not up unto a conformity to the law: sin is not mortified, no, nor the power of it weakened; but what it loses in sensual, in carnal pleasures, it takes up with great advantage in blindness, darkness, superstition, self-righteousness, and soul-pride, contempt of the gospel and the righteousness of it, and reigns no less than in the most profligate sinners in the world.

2. The strength, efficacy, and power of this law of sin may be farther evidenced from its life and in-being in the soul, notwithstanding the wound that is given unto it in the first conversion of the soul to God; and in the continual opposition that is made unto it by grace. But this is the subject and design of another endeavour.

It may now be expected that we should here add the especial uses of all this discovery that hath been made of the power, deceit, prevalency, and success of this great adversary of our souls. But as for what concerns that humility, self-abasement, watchfulness, diligence, and application unto the Lord Christ for relief, which will become those who find in themselves, by experience, the power of this law of sin, [these] have been occasionally mentioned and inculcated through the whole preceding discourse; so, for what concerns the actual mortification of it, I shall only recommend unto the reader, for his direction, another small treatise, written long since, unto that purpose, which I suppose he may do well to consider together with this, if he find these things to be his concernment.

"To the only wise God our Saviour, be glory and majesty, dominion and power, both now and ever. Amen."